A JOURNEY OF FAITH

Effie Irvine · 2004

A Journey of Faith

by

REV. EFFIE IRVINE

SERENDIPITY

© E. C. H. Irvine, 2003

First published in 2003 by
Serendipity
Suite 530
37 Store Street
Bloomsbury
London

British Library Cataloguing-in-Publication data
A catalogue record for this book is available from the British Library

ISBN 1-84394-041-8

Printed and bound by Alden Group, Oxford

*To the memory of my Mum and Dad and
my husband Alex*

Acknowledgements

Thanks are due to many friends who supported and encouraged me to write this book. Especially, Councillor Nancy Jackson and her husband Harry. These two good folk read the book chapter by chapter, edited it, corrected it and encouraged me. Harry introduced me into the world of word processing. Teaching me how to use the machine, his patience was unbelievable. The fact that this book has reached the finishing line is due to the help, understanding and advice offered and gratefully accepted from Nancy and Harry. Without their help this book would never have been published.

Thanks are also due to Mr Bill Coffey, of *The Herald* (Glasgow), as a journalist his advice regarding the layout of the chapters of the book was very valuable. Thanks to a few very good friends who knew about the project, kept their knowledge to themselves and encouraged me, especially in the early days when things were not progressing as quickly as I would have liked.

Thanks to my own family for their forbearance over the months.

Preface

More than 30 years ago, the Revd H. C. Euphemia Irvine was called to be the Church of Scotland's first woman minister in a parish. She was in her forties, four feet ten inches high, and a new era in her life and in the life of the church had begun.

The call of Effie Irvine was doubted by many but never by Effie, who, with the encouragement of family, friends and far-seeing teachers and clergy, overcame all obstacles put in her path.

The evidence of lives touched by God through her ministry is overwhelming. Effie is not a crusading figure but her story, simply told, lays out the evidence of God's hand every step of the way. Her life is an example of the rich diversity of experience and fulfillment which comes from following the path God has chosen.

An elder at Campsie Trinity church said to Effie after her very first communion service: 'We did not see you as a woman this morning, we only saw you as our very own minister'. This is a reflection which, thanks to the faithful ministry of Effie and those who followed her, now rings true in parishes the length and breadth of Britain.

The church today is very different from the one Effie was ordained to minister in, and this record of one woman's ministry over thirty years, will challenge some who question whether God is calling men and women as equal partners in the ministry of His church.

Alistair McCabe
Chairman
McCabe Pilgrimages

Chapter One

It was September, 1967, and I was standing at a bus stop in Danes Drive, with Scotstoun showgrounds behind me. I am quite sure that nobody would give me a second look, a very ordinary looking character. Dressed conservatively in a short coat, tartan skirt, with two pleats at back and front, to give freedom of movement, and of course, flat shoes, I liked comfort more than style. Spectacles were a necessity, blue eyes, which at that time were not taking in my surroundings, I was impatiently waiting for the appearance of the bus.

I waited, fears began to develop: should I make this journey, or forget it and head for home? My mind was restless, I was feeling rather tired, the steel corset I was forced to wear was rigid; it restricted my breathing, but it kept me straight and tall, all four feet ten inches of me, I was like a wee tin soldier. There were no keep-fit classes for me, no touching toes, in fact I could not bend from the waist at all.

Why the straitjacket? Eighteen months earlier I had boarded a bus for a visit to the Western Infirmary. My father-in-law, better known as 'Faither' to all the family, was quite ill, my husband Alex and I were concerned about him. As I got up to leave the bus that day, preoccupied with the news from the hospital, a fellow who was a little inebriated was pushing his way up the bus. He was quite a bit heavier than me (not surprising, since I weighed six stone ten pounds). He staggered into me; I had no chance, I fell and hit the tail end of my spine on the edge of a seat. I scrambled to my feet and got off the bus. For the moment the injury was quite painful, but I had to do this visit at the hospital, the pain certainly did ease, so I thought no more about it.

After two or three days the pain came back, it steadily got worse. When the gnawing discomfort continued to plague me, I went to see my GP, He prescribed painkillers; they did help a bit, but the ache never really went away. Some more weeks passed, the GP was once more visited, and this time it was suggested that a physiotherapist would be the person to help. Clydebank clinic was the nearest place for me. Several sessions did seem to help. It came to the last treatment, I was advised not to lift anything, not to stretch, and to 'walk tall'. For a few weeks things were quite good, but ever so slowly the pain returned. I put up with it, painkillers became a way of life. Then the day came when I was tripping over things, and my shoes were getting worn at the toes of my left foot. My mother had been in Australia for two years. She arrived home about eighteen months after my fall, she took one look at me, and said, 'Doctor.'

I went with her like a child to my GP. Mother asked that I should have the opportunity of an X-ray at the Western Infirmary. I had to wait for an appointment, but within a week, I saw a consultant. It transpired that the lower part of my spine was bent. The doctor said that day that I'd had the injury too long, and did not think they could do much to help me; further to that, my age was against me. I was forty-two years old, and I felt I had a lot still to do with my life. The next day found me at the Western Infirmary again to have a 'plaster jacket' fitted; it was solid from just under my arms to my bottom. It was quite an experience, but within a couple of days, the pain began to get more bearable. It was a marvellous relief, but brought with it many problems. I could not wash my feet, I could not wash my hair; I needed help to get into bed, but was able to roll out of bed in the morning. The plaster was removed after six weeks. I was measured for a steel corset, then I had to lie in bed for two months until this corset was made for me. I was advised that I would have to wear the corset for the rest of my life. While in bed, I had my doubts about studying. However I phoned Clydebank Technical College and asked if they would accept me to study Higher English, and Higher History. You have missed three months was the reply, but if you would like to come in to College at the beginning of January, you could try. The exams will be at the end of March, you could sit the two Highers; if you fail you may take the resits later. I did go in to the college in January, sat the two Highers and passed both; that really did help me.

But back to the present, the bus was slow in coming. Still time to change my mind. My future depended on the decision I was to make that day. Under my arm was a brown envelope containing papers that I hoped would give me the opportunity to alter my way of life. My faith was strong, not in myself but in Jesus Christ, I believed I was called to serve Him full time, I was totally committed to this venture of faith.

The bus did arrive, and in spite of the steel corset, I went upstairs to my favourite seat at the front with a bird's eye view. I knew the route well: Danes Drive to Victoria Park Drive North. Whiteinch Park on the right, with the pond where we played as children, paddling in the summer and sliding on the ice in winter. We rolled our hard boiled, painted eggs down the big hill every Easter time. We played cowboys and Indians in the famous fossil grove, and were chased by the park ranger. My Dad was a joiner; he made a small yacht which he sailed on the pond. A number of men formed the Victoria Park Yachting Club. They held races with these beautiful, small ships, and the winner received a silver cup. My young brother Douglas and I had a very important job to do when Dad's yacht was on the pond. We each had a long pole, and had to run round the perimeter of the pond. The edge of the pond had jagged pieces of stone cemented all the way round, and if the yachts touched the edge of the pond, they would have been damaged. We had to use the long pole to turn the yacht into deeper water. This helped to keep us out of mischief, and also kept us fit.

There was a bandstand in the Park, and concert parties entertained in the summer evenings. If you didn't have the money to get in, you could stand at the back and watch over the railings; it was always good entertainment. The bowling green was nearby, where the old men enjoyed a very gentle sport. Now it's a young person's game, and women bowlers have become very good players. Another game in the park was the cricket, again it was a more gentle sport then; the fast bowlers had not emerged till some years later.

The paddle-boats were a real treat, one penny for four folk, and make sure to come in when the boatman called your number. One day, out of sight of the boatman, we took on a non-paying passenger, the boat sank. Naturally we all got soaked, the boatman was furious and so was my mother when I arrived home and dripped dirty water all over her freshly polished lobby floor. Years later I would play hockey for the Jordanvale Church Girl Guides and go home with skinned knees from the black ash football pitch. The memories eased the tension, all the time the bus was drawing closer to my target.

Leaving the environs of the park, crossing over Balshagray Avenue into Victoria Park Gardens South to Crow Road, Broomhill Cross, then into Clarence Drive. We passed Balshagray Church, Ross's Dairies offices, to the railway bridge. Tramcars came thundering down Clarence

Drive in those days, I remember the day when the front wheel of my bike got stuck in the tramline. I couldn't move it, but a good Samaritan dived off the pavement and rescued me and the bike. I got a real tongue bashing from this very concerned gentleman: rather him than my mother, but of course I never related that incident to either of my parents. It was just a good thing that there were no tramcars coming.

The bus made its way along to Byres Road. As teenagers we'd go there on Sunday afternoons and walk up and down making eyes at the boys. We thought it rather daring, but we never seemed to hit it off with any of them. Over Byres Road and into University Avenue. Panic rising to the surface again. As the bus approached my stop, I gingerly got myself down the stairs of the bus. Wellington Church towered above me, I asked a few folk where the Faculty of Divinity was, and eventually I was informed, just up there. I turned up Southpark Terrace and made my way to the Faculty of Divinity. My steps slowed as I walked up the path, I was just a wee bit out of breath. I stopped at the entrance, then gently opened the door. It was a dismal kind of place, dark wood, lots of doors, and the inevitable green linoleum. There was only one person there, a wee woman wearing a bright floral apron. She was polishing the floor for all she was worth, using a big, heavy polisher, too big for her really, but she hefted it back and forward until the floor gleamed. She stopped, conscious of my presence, and in her best Glasgow vernacular, asked: 'Can I help you, hen?'

'I don't know, I was hoping someone would be in the building, I am looking for a bit of advice.'

She looked up at the wall. I followed her eyes to a large, brown board with names printed in gold leaf.

'Take your pick, hen, there's two of them in.'

The first name, Professor John Mauchline, meant nothing to me, but I did recognise the other one. Professor William Barclay, I'd seen him many times on the TV. 'I'll have him.'

She said, 'Upstairs.'

I went up the stairs as if there was no tomorrow, got to the Professor's door, gave a gentle knock. I was so breathless, the steel corset was feeling very tight. I knocked a wee bit louder a second time. A deep, gruff voice was saying, 'Come in, come in.'

I pushed open the door, and in absolute fear and trembling came face to face with this quite rotund figure, looking over his specs at me, and at the same time fiddling with a hearing aid control in the top left hand pocket of his dark suit. He had a huge desk, littered with papers, and books everywhere. He motioned me to a seat at the other side of his desk, I followed the direction of his hand, found the seat, and was very thankful for the rest. He said, 'What can I do for you?'

I passed over the brown envelope, saying, 'These are the qualifications I have managed to get. Advanced level in Biblical studies, O levels in English, English Literature, and Geography, all London University, all acquired through a correspondence course, plus a Higher English (grade B), Higher History (grade C), Scottish Certificate of Education.'

Professor Barclay gave them a quick scan. I am sure he had seen better, much, much better qualifications before.

He said, 'What do you want me to do with this lot?'

'I wanted to be a teacher of religious education, taking a B.Ed degree at Jordanhill College of Education, but I received a letter this morning telling me that they were not accepting me for the course. No reason was given. My minister advised me to come to the University. I chose Divinity because I did not know where else to go.'

Again the gruff voice: 'Do you know anything about Greek?'

Answer, 'No.'

'Do you know anything about Hebrew?'

No. I was tempted to say, 'Sir, I'm just learning English.'

'Are you willing to work?'

'Yes.'

The gruff voice was taking on a kindly tone. I began to feel a bit more at ease, but still I thought, 'I haven't a hope, at forty three years of age, who will want me?'

The professor was turning over the certificates again; perhaps he'd seen worse.

Out of the blue, he said, 'I'll take you for a BD. You will study Scottish History and Logic at the Arts Faculty of the University. That will be your first year. It will be a four year degree course. You will also have to study, sit and pass New Testament Greek for entrance into Trinity College next year. You can take a Greek class at Trinity College in the afternoons. You should be able to manage that.' He put the certificates back into the brown envelope, then he handed it to me. He rose from his desk, and walked to the door; the interview was over.

I had not really taken in all that the Professor had said. My voice was speaking and I heard myself say, 'When will I know if I'm accepted?'

'You know now,' he said. 'You're mine. You will be at Trinity College on 3 October, don't be late. You will matriculate on that day.'

I wondered what that big word meant.

I left Southpark Terrace on cloud nine, and crossed University Avenue to the gate of the University. It would be a great shortcut for me if I could get down to Dumbarton Road through the University grounds. The gateman stepped out of his little house.

'Can I get to Dumbarton Road from here?'

'Yes, just follow the road round and you will get there, you can't go wrong.'

It was downhill all the way, that was a relief. I wanted to shout to the world, 'I am a student!' My hope and my prayers had been answered, it was the beginning of a marvellous adventure that was to change my life.

I hopped on a number 9 bus. I was urging the driver to step on the gas, he was going too slow for me. Patience, patience. On the bus on the way home, I could hardly believe what was happening. I was so excited. We had reached Partick, so much traffic, the driver of the bus was having difficulty; unfortunately for me, it was a busy time of day. I was itching to get home with the news. The Rev. Kenneth McLean Bethune would also be waiting for a call from me.

Especially as he had been a major driving force in the achievement.

Today had begun like any other day. Husband Alex left for work about 7.30 a.m. He worked at Anderson Strathclyde, an engineering works in Bridgeton, where he was a staff inspector. After that it was breakfast for the rest of us, and Faither took Dougie the labrador for his morning walk.

Just a normal day, until 8 a.m. when the post came through the letter box. I had applied to Jordanhill College to take a Bachelor of Education course which would see me qualified for the job I really wanted to do: become a teacher of religious education. I heard the rattle of the letterbox and was there just after the brown envelope fell to the floor. I looked at it for a few seconds, then lifted it and opened it. The verdict straight and to the point.

'This is to inform you that we are not accepting you for the course of B.Ed.'

It is difficult to find the words to express how I felt at that moment. Dejection and despair come readily to mind. And later on, after reading that curt rejection many more times, I think that a bit of determination emerged. Why had I been refused? There was no reason given. My qualifications met the requirements for the course. I had not had an interview at the college, so I had done nothing wrong there. The reason became increasingly obvious. I was too old.

I did not tell my mother about the letter. I did not want to worry or upset her. I phoned Rev. Ken, my minister.

'Drop everything,' he said. 'Come up to the manse, bring the letter and your qualifications with you.'

I had no idea what he intended doing, but I obediently set off for the manse. It was quite a walk for a wee tin soldier, and uphill most of the way. It was not the first time that my scholastic endeavours had been frustrated. A couple of years before, I had studied, by correspondence, at the University of London. Then I found out that these qualifications would not be enough to get me into a Scottish college. But adding the Scottish qualifications should have been enough to get me into Jordanhill College.

I was out of puff as I approached the manse. My corset was acting up as usual. I hoped there would be a cup of tea, and a wee bit sympathy at the manse. I certainly got the former, but the latter was in short supply. The Rev. Ken understood just how disappointed I was. He knew of my belief that God had called me to full time service. I was feeling a bit sorry for myself, but if I thought I was going to a safe place where I would be able to lick my wounds, I was wrong.

He told me, 'You're not going to give up just because you've hit a hurdle. Take your papers and the letter and go to the University and see somebody there.'

I replied, 'I don't know anyone there, not even a student.'

'Just go,' he said.

And now I was getting off the bus to walk back to Lime St, and my whole life was changing. I felt numb. Had I really heard Professor Barclay right? I had, I knew that I had, but it was all like a dream. I was to report to Trinity College on 3 October, I would study at the Arts Department, Scottish History and Logic and Greek at Trinity College. There would be no short cut to the end product; if the call to serve was valid, this was the opportunity. The door was wide open. The question invading my mind at that moment was this, did I have the capability to see it through? I was on the verge of taking cold feet.

As I opened the door at 16 Lime St I realised that my mother would be worried. I had been away for hours, without any explanation and, well, mothers do worry about their family, no matter what the age. Mum was home, and as soon as I got in the door, I forestalled the question, 'Where have you been?' The story came tumbling out, she was caught up in my enthusiasm. I finished the story with the words, 'It's true, Mum, it's true.'

As we moved into the living room, she said, 'I hope you will manage. I'll do all I can to help in the house.' There was a wee kiss and a cuddle. Mum never knew how much that meant to me. Suddenly, I remembered there was something I must do. So I hurried to the bookcase, grabbed a dictionary, and hurried through the Ms till I found it.

Matriculate: To be admitted to the privileges of university.

I was learning already.

It wasn't long until Faither came home. I told him the news. 'Aye, well done,' he said, sitting down with his newspaper. 'I hope you get on all right.'

I could hardly wait for the Quiet Man to come home, Alex, my husband of sixteen years, an elder in the kirk, my rock. I watched for him from the room window, excitement rising in me again. He was hardly in the door before I began to rattle it off nineteen to the dozen. Gently, he guided me into the front room. 'Begin again,' he said, 'start at the beginning. Tell me slowly.'

As I finished the whole story, there was a big smile on his face and his eyes were shining. 'That's just great news,' he said. I knew then that with Alex beside me I had all the support I needed.

Slowly, word got round our friends. Margaret and Frank Cowan, who lived at the foot of our street, came up to see me. Could you use a wee desk? Yes I certainly could, thank you very much. Then they brought a bookcase, and later on they even bought books for me. Such good friends and what a great support. There were others who were not slow to point out the drawbacks and potential downfalls.

The Rev. Ken was overjoyed. He and his wife were a great support. Rev. Ken was a Greek scholar, and offered to tutor me in that subject.

The news filtered through the congregation of Jordanvale Parish Church. Some were in favour, but quite a few were against the very idea. The thoughts of some were that I was now aged forty-three, too old to study, should have started years ago. I had little education, having left school at fourteen. My health was not all that good, steel corset and all that, etc, etc. Sometimes it's good to have opposition. You can harness that force, turn it on its head, and use it to drive yourself on when times are tough.

On the Saturday, his first day off work, Alex disappeared into town. He came home and handed me a parcel which contained a shiny black leather briefcase. Said he, 'That's something I'm sure you are going to need.' I still have that briefcase; it is still used, a bit shabby, the shine is gone, the handle is held together by sticky tape, but I would not part with it for anything.

Alex said that day, 'Never mind the doubting Thomases. I believe you will make it, I have no doubts.' These very important words at that time were the encouragement that I needed. I soon learned that my struggle to make the grade would be against all the odds.

There was one thing that I disposed of early, despite medical advice against it. I only wore the steel corset for nine months. Then it was consigned to the back of a drawer. My GP was not amused, he wanted me to go back to the hospital. I had not worn it for three months. The patient was issued with a new corset once a year, and mine was now due. I promised the doctor I would return if the pain came back. As I left the surgery I said to the doctor, 'The age of miracles is not over.' He laughed, and said, 'I sincerely hope you are right.' I must have been, I've never worn any corset from that day. The first sign for me that all would be well in time.

Chapter Two

Preparing for university, my mind flew back to another first day. Radnor Park School, my earliest memory. Mother said I was desperate to go to school. The great day came. I remember the playground quite clearly, wee tots all a bit anxious, mothers hovering in the background. Some of the wee ones were tearful, clinging to Mums. Me, I was trying to comfort a wee girl who was crying quite sore. Her Mum had left thinking everything was all right. Seeing the others weeping my wee friend joined in the chorus. My mother said she watched me, feeling a bit left out. As the other mothers fussed, she left the playground and went home. She said, 'I knew you would be all right.'

I was born at 277 Kilbowie Road, Clydebank, on 28 August 1924, at 5 p.m. There were Mum and Dad, Elizabeth and James Brysland, (Liz and Jim). My big brother Tommy and wee brother Douglas joined us about three years later.

My time at Radnor Park School only lasted about six months. Mum and Dad had their name on the housing list of Glasgow Corporation. We were allocated a house at 11 Fulwood Avenue in Knightswood. It was supposed to be a new start for the family. There would be a bathroom with hot and cold water, a bedroom for the boys, one for Mum and Dad and one for me. A great improvement from a room and kitchen. My next primary school was to be Bankhead in Knightswood. I don't remember anything about it because I was only there for a few months.

Dad was a joiner, a skilled tradesman who was not afraid of hard work. But the country was then in the clutches of a depression. He was out of work more often than he was employed. We were no sooner in Fulwood Avenue when all the men at Dad's work were what was called 'laid off'. The rents were too high for those on unemployment benefit. The family would have been in debt very soon. Mum and Dad decided to give up the house at Fulwood Avenue. We moved again, this time to friends, Auntie Cathie and Uncle Robert Flynn's home. Robert and my Dad grew up together, Aunty Cathie and my Mum had been friends from childhood. They had a room and kitchen in Whiteinch where Mum and Dad came from originally. They gave us their front room, and they lived in the kitchen. They had one child. At that time my older brother would be about eight years old, I would be about six and our wee brother almost four years. It was a tight squeeze. Times were hard. Robert was also out of work, as were many men in 1929.

One day when Robert and my Dad got their 'buroo' money they went to the fruit market and bought a case of apples, which they sold at the Central Station, and doubled their money. The two wives had no idea where they were, but when they came home with the fruits of their labours, Cathie and my Mum were overjoyed; we were all well fed that week-end.

A few months later, Granny Cosh, on my Mum's side, spoke to her house factor, and we were given a house to rent at 5 Medwyn Street, Whiteinch. A room and kitchen, plus a bonus, an inside toilet. The house was in a terrible state. I can still remember the ceilings were painted red. Family and friends rallied round to help and very soon we were in our own home: sparsely furnished but it was ours. There was a hole-in-the-wall bed space, a big black range (fireplace), and a white sink at the window with a cold water tap, no hot water. The coal bunker was at the kitchen door. The house was lit by gas with a penny meter. It was like a palace to us.

Money was always scarce. One day during school holidays when I rushed into the close, Mum was scrubbing the white wood doorstep.

'Can I have a penny for the swimming baths?'

Mum rose from her knees. I followed her into the kitchen. On the high mantlepiece was Mum's purse; I called it a concertina purse, it had a whole lot of pockets in it, Mum lifted down the purse, opened it. There was one penny in it.

Mum said, 'That penny is for the gas meter tonight or for you, which is it to be?'

I turned and walked out of the kitchen. What a marvellous psychologist. I learned a great lesson that day. That happened on a Wednesday, Thursday was the day Dad signed on for the 'buroo' money.

Our house was on the ground floor of a three storey tenement. The door was seldom locked. There were very few homes where the door was locked as there was nothing much to steal, during the depression; we were all in the same boat. Up our tenement close there were

Mum and Dad with Fiona Mackenzie.

twelve homes and at one time there was only one man employed. He was an insurance man who sold penny policies. If there was any occasion for our door to be locked, we just climbed in the kitchen window.

My Dad was a very cheery soul, all of five foot tall. He was very musical, but he could not read music; he could play the piano, the accordion, the tin whistle, the mouth organ, the Jew's harp, and the drums. He whistled, he said, because he could not sing.

Both parents had a sense of humour, but sometimes there were rows, because I think it was a constant struggle for them to keep their heads above water, to feed and clothe three demanding children. We owe our parents a great deal of respect. I'm sure many of my contemporaries would say the same: the one thing we never lacked was love. That love was shown in their caring commitment to do their best for us, as children. It was obvious that we came first in their every thought and action.

We all attended Church, and Sunday School. Every night our prayers were said at Mum's knee: 'This night as I lie down to sleep, I pray the Lord my soul to keep, if I should die before I wake, I pray the Lord my soul to take.' Then there was a great long God bless every relative's name one could think of. We extended the list very often to keep us out of bed longer. The Brownies were very important to me, then the Girl Guides. Being the smallest Guide in the company, when the order was given, "Tallest to the right shortest to the left," I just walked to the end of the line. The boys had the Life Boys and then the Boys Brigade. Mum sang in the choir, and she was a member of the Thursday afternoon women's meeting. Dad was in the men's fellowship. At times he was called upon to help out with Church fabric repairs, especially when it was to do with wood.

Some funny things did happen in our family. Dad pointed out to Mum one day that our kitchen floor linoleum was a bit faded, in fact with the wear and tear of so many feet the original pattern was almost non-existent. There was a shop in Partick selling linoleum paint at sixpence a tin, too good a bargain to miss. Dad was sent for the paint. The great night came, and we were sent to bed early. Supper was for the first time, like a picnic, served in bed. Mum got everything ready for the morning, the kitchen as far as possible, cleared of furniture. Dad was very methodical, he put a jam jar under the hole in the wall bed, with turpentine in it for the paint brush when he was finished. His pyjamas were laid on his pillow; Mum was urged to get into bed.

The painting job began at the window, the colour was cardinal red. Slowly, bit by bit, Dad made his way towards the bed. The doors in the room and kitchen were always left open for fresh air during the night. When the painter reached the bed, he left a square, so that he could change into his pyjamas, leaned out the bed, painted the last of the floor, put the paint brush into the turpentine and lay down with a sigh. By this time we had electric light. Mum said, 'Jim, you forgot to put out the light.' The kitchen door was open and Dad was able to stand on the bed, get one foot on the handle of the door, swing himself over to the light switch, turn off the light, swing back and fall into bed.

All was well, except there were three excited children who were awake very early, and were desperate to see the new floor. No slippers, we ran into the kitchen; alas the floor was still tacky. Consternation. Mum tried everything to get the paint off our feet to no avail, it just had to fade slowly. We had great fun taking our socks and shoes off to let our pals see our feet. They called us the redskins of Medwyn Street.

When I was about ten years old, my Mum was quite ill with gastric flu, money was tight, there was no NHS. We had to pay 2s.6d. for the doctor's visit, and also pay for the medicine. There were no antibiotics in those days. Dad said to me, "Look after your Mum, there's something I've got to do today." It was a Saturday morning. Dad did not come home till lunchtime. He had a big black box, and inside was a piano accordion. He took it out of the box, and began to play; it sounded great. Mum was crying, "Jim, what have you done?" Dad was trying to comfort her. He had bought the instrument in Cuthbertson's in Sauchiehall Street. It was to cost 1s.6d. a week. Where are we going to get 1s.6d. a week? But Dad had it all worked out. He had taken on a dancing class; he was to play for one class on a Saturday morning, and a week night class. He would be paid, 2s.6d. for each class. I was to get dancing lessons free. So 1s.6d. went to Cuthbertson's, but Mum received 3s.6d. a week, which was a lot of money. The accordion was to make life a lot easier for all of us. Eventually Dad got a few other engagements and it all helped the family financially.

Up to this time, our front room had no furniture in it, except for the hole-in-the-wall bed where the boys slept, plus my bed chair, which was folded down each night. It was decided that a start could be made to make the room really like a front room. Dad began by building a tile fireplace, which meant it had to be laid out on the floor and a frame made, which was filled with cement. The tiles were then fitted on top of the cement. The idea was that once the cement dried, which took some time, the frame was taken away, and the fireplace was then ready to be placed in position. It was a great job, well done and it worked. We had an oriel window in that room. Dad then built that in making a seat with a lid that lifted up giving us some storage space. Granny Cosh then made cushions to fit; it looked lovely.

The room began to take on a different appearance. It was papered and painted. We were overjoyed when our three piece suite arrived. There was still the hole-in-the-wall bed, and the boys still had to sleep there, but it was curtained off during the day; that way, the bed wasn't seen when we had visitors. My bedchair was moved into what was known as the cloakroom, it became my very own wee bedroom. There was only one drawback: when anyone needed the toilet, they had to pass through my bedroom.

Two great folk I remember well, who were the salt of the earth. Each Friday, Paddy Walker, who was our local butcher, sold shilling parcels to help those whose husbands were not working; there were many in that situation. The parcels contained a bit of boiling beef, some mince, two sausages, and a bit of bacon. It was amazing what my Mum was able to do with that. The boiling beef went to make broth, then the beef was taken out the soup, and made a pot of stovies, marvellous on a cold day. Jessie, who owned the fruit shop next door to the butcher, sold vegetables for soup: one penny bought carrot, turnip, leek and cabbage. We could also have chipped fruit, consisting of a few apples or pears, with sometimes an orange in for good value. There was always a queue at these two shops on a Friday morning ... There was porridge every morning. We were never allowed to say, 'I don't like that.' If you did not eat what was put down in front of you, it was quite simple, you went hungry.

We had a cousin called Bertie Turner, who was a bit older than us. He and my Dad decided to make a wireless set (radio). Dad had made a cabinet that was to house this radio. Come the great day, it was a Sunday afternoon. The homemade wireless set had something called 'cat's whiskers'. There was also a set of earphones. Dad was sitting twiddling with buttons, and we were in a high state of excitement. Suddenly, Dad says, 'Wheesht, Wheesht,' he shouted, 'I'm getting a station.' Music, it's getting louder. It was, and we were all hearing it, but it turned out to be the Salvation Army band going through their repertoire in our street. Eventually that wireless set did work.

Mum and Dad had some friends who came to visit every fortnight. One of the nights they were expected, they did not turn up at their usual time. Mum had the room fire lit, everything was ready, but there was no sign of the guests. Mum said to Dad, 'They're late tonight, I'll go into the room and watch for them at the window.' She went into the room and the friends were already there, sitting quietly. They had all climbed in the window, they were a daft lot.

My mother was a hand chocolate coverer to trade. Before Christmas and Easter, she would be called into Birrell's chocolate factory at Anniesland to help out in the production of Christmas boxes of Milady Chocolates, and Easter eggs. That really did help. One of the times Mum was doing this, Dad had got a job. Mum used to prepare the dinner the night before. I had to put the dinner on at a certain time. Douglas was to do any messages that were needed, and we were to light the fire. Sometimes the fire was difficult to light, and if the sticks were damp it was even more difficult. On this particular day we could not get the fire going. We knew that Mum had some firelighters, but we had been told not to use them. However that day we decided needs must. That would have been all right if we had just used one, but we put three firelighters in the fire. Of course, the flames shot up the chimney, and before you could blink we had a good going chimney on fire. Remember we were at the bottom of a three storey tenement. Douglas ran for a pot, filled it with water and threw it on the range; by this time burning soot was falling down. I ran outside into the street. As luck would have it, our Uncle Tommy was coming along the street. He was out of work, He was the type of person who was so laid back it wasn't true. He was looking up at the chimney, which was now belching black smoke, and said, 'Somebody's got a rare going lum on fire.'

I said, 'Aye it's ours, come on quick, Douglas is going to get burnt,' I'd never seen my Uncle Tommy move so fast. He near had a fit when he saw the range, it was almost red hot but he was on the ball that day. He soon had the range damped down. He then helped us to clean up the place, he carried bucketfuls of soot out to what we called the midden, and even washed the floor for us. Uncle Tommy was my hero. The outcome was that firelighters were absolutely forbidden thereafter; they were not even allowed in the house.

School was always a delight to me. I was never at the top of the class, nor at the bottom, maybe just above the pass mark for all subjects. I disliked arithmetic, still do, but loved English, History and Geography. The strap was used on me very often for talking. I do remember that my Mum had to buy our books, Tommy was first to use them, then they were handed down to me. When Douglas was preparing to go to school my Mum realised that the books were getting a bit worn. There was no way she could buy books for the three of us. If you wanted free books, you had to get a form from the head teacher. Mum wasn't very happy about this, but she did go to see Miss MacLaren, a very understanding lady. Mum poured out her story. Miss MacLaren said 'Don't you worry, Mrs Brysland, from the beginning of the next term all school books will be free.' A great burden had been lifted.

My time at primary school came to an end. I had passed what was known as the quallie, and was due to go to Hamilton Crescent School in Fortrose Street in Partick. Another exciting day. It was decided by my Mum that I would take the commercial course: Shorthand, typewriting and book-keeping, with the idea that an office job would be the right vocation for me. Algebra was introduced into our curriculum. I did not understand why we had to add, x,y, or z, when we could add 1,2, and 3. I approached Miss Miller our mathematics teacher and told her that I could not understand algebra and did not think I would be able to cope. To my great surprise, she agreed and she never mentioned it to me again and I never learned algebra. I left secondary school aged fourteen, and set about looking for a job. An Office Job????

Chapter Three

Time to find a job. It had to be an Office Job. I had no real qualifications, just the fact that I had become familiar with type-writing and bookkeeping at school. Forget about the shorthand, I had lost interest in that from day one, it was like the algebra. A plumber's shop in Whiteinch, next door to Gordon Park Church, had a notice in the window, Office Girl wanted. I went in. It was a dreary place. The shop window was painted white on the inside, half way up. This made the small office a trifle dull. The rest of the shop was used by the plumbers as their store and workshop. Lead pipes were lying about the floor, water taps, bits of plumbing equipment, and even an old bath, plus the men's tools. There was one long work bench with a vice at each end. It was the most untidy place I'd seen in a long time. The boss was Mr Gray and there were three workmen on the premises; two were journeymen, the third was an apprentice. The door of the office was closed. I knocked, the door opened. I asked Mr Gray if the job was still open. He asked me a few questions, I was not very fussy whether I got the job or not, but I answered as best as I could. Then the boss said that the wages would be 8s.6d. a week, with two pence off for an insurance stamp. Hours would be 9 a.m. to 5 p.m. I would be expected to answer the phone, getting the names and addresses of the customers, and their requirements. I would be expected to keep the books up to date, and type the invoices, and send them out. Then he said in an offhand sort of way, 'The job's yours if you want it.' I didn't really want it, but thought I'd better say yes till I could get something more exciting. Oh, and I would be expected to keep the office tidy. I thought that would be the most difficult task of all.

Mother was thrilled; the fact that it was an office job was all she wanted. I would learn from this wee job, and in time would climb the ladder of success to a bigger and better office. It was not long before I was bored, and knew for sure that office work was not for me. I was more interested in what the men were doing. The men were lumbered with another apprentice, me, I learned quickly. One of the men taught me how to make a lead pipe joint with a leather wipe and a blow torch. That was for me, and working with my hands kind of changed my mind about the office job. I stuck it out as long as I could to keep Mum happy.

The year was 1938. My Dad had had a job in John Brown's shipyard in Clydebank for a good few months. It seemed to be the beginning of a steady job, something Mum and Dad had not experienced for years and years. The ship involved was the *Queen Mary*. Dad had a mate working with him who was called big Bill McLean, Bill was from Northern Ireland and was living in digs. Although there was no chance of Bill sharing our home, Mum very often gave him a meal; he was made welcome and enjoyed the Scottish hospitality. One night, Bill asked Mum and Dad if we as a family would like a wee holiday in Lisburn, his home town, in Northern Ireland. His wife had offered to take us for two weeks, because he had been made so welcome in Scotland by our family. Mum and Dad accepted the invitation; my older brother Tommy did not want to go, so he was left with Granny Cosh. There was great excitement, preparing for the first holiday we had ever known, we began to save all our pennies, Douglas was always better at saving than me. Of course it had to be organised for the Glasgow Fair fortnight, that was when most of the works closed. John Brown's was no exception. I had to ask Mr Gray for time off to be with the family. It was July 1939, Fair Friday, that we went to the Central Station on the tramcar. The train to Stranraer, then the boat to Belfast, last of all, a bus to Lisburn; the journey itself was a new experience for all of us.

We had a wonderful holiday. The Irish folk were more than kind to us. The McLean family were like a large tribe of people; every member of that family wanted to entertain us. They took us to Bangor, to Belfast to the Zoo, and to the Mountains of Mourne. We had picnics, visited a friend's piggery, what a smell, and the linen factory, where some of the family worked. It was just a very wonderful two weeks for all of us. As I said already, Douglas was very good at saving his pennies. When we were ready to set off for our holiday, Douglas gave his holiday money to Dad for safe keeping. Each day of the holiday he would ask Dad for some of his money, and Dad handed it out. When we were coming home on the boat, Douglas asked Dad for his money. 'You have spent it son, every time you needed money I gave it to you.' The boy answered, 'If I had known that was my money you were giving me, I wouldn't have spent it.'

We returned from Ireland, refreshed. Life was changing for us as a family, we were not to know just how different things were going to be, not just for us but for Britain itself. Dad of course started back at John Brown's. With reluctance; I went back to the office, oh how I detested that place. After a couple of weeks I'd had enough. Mum woke me for work one morning.

'You'll be late for your work if you don't get up now.'

I had the temerity to answer back, 'I am not going back to that so called office, I hate the very sight of the place.'

When Mum had calmed down, I said, 'I am going up to Barr & Stroud at Anniesland, they are looking for workers.'

'That's a factory,' said Mum.

'I don't ever want to work in an office again.'

She let me go, and provided me with the bus fare, otherwise I would have had to walk it. I think Mum realised I had made up my mind about office work.

Barr & Stroud made periscopes for submarines, rangefinders for the Army, Navy and the Air Force, and binoculars for all the services. When I reached the big doors of the factory, a tall man in a fawn raincoat and felt hat, looked down at me from a great height; later I was to learn that he was the works detective. 'Yes?' he said.

'I'm looking for a job.'

'My goodness, you are in luck, Mr Hislop is interviewing this morning, there's two other wee lassies waiting in there, you might as well join them.'

In I went and joined the other two; they would be thinking the same as me. Who would get the job? We need not have worried. Mr Hislop came in, in a white coat, with dark blue epaulettes on his shoulders, the sign of a foreman. He seemed a very kindly man. We were all asked the same questions, where we lived, our age, if we had worked before. He gave each one of us a form to fill in, and left us alone for a wee while, when he returned he took the questionnaire back, sat down and said, 'I think you all deserve a job, we will just employ the three of you. You will start in the West Works, across the road. You will be message girls for a year, and then have the opportunity to work at a bench.' Marvellous. We were to start on 11 September 1939.

Before we started work, World War Two had begun on 3 September

1939. When we arrived to begin our 'message girl jobs', we discovered that soldiers were stationed outside and inside the factory. They were suitably attired in khaki battle dress. The West Works was where the periscopes, rangefinders and binoculars became finished instruments, ready for use in the services. The three girls employed by Mr Hislop in August, Jessie, Jean and Effie, were all about the same height and were nicknamed, the 'three smart girls'. We were teased without mercy, sent for tartan paint, a long stand, etc. I had had enough. I was given a card for a rubber headed hammer. I refused to go, there was no way I was going to be caught again. One of the women enlightened me, saying that there was such a thing as a rubber headed hammer, it was used to tap the lenses into position on periscopes. I went for the hammer and said to the man who sent me, sorry.

After a few months 'the three smart girls' were separated. I was sent to the rangefinder department. One of my jobs was to carry the finished instruments to the paint shop, one under each arm. My first time in the paint shop terrified me. The girls who worked there were a bit rough; they had to be, it was a rotten job. They used spray guns to paint the rangefinders, and never used masks, so they were breathing paint spray into their lungs day in, day out. They used to shout and tease us mercilessly. "Does yur mammy know yer oot, wis yur hair cut wi garden shears, where did ye get they legs?" Eventually they dubbed me "football legs" and it stuck. One day was the Daddy of them all. I was always very pale but very healthy. I went into the paint shop, by this time, used to the banter. The voice came over loud and clear.

'Hey, fitba legs, gonnae len us yur face ti we get hame seek.'

After that nothing surprised me, and in time they became quite friendly, leaving me alone. I certainly got an education in Barr & Stroud.

As promised, after a year as a message girl, I was called to Mr Hislop's office. He asked me if I was happy working in Barr & Strouds. I answered in the affirmitive, I could not see myself in an office ever. 'That's good, because it's time for you to start work at the bench. Is there any particular job you think you could manage? If there is you will require some training.'

That was the best news I'd ever heard. 'Yes,' I replied, 'I'd like to work on focus and diaphram.'

'You can begin next Monday, Miss Briton will take you under her wing. If you have any problems you can come and see me.'

The new job meant I would be working with and fitting lenses to rangefinders. First of all I had to learn how to handle and clean the lenses before fitting them. I had to become familiar with a drilling machine, work with rivets – the heads were like pin heads – use screw drivers, files and a rubber headed hammer etc. Dad made me a toolbox with its own key; you had to buy your own tools. I was extremely happy, working with my hands. I learned quickly, and was overjoyed to find in my pay envelope the handsome sum of sixteen shillings, a rise of six shillings. I was rich! I was proud to hand over my pay packet to Mum. I got a shilling pocket money and my bus fares. I was very contented with my promotion and happily looked forward to a long time in Barr & Strouds.

To begin with our working hours were quite good. Once I had managed to convince the boss that I could now manage on my own, I was advised that I would have to do wartime hours. We worked 8 a.m. till to 5 p.m., and three nights 6 p.m. to 9 p.m. As the war progressed, it became every night till 9 p.m., and when it came near the end of each month, if our quota was short, we worked Saturdays 9 a.m. till noon, and Sunday 9 a.m. to 5 p.m. I remember saying to my chargehand. 'I can't work on a Sunday, I go to Church on Sundays.' The answer was, "Forget it, there's a war on." I went to Church in the evening. When I was seventeen I was put on nightshift; the shift was 8 p.m. till 8 a.m., month about. Nobody liked nightshift, but we did get used to it. It turned out that we spent more hours in the factory than we did at home. We were a happy bunch, there was always somebody acting in a farcical way. Of course there were many sad times, when one of our colleagues would get word that a relative was missing, wounded, a prisoner of war, or killed in action.

One day there was a request on the works notice board asking for a volunteer to help the nurse in the ambulance room. When a hooter sounded, it meant there was a serious accident. The first aider had to stop work and run to the ambulance room, so that the nurse could be free to deal with the serious situation. Having all my first aid certificates from St Andrew's Ambulance Association. I applied for the job, and got it. I was pleased to be told I would get an extra penny added to my earnings; that was a bonus I did not expect.

The union in Barr & Stroud called a strike, asking for a rise of one penny a week. Lots of us did not want to go on strike, but we were told strike or else. We were out for six weeks, and went back to work for one halfpenny. In this day and age, all this sounds laughable. It meant that we had no pay for six weeks. My mother had a friend who worked in the box office of the Alhambra Theatre, who asked me if I would like to work in the theatre while I was on strike. A circus was on at that time. I became an usherette with a gold apron, selling programmes and showing folk to their seats. I was located in the dress circle. I got quite a lot of tips. Mum still got my wages and my pocket money went up to one an sixpence. Night after night I was entranced by the performances of acrobats, gymnasts, trapeze acts, tight-rope walking, dancing and singing. Everything was timed to the second, hard work. but great entertainment.

My older brother Tommy joined the Black Watch. He was stationed at Milnathort in Fife for his training. He was almost eighteen years old. That was bad enough, but just after his training was completed, he volunteered for a group called, Wingate's Chindits. He had also become a paratrooper. Mum and Dad received word from the War Office that they would not receive any letters from Tommy for some time to come. They of course were advised to write to Tommy and the War Office would make sure he got their letters. Of course, we were not advised where Tommy was serving. It turned out that they were headed for Burma; they had also been trained for jungle warfare. The War Office sent a letter to Mum and Dad once a month to let them know that their son was well. The young volunteers of Wingate's force were flown into the Burmese jungle by glider and dropped by parachute. There were a lot of these young men never came home. Tommy did, and we were shocked when we saw him, he was a shadow of his old self. The food they ate was dehydrated, dropped by planes, and stored in tins. His hair was almost non existent, and his skin was yellow because of the anti-malaria tablets they had to take.

Tommy came home for three weeks leave, expecting to be posted back to Burma. These three weeks were very difficult for the family. Tommy acted like a recluse; of course we had no idea at that time how much these young men had suffered, nor did we know how many of their comrades had died. Tommy never spoke about his experience, sufficient to say he suffered many nightmares even after he was married. He was due to report back to London when his three weeks leave was up. We saw him off at the Central Station. A few days later the Military Police were at the door. Tommy was missing. The MP believed he had gone AWOL. Our minister, Rev. Paul Hind, was going to London and he offered to look into the situation. Our minister was able to convince the army authorities, we don't know how, that something was wrong. The War Office, began to enquire into the matter. Tommy was found in a civilian hospital in London. He had taken ill on the train with malaria, collapsed and had been taken to hospital. He lost all his kit, and nobody had the wit to inform the army. He had been very ill, and when he was able to travel he was sent to the army barracks at Stewarton, not back to Burma. Lucky for Tommy as he met his future wife at Stewarton; she was Anne, an ATS girl, who came from Kilbirnie in Ayrshire.

When the war started my young brother Douglas was twelve. He was evacuated to Balmore, north of Glasgow. First of all, the children were taken to Balmore Church hall, deloused, if it were necessary, examined, and then picked up by the persons who had volunteered to take these children into their homes. Douglas was very fortunate to be accepted by a Miss Elder, who lived in a bungalow called White Heather. He was her only evacuee, so was a bit spoiled by this very fine lady. He was very contented there, but unfortunately Miss Elder's nephew was killed in 1939. Douglas had to move. Miss Elder felt she could not carry on with the responsibility of children. My wee brother was in four different houses altogether. At one of those houses, a cottage just off the Balmore Road, the lady made porridge every night, she poured it into a drawer. No, Douglas did not get it in the morning, he got the porridge when he returned from school. Then he went to a farm cottage, where the Tinto sisters were his last carers. They boarded cats and dogs, and they had pets of their own plus a parrot which had the freedom of the house, but it was quite tame.

While there, Douglas got the opportunity to go, 'tattie howking'. He earned 6s.8d. for the day; he only survived one day, because his back was killing him. Coming home from school one day he and some of his chums were guddling for fish, but the gamekeeper caught them and confiscated the fish. Douglas had not been there very long, when a landmine exploded two fields away. He had reached the age of fourteen, and Dad decided it was time he was home. When Dad went to collect him at the bus station, he could not understand why his case was so heavy. Douglas had gone to the field where the landmine had fallen, and picked up quite few bits of shrapnel, plus part of the parachute to bring home as souvenirs. He was only home a couple of days when he got a job in a grocer's shop as message boy. He was delighted, a message bike went with the job.

I remember well the Clydebank blitz in 1941. By this time there were brick air-raid shelters in Whiteinch park. When the sirens went off we had to make our way to these shelters. The night of the blitz, my Dad and I stood outside the shelter and watched the German bombers drop their cargo over Clydebank. It was a beautiful night with clear skies, perfect for the air-raid. The landmines dropped attached to parachutes. As they floated down, they were like huge chandeliers, then came the crump as they struck their targets. It was terrifying, yet we felt compelled to watch. Clydebank was devastated, and the bombers returned the next night. Many, many souls died on these nights, and many were left homeless.

We were all busy during the war, mostly on the war effort, and we put up with quite a lot of rules and regulations. There was the black-out, baffle walls, ration books and clothing coupons. We managed to accept all these things and still smile and have fun, and looked forward to a day when all the servicemen would return home. In 1945 there was great rejoicing the war was over, at least we celebrated VE Day. The far east war took a wee while longer. The house we had lived in at 277 Kilbowie Road Clydebank was blitzed, and the house we lived in for a few months in Knightswood, 11 Fulwood Avenue, was also damaged in an air-raid.

Barr & Stroud changed from war work to making bread wrapping machines, and toffee wrapping machines. The men who were the real instrument makers returned from war service and were re-employed. I became a progress clerk (a chaser). My job was to chase the parts for the new machines through the machine shop. One day I was a bit frustrated. About fifty machines were waiting to be completed, short of two parts each. I went to the machine shop and the parts were ready, but we were not allowed to touch a barrow; that was the labourer's job, demarcation was the name of the game. I shouted at the charge hand, 'Get me a barrow and I will move the finished parts myself.' Of course there was no way that was going to happen. I left in disgust, another day wasted. Next day, back to the machine shop, my boss was now shouting at me for these very important machine parts; there was a deadline. When I arrived in the machine shop, the charge hand had the special parts on a barrow, with a labourer ready to move. The men on the machines suddenly gathered round and the boss made a speech, and presented me with a tiny replica barrow. It said on it, 'wee Effie's barrow'. I still have it.

In 1945 I had reached the ripe old age of twenty one. I had a lovely birthday party at home. Things were slowly getting back to normal. There was still rationing, but Mum made a lovely cloutie dumpling; it was indeed a luxury, I think she had been saving the ingredients for some time. We had moved house when I was twenty. We expected Tommy home from the army. Our room and kitchen were too small. We moved to 15 Scotia Street at St George's Cross. It had a big front room and kitchen, I had a bedroom to myself, and Douglas also had a wee room which he would have to share with Tommy. We did not change our church but travelled to Whiteinch every Sunday morning, and spent most of our week nights there also.

Life was taking on a whole new meaning. The overtime work was finished; we felt free to have week night activities. We were still church orientated. Most of our friends were also involved with church life. Dad had worked down in Southampton when the *Queen Elizabeth* came home for refitting, after having been a troop ship for some time. All that travelling was over, and Mum and Dad were also getting back to a more normal family way of life. We all looked forward to a fresh start.

Chapter Four

Slowly but surely, life began to take on a new meaning. Sunday School work, which had been a bit sporadic, became more organised. A young man who had been in the Air Force ground crew had just become the Sunday School secretary. His name was Alex Irvine. He had just been demobbed, having served in France and Germany. He had been attached to the transport division of the Air Force. His Dad was an elder in our church, I knew him quite well, but did not know Alex at all. He was a very good secretary to the Sunday School, but he was so shy, it was unbelievable. It took a long time before Alex relaxed with the teaching staff of the Sunday School; at teachers' meetings he sat in the background and agreed with all the decisions made. Bit by bit we became acquainted with one another, but it was hard going. I discovered that Alex's Mum was almost blind because of blood clots behind her eyes. Being an only child, Alex was very concerned about his mother's health. He spent most of his time at home. This meant that he was not meeting other folk very often.

Sometimes Dad took me to Firhill to see the Partick Thistle football club play. Dad had been a fan since he was a boy when the 'Jags' football ground was in Partick. One Saturday, Dad and I were at Firhill. Alex appeared at our door. Of course Mum knew who he was. He asked if Effie was in; Mum told him where I was, and invited him in. She entertained him for most of the afternoon, and he hardly uttered a word. It must have been hard going for Mum, but she was never really stuck for words. I was most surprised when I got home. He was the last person I ever thought would come visiting me. The next day at Sunday School he asked me out. That was the beginning of our romance. At first, I found it very difficult to keep a conversation going, but slowly, Alex began to respond. Many a time I did not want to make the effort to talk to him, but over the weeks and months, I discovered the worth of this quiet man. Quite unassuming, with a droll sense of humour, very patient, never in a hurry guy, a real good man. We became an item.

Alex and I enjoyed the same things. Live theatre, especially plays, Citizens Theatre where we first saw Duncan MacRae, and Stanley Baxter. The Five Past Eight shows at the Alhambra. The Glasgow Empire for the variety shows; it was there we saw Danny Kaye. We enjoyed walking, sightseeing and just being together. Alex had a Ford eight car, a Popular model, and hand signals were the order of the day. It had running boards on it, and there was no boot. He had bought the car really to get his mother out of the house; it was her only means of transport and made her very happy. I enjoyed it too. Mrs Irvine had a travel rug in the car; believe it or not, I still have it in my car. They don't make them like that today.

Alex's Mum died in 1948, and it was a very sad time for the family. At one time there was an Irvine's dairy in Whiteinch, but because of Mrs Irvine's illness they sold the dairy to Sloans dairies, but Mr Irvine kept his own milk run. That way he could look after his wife, because he was free from about 12 noon. He was a very fit character, but housework was not one of his strong points. So it was that I became more and more involved.

The romance between Alex and me developed against all the odds and we were engaged on 25 December 1949. One of the things I always wanted to do, was drive a car. Alex suggested that I learn before we were married, and so the lessons began. He was a very good and patient teacher. I took to it like a duck to water; there was not so much traffic in those days, but we were faced with horse drawn vehicles, tramcars and buses. Alex also paid for me to have ten lessons at a driving school, that cost £1 for each lesson, quite a lot of money at that time. On the day I was due to sit my driving test, Alex said, 'You pass it now or never, because I can't take another day off my work.' These words worked wonders. I passed first time.

Alex and I were married on 17 February 1951, at Jordanvale Parish Church, Whiteinch. The reception was in the Prince of Wales Halls in Sauchiehall St, Glasgow. It was cold with flurries of snow, but we were happy. The honeymoon was spent in London; our hotel was in Sloane Square. We only had one week so tried to take in as many of the famous places and buildings as we could. Every day was bright and sunny, we were so fortunate with the weather. On and off buses, learning about the extent of the Underground, it was over all too soon.

We came home to auld claes and porridge literally. We had been unable to find a home of our own. It was decided that we would live

Alex and me.

in Faither's house for the time being. While we were on our honeymoon my Dad and young brother Douglas papered and painted the upstairs; bedroom for us coming home. There was only one bedroom upstairs; Faither's bed was in the living room downstairs. As usual, in these days, it was a hole-in-the wall bed. We did have a bathroom and a kitchen, that was it. The house was rented, we paid half the rent. It was a small terrace house at 23 Victoria Park Street. When we came back from honeymoon we had to begin to put this wee house in order. We were not able to buy our own furniture because we were looking forward to having a home of our own. It was to turn out to be a few years later.

After marriage, women did not go back to work in these far off days. The days were quite long to begin with, but I soon filled in the time. The first morning home, I was up at the crack of dawn, or so it seemed, to get breakfast ready for Alex and Faither, but they had been so used to fending for themselves over the years that they said I would only be a nuisance in the morning. That was the first and only time I ever got up for them in the morning. Faither came home about 12 noon each day, and usually slept in the chair for an hour or two. Alex was home about 5.30 p.m. Dinner was always ready for him. Time was going on, the bowling club was about to open. Faither said, 'Why don't you join the bowling club, you would enjoy that.' Alex said, 'Why not.' Mrs Irvine had been a very keen bowler; her name was up on the champions board seven times. Alex himself was not interested, but had no objections to my becoming a member, so long as I did not involve him. I joined, and did enjoy it very much. I never did win the Championship, but did win the President's trophy three times in a row. Faither bought me a set of bowls, Alex bought the shoes; I was being spoiled.

Once the house was in a reasonable state, Alex and I decided to have a house-warming with a few friends from our church. Mum offered to invite Faither to their house for his tea that night, and try to keep him as long as possible so that we could have some time on our own with our friends. It was not to be; Faither came home at ten o'clock, he knew all of our visitors. He made himself comfortable, and when he had exhausted the conversation undid his tie and said, 'I'll just get ready for my bed now.' As I have explained, his bed was in the living room, so our friends had to scarper, the old devil.

As a group, we attended each other's works dances. Alex works dance was to be held in the Grosvenor Hotel in Gordon Street. There were ten of us going. It was white tie and tails for the men, evening dress for us girls. It was lovely to see so many dressed in this attire, but the men's white shirt fronts were very stiff and quite restricting. On the night of the dance it was teeming rain, dark and rather dismal. Alex went out to the car. I waited for him to tell me the car door was opened, but instead of that, he came back into the house to say he had dropped the car keys and they had gone down the drain. There was only one key in those days. He could not bend in this monkey suit. Their was only one thing to do: Alex went round to one of the group, Alastair Elliot, to see if we could go in his car. It was even smaller than our Ford; his was an Austin Seven. We had to pick up Alastair's girlfriend Christine, then we arrived at this very posh hotel in our small limousine.

Faither was quite a character. He knew I was very fond of animals. He came in from his milk run one day, had his lunch, and said to me, 'Get your coat on, we're going out.'

16 Lime Street.

'Where?'

'Never you mind, just get the coat on.' Off we went on the tramcar into town, then a bus out to a road beyond Maryhill, then we walked to a farm which had dog kennels. There he bought a wire haired fox terrier puppy for me. I had never asked or mentioned that I wanted a dog, but he thought it would be good for me to have one. He was called Dougie after my wee brother, and was a very lovely natured wee dog.

We were doing up the living room. I was contemplating papering the ceiling, it was badly needing done. Faither and I were standing in the living room and I said, more to myself than him, 'If I had a decent pair of stepladders I'd paper this ceiling myself ...'

Faither left the house, and was back about ten minutes later. He had gone into the emporium at the foot of our street and bought the highest pair of ladders he could find. I did manage to paper the ceiling. It cost quite a lot of money, because a lot of the ceiling paper was wasted, before I got the hang of it. These ladders were so high there was nowhere to store them in the house. They had to be kept outside; it was a good job they were aluminium.

We lived in Faither's house for six years. There was a mid-terrace house for sale in Lime Street just two streets away from Faither's house. Alex put a bid in for it, and I'm happy to say we got the property. We were over the moon. Alex took out a mortgage, and we waited impatiently for the move. We were looking forward to a home of our own. Prior to us moving in, Faither came round to see the house. We had two bedrooms upstairs, a good sized front room, a living room, kitchen and bathroom.

Faither came upstairs with us, looked at the small bedroom, and said, 'This wee room will do me fine.'

I replied, 'I'll be looking after you in your own home.'

'Too late,' he said, 'I have already told the factor that I was giving up the house at Victoria Park St at the end of the month. I won't be paying any more rent.' That was that. I wasn't to know I would have Faither with us for another twenty one years.

We moved into our new home in early 1957; it was a very good move and we loved it. We had furniture of our own choosing except, to please Faither, we kept his bedroom furniture which was really quite nice. Alex set about making the garden look a bit better. He planted a hedge, bought roses, laid slabs; he was no gardener, but the garden became a place one could sit in and enjoy.

We both gave our church a lot of our time. Alex became an elder. He was the convenor of the fabric committee. Every Saturday night he went to the Church and put the heating on for the Sunday services. We were still involved with the Sunday School. I became the flower convenor, arranging the flowers on a Saturday afternoon. We were both members of 'The Stage Club'. Pantomimes were produced for the Christmas season. On more than one occasion, I played the dame. There was one panto when I was the dame by the name of Aggie. I had to sing 'I've got a lovely bunch of coconuts'. Now I was not famed for my singing prowess, and the second night of the show, as I was about to sing, the pianist shouted up to me on the stage, 'It was the wash house key last night, what key would you like tonight?' I replied smartly, 'I'll have the Yale key tonight.' That seemed to get the audience laughing so we kept it in as part of the script.

Alex was also involved with the stage club, he became the stage manager. I became the producer of the three-act plays which were produced early in the spring. One of the plays was called 'Ghosts and Old Gold'. One of the cast had to wear a suit of armour. Bambers, at Charing Cross, were the theatrical people; they hired out costumes, stocked the scripts for plays and pantomimes, and all theatrical make-up came from them. The producer of the stage club was responsible for hiring and buying from them, I had ordered two suits of armour and had to pick them up on a certain day. The Grand Hotel was straight across from Bambers; it was a busy corner. I parked our wee Ford Popular outside the shop, and went in for the armour. It took a wee bit time to get it organised; two suits are a lot of metal to carry. I clattered my way out to the car, to find the biggest policeman you ever did see, leaning on the car roof.

'Is this your car madam?' His eyebrows raised slightly as I struggled to open the car door. 'Wait a minute, I'll give you a hand with that.'

'I've still some more to bring out, it's lying inside the door of the shop.'

Off he went and brought the rest of the armour, and put it in the car. He passed a remark about sending a wee buddy like me to lift all that metal. Then he said, 'I was about to book you, but your height saves you, on your way. Don't park here again.' You see, being wee is not always a drawback.

Another play we had, was 'Wild Goose Chase', I was advised by a butcher to buy a goose at the fish market at Stockwell Street. It was to be fresh, because it had to be thrown about the stage for the duration of the play, which was one week. I duly went to the fish market, and asked for a goose. The man wrung its neck in front of me and put it in a brown paper bag. I was feeling a bit queezy, about to turn into Argyle Street, when the bird in the bag went into its last throw of life. I stalled the engine of the car, no syncromesh gears in those days, and almost ran onto the pavement, but managed to steady myself up in the nick of time. People were beginning to offer help? I don't know how I managed to drive home, but got to the Church Hall with my dead goose. I was told to hang the bird by the feet, and it would keep all right for the week. That night was the dress rehearsal. I did not tell the cast that the bird was real, so they all stroked the white feathers. Eventually I had to tell the truth, and at first nobody wanted to touch the poor thing, but the play went on for the week. The butcher was right, it was in very good condition by the end of the week. The play over with no mishaps, our butcher plucked the goose, and we had it for our dinner; it tasted beautiful.

Douglas married Sheila Keatinge in 1957. Sheila's Mum sang in our Church Choir; she was also the President of the Thursday afternoon women's meeting. Isa Keatinge and husband Willie were members of the bowling club. The family union was a very happy event.

Sadly my own Dad became quite ill. He suffered from emphysema of the lungs, his breathing was very poor. He deteriorated slowly, and died in November 1958. He was much missed, by all of us. Mum was bereft, and we felt her pain. Dad was only sixty two years old. Dad and I had always been close, and I certainly missed him; a light had gone out in my life. I remember playing a bowling tie. It was the final of the championship, and I really wanted to win; I wanted to see my name on the winners' board in gold letters. Dad had come into the bowling green to watch the tie. I was well and truly beaten. As I walked off the green, dejected, Dad said, 'You didn't deserve to win that tie, the other lady played better. You took it for granted that you would win, you can't do that, you were not good enough. Keep trying, your day will come.' I never did win the championship.

One Thursday night sitting at our dinner, Faither asked me if I was going to be out on the Friday at two o'clock. 'Why?' was the question. Faither said, 'Never mind, but you need to be in.' I knew he was up to something, but there was no use trying to find out; he had another secret. Friday came, two o'clock, a big van drew up at the door. I could not believe what came out of the back of that van. It was a beautiful piano. The problem was, not one of us could play it. I asked Faither, why he had bought this lovely instrument when there was no one could play it. His answer was that a front room was not a proper front room without a piano.

Alex and I had a very happy marriage, except we were not blessed with children. That would have been the icing on the cake, but it was not to be. My young brother Douglas and his wife Sheila had two sons, Graham and Crawford. From the time they were babies I was privileged to look after them one day a week; that was lovely for us. As the boys grew up, they looked on our home as their second home. It was a great joy to watch them develop into quite different characters. They were always very good chums. Graham was the quiet one, Crawford the mischievous one. Going into church one Sunday, one of the teachers came to me and said, 'Your Graham has swallowed his collection threepence piece,' I said that it would not be Graham, it would be Crawford. I went into the Sunday School, went straight to Crawford and asked to see his offering. He immediately took the coin out of his pocket, I had been wrong. Graham shouted, 'It's me Auntie Effie.' Sheila and I took Graham to Oakbank, the Sick Children's hospital at that time. They x-rayed him and saw the coin, and kept him in overnight. The outcome was, we just had to wait till the coin passed through him. I think Sheila still has that threepenny bit.

The boys were both members of the Junior Brigade in the Church, They had a football team. Crawford asked me and his mum to come on the Saturday morning and watch the match. Crawford was very small and the football strip was too big for him. Graham was also in the team, but he was able to get a kick of the ball. Wee Crawford ran his heart out but to no avail. The rain was making things very difficult. Half time came, the players all got a bit of orange, then it was back to the game. All of a sudden the wee bedraggled figure of Crawford came off the pitch, looked up at his Mum and said, 'Let's go home.' His mum replied, 'The game's not finished yet.'

'No, but I am.' That was it, we took him home and put him in the bath.

Sunday by Sunday we attended the church. I sat in the Irvine pew, Alex was a member of the choir. Rev. John Graham was our minister. It was the Sunday of Communion, always very special for me. At the end of the service Rev. John leaned over the pulpit and said, 'Jesus Christ has done all this for you, what are you prepared to do for Him?' For me, these words hit me like a sledge hammer. I had always been a follower of Jesus, but I realised at that moment that I was totally involved because I liked it. It was a way of life for me. On that Communion Sunday my Christian outlook changed. I had a word with Rev. John after the service, asking him what I could do to alter my way of service. He replied that I should let it be, I had been called to a different kind of service, time would tell what it is to be. He also said, 'God will claim you in His own time.' How true that was to be. In the meantime, it had got round the congregation that Effie Irvine had gone religious. The secretary of the afternoon women's meeting asked me to speak at one of their meetings. What could I talk about? Just tell them about the experience you had in Church on Communion Sunday. I don't remember much about that talk, but a few weeks later, I was stopped in the street by a stranger who asked me if I was Effie Irvine.

'Yes I am,'

'Could you come and speak at our women's meeting at the Wesleyan Methodist Church in Partick?' I told her that I did not go out speaking. Her quick reply was that I had done it at Jordanvale and I could use the same talk at her Church. I accepted. The speaking engagements snowballed. Sheila's mother Isa Keatinge was a very lovely singer. She offered to go with me on these engagements and it was a great help. Isa sang before I spoke and after I finished. It worked perfectly well.

I realised if I were to be doing this kind of speaking, which involved a gospel message, I'd need to be educated. I said to Alex at dinner one night. 'I think I'll study for a Higher English.

'What are you going to do with it,'

'We will see if I am clever enough to get it first.

I wrote away to London University to be accepted for a correspondence course, taking English, English Literature, Geography, and an A level in Religious Knowledge. That was the beginning of the long road to fulltime service in the Name of Jesus.

Eventually I did get the qualifications. It took a long time, but despite the setbacks, and there were many, I entered the University of Glasgow on 3 October 1967. Professor William Barclay had opened the door. It was the first time in the history of the University that a BD would become a first degree, before this time one had to have a prior degree first MA or BA.

Chapter Five

The day of "Matriculation" came all too soon, I was not ready. Alex had left at 7.15 a.m. for work He put his arms round me, a big hug, a wee kiss, and he was off. His parting shot was, "Don't worry, you'll be fine.' Mum was up and about; she was going to be the cook for the family, that eased my mind. Mum was a very good old fashioned cook. Mince and stew, soup, apple tarts, coffee buns, clootie dumplings and sultana cakes. My father-in-law, better known in the family circle as 'Faither' would walk the dog, big Dougie the labrador. We had all accepted a completely new situation, support was there for me; all I had to do was get this BD degree.

First lecture was to be Scottish History at 9 a.m. I walked out the door of 16 Lime Street at 8 a.m. The black brief-case stood out like a sore thumb, I was conscious of its newness and hoped no one would see me setting off. Any bus would take me to the University, but this time I needed to walk up the hill, that's why I had left home so early.

Happy to relate, the wait at the bus stop was short. I climbed aboard. There were very few people downstairs, and no one I knew. Much relieved, the tension eased a bit, but as I sat down, the nerves began to jangle again. The corporation buses in those days did not have doors at the front. You entered at the back of the bus on to a platform. If the bus was busy, the clippie (female conductress) would advise you upstairs only. It was always the right thing to obey the clippie. That morning, for me, with the brief-case, the steel corset and the nerves, it was safer to be just inside the door. There would be no hassle getting off the bus later on. As we travelled through Whiteinch, to Partick, then Partick Cross all the old familiar places of my childhood days flashed before me. I could have gone blindfold to my destination. My bus stop was just beyond the University gate.

Excitement was rising. There were quite a number of folk heading up to University Avenue. I guessed that most of them would be students. There were very few of them older than myself. Reaching the environs of the University, there were even more folk crowding the Avenue. I never realised there would be so many students in the halls of learning. How young they looked, full of confidence; some of them would be going into their second, third or even their final year.

Back to the gateman who had directed me to Dumbarton Road in September. 'Could you point me in the direction of the Faculty of Arts, please.'

'Over the road, you will find it easy enough.' I did find it easy, I more or less followed the crowd. On reaching the lecture room, I was asked for my name, full name. Euphemia H C Irvine. 'You are one of the divines.' 'Thats what BD students were called. The desk person spoke again, 'There is another BD student over there, there will only be two of you in this class.' Sure enough, there were only the two of us, the other one was called Eric Lacey.

We seemed to hit it off right away. Eric was a bit younger than me, but still a mature student. He and his wife were giving up quite a lot financially so that Eric could study for the Ministry. The great thing about Eric, he was a taxi driver, very handy. He gave me a lift to the bus stop when I needed help. We were also the only divines in the Logic class.

The class of Scottish history, we discovered, numbered over two hundred students. Both Eric and I felt a wee bit in the minority. It was a very different atmosphere from schooldays. The lecturer entered the room, and walked to what could only be called a dais with a high desk. He lectured for an hour, and walked back to the door. That was it, no conversation. We were supposed to take notes; if you could write in shorthand, things would have been easier. Class over, we left our desks, and on the way out we were handed a list of required reading. The Logic class was at eleven o'clock. We had time to gather our wits about us, have a cup of tea. We presented ourselves at ten forty five and registered together. The Logic class was exactly the same format, the only difference being that there were less than a hundred in this class. We listened again for an hour, trying frantically to keep up with the lecturer; frankly, we did not understand the logic of it.

At twelve noon, Eric drove us over to Trinity College, at Park Circus, to register for our Greek class. We discovered that there would be twenty six students in our year: twenty four men and two women. Sixteen were studying for a BD degree. Five were studying for an Licentiate of Theology which was a church diploma, and five were mature students. The BD students had to study Hebrew and Greek, the Licentiate of Theology students had to study Greek; the mature students did not require the languages: for entrance they had to be over forty with one university degree, an MA or BSc. I was very glad that Professor Barclay had guided me to the BD degree; it was a tough assignment but well worth the study. We attended our first Greek class that afternoon. It seemed like double dutch to most of us.

The boys in our year were all very courteous and kindly. After our lecture, we were shown round Trinity College, especially the library where we were expected to spend some time studying. Four o'clock came, we all moved off in different directions. Eric gave me a lift to the bus stop. Again we were given a book list. A Greek New Testament was a priority, and a Greek dictionary. The bus home seemed to take an age, it had been a long day. I was just a wee bit tired.

Mum was busy in the kitchen; she was preparing our dinner. Alex would be home about five thirty. Mum was anxious to hear how the first day had been. Would I be able to manage? All I could tell her was I'd do my best. She was afraid from the word go that my health would suffer; after all I was wearing a steel corset. Sleep did not come easily that night. Mum's words kept coming into my mind; the problem was, she could be right.

Alex arrived home, and laughed when he saw what was in the brief-case, three notebooks, one for each lecture, plus a list of required reading. We had dinner then out with the dog. It was getting dark. Alex told me on that walk, 'I'll back you all the way, I think this is meant to happen. Don't worry about anything, just get on with the studying,' and then the gem of wisdom, 'It's only four years.' Alex was my greatest support, he never did let me down, and I realise, looking back over that time, I could never have attained that degree without his constant help. He was my anchor over the years.

We were able to buy some of our books in Trinity College book shop. Alex paid for most of them. The expensive books he covered with clear plastic film. I still have some of these books; the plastic covers have lasted over thirty years. Alex would say, 'If it's worth doing, it's worth doing well.'

Home life was made easy for me, our wee family seemed to draw together in a common cause. I still did washing, ironing, hoovering and dusting. The Church was still the focal point of life. It was amazing how many of our church friends reacted positively. Genuine encouragement and a caring concern was there for me. I was forever getting notebooks and pens as wee gifts, I even got a rubber. On the other side, I was aware of some derision. 'Big-headed, she will come down to earth with a bang.' Somehow, it didn't bother me, I was too busy working my way through the mountain of material lying before me.

I had been a Sunday School teacher for twenty four years, beginning when I was fifteen, the last four years of that time as SS Superintendent. Our very wise Minister Rev. Ken Bethune advised me to resign every-thing that would come between me and study. The first resignation was the Sunday School. I was producer of our Stage Club, three act plays were our forte. I did enjoy that club, it was good fun. It had to go. Church flower convenor was next on the list. That entailed arranging the flowers each Sunday for the Church Service. Don't get me wrong, I did not arrange the flowers because I was good at it, but because there was no one else who wanted the job. Another resignation as treasurer of the Womans' Guild. Time was of the essence, and believe it or not, all these voluntary occupations were immediately filled, which brought me a great deal of comfort and relief. I was also a member of Victoria Park Bowling Club. The bowls were sold, the shoes binned. The decks were cleared. It was to be a totally different life-style.

The first week at University was a bit of a nightmare. Lectures had to be written as quickly as possible, lecturers very seldom repeated themselves. Read the books, read the books. You will get some of them in the library. That was a laugh, especially history books; there were not enough of them to go round. Buying the books was the best option. Trying to get your mind to switch from History, to Logic, to Greek was a minefield, but as the days went by I began to settle to a new way of life.

I was happy to reach Trinity College each day after the noise and bustle of the University classes. Trinity was more peaceful. Some of our students were young enough to be my sons. There were four mature students who were older. One was called Adam, you could not get older than that. To begin with, the boys called me Mrs Irvine, then Euphemia, then Effie, and when it reached 'hi you' I knew I had become one of the boys.

The schedule for a day ran something like this. University at 9 a.m. for History class, Logic at 11 a.m., lunch at Trinity, where Professors, lecturers and students very often had lunch together. Afternoon Greek, then into the library, a very peaceful place to be and an opportunity to go over the day's scribbling before it escaped from your mind. I usually left Trinity about 4 p.m. Dinner at 5.30 p.m., began studying about 6.30 p.m. till 10 p.m. Then Alex would shout, 'Walkies!' That was not just for Dougie, it was also for me. On these walks we had an opportunity to talk over the day's events, then came some supper, and back to the desk, very often till midnight. That was the pattern, Monday till Thursday. Friday evening we either had friends visit or we went out. Saturday I worked in the afternoon, but not in the evening unless I was behind with the reading. Sunday was church time, no study except when I was pushed for time.

We had class exams to sit within three months of our first lectures. The first time we had to present ourselves for a class exam, Scottish history was the subject. I had not sat an exam since 1938 in a class of about thirty. Now we were faced with over two hundred students milling about outside the lecture room waiting for permission to enter. Five minutes to go, the door opened, we all trooped in. Once inside and we settled down, we were allowed to turn over the paper and read the questions. Then the voice from the front of the class, the invigilator, said, 'Begin.'

I couldn't hold the pen. There were ten questions, we had to answer five. It took me another five minutes to compose myself. I don't remember the questions. The Logic exam was next, it was even more difficult. On leaving the exam room there was the feeling of despair. At the end of the day there was enough information on my two class exam papers to give me very low pass marks on both subjects, but I was advised in red ink on both occasions to put more material into the answers.

Strange as it may seem, I did get a good pass mark in my entrance Greek. I still have the pass ticket. That result was due to Rev. K. Bethune who tutored me for the Greek exam. The fear of failure was always there, in the back of my mind. I had passed, but by the skin of my teeth.

Of course the time came in April 1968 when we had to sit the degree exams which would enable us to enter our first year at Trinity College. I was not looking forward to sitting History and Logic. When the results came through I had failed both; depression set in. The doubters were right. I had worked hard, it was futile, a time wasting exercise. Alex, of course, in his own quiet way tried to reassure me. Give yourself a chance, the resits are in September.

That year, some of our class attended the General Assembly of the

Church of Scotland in late May. I was still trying to come to terms with failure. There was the students' gallery; we sat together, commiserating with one another, I was not the only one to fail, that did help a wee bit. On that particular day, the ministers and elders were debating 'women in the Ministry'. Valid arguments were put forward, for and against. Discussion on this matter had been sent down to Presbyteries; they had already voted 47 in favour and 17 against. Despite this majority decision strong opposition was still being expressed. For example, in Life and Work for July 1968, a letter from a female reader in Glasgow stated: 'The General Assembly has now decided that women may enter the Ministry. I am disgusted to hear this and now have no wish to join the Church of Scotland as a member, nor do I ever have the intention of listening to women "preach" or speak in Church.' In May 1968 The General Assembly announced that "with the consent of a majority of Presbyteries ... women shall be eligible for ordination to the Holy Ministry of Word and Sacrament on the same terms and conditions as are at present applicable to men.' I knew instantly. It's the Ministry for me. Excitement was high, then I remembered: the exams were a disaster, two resits in September? What to do? Professor Barclay would be the one to speak to, and a decision was made: I'd try to see him tomorrow ...

I arrived at Trinity College at 8.30 in the morning; the Professor was always at his desk early in the morning. I knocked at the door, and was about to move when the door opened. Before I could say a word, he said, with a twinkle in his eye, 'It's the Ministry, I expected you to come.'

I said, 'I've failed History and Logic, the resits are in September.'

'I know, I know.' That kindly gruff voice. 'You got the Greek, you will manage the resits,' that was that. If he thought I could do it, it just had to be done.

September came, I swotted all summer, sat the resits, and passed both. Strangely enough, I never did fail another exam. Was my call valid? I believed it was. In the meantime, I was advised to seek acceptance for entry into the Parish Ministry. All students for the Ministry had to pass through a Selection School. Two days of rigorous testing. There were eighteen of us at that school, and we were interviewed, first by two ministers. Why did we wish to enter the Parish Ministry? What was our church background? They actually tried to put us off. Then two psychologists took us back to our childhood. They were trying to find out if we were stable characters. These two made me feel a bit edgy. We were interviewed one at a time. We were then each presented with a letter to write. My letter was to be sent to a family who were very good members, but had had an altercation with their elder. The idea was to bring both sides together, trying to keep both parties as members of the congregation. Quite a difficult letter to write. Next was to be the Moderator of a Kirk Session, with a difficult debate to tackle, difficult, because very few of us had ever been at a Kirk Session meeting.

While we were having our meals at the Selection School, and while we were interacting with one another, the ministers and psychologists were, in a sense, analysing our personalities. Before we left the selection school, the chairman interviewed us, again, one at a time. He advised us that we would have to wait at least ten days before we would know whether or not we had been accepted for the Parish Ministry. He also advised us that we would not be told why we were not being accepted. If we failed we were at liberty to try again.

My letter arrived, It just said, 'You have not been accepted for entrance into the Parish Ministry. You may try again in the future.' I was devastated, humiliated, knocked back once again. What would the family say, what would Alex say? How do you tell your family and friends when they are doing all they can to help you? How do you tell them, you are a failure yet again. Not accepted. What about Professor Barclay?

I was about to find out. My next year was the first in divinity proper. We had to present ourselves before Professor Barclay. My turn came, I felt the usual coldness inside. The great man looked up from his desk.

'Effie, you passed the resits, you managed the Greek, good, good.'

'Yes, but I have been turned down by the Selection School.'

He looked at me, there was a challenge in the look. 'Are you going to give up now?'

My reply was one word, 'Never.'

The Professor seemed satisfied, so was I. As I walked away from his desk, I thought to myself, You will make it, because that man thinks you'll make it, and you will not let him down. The other thought that was always with me: I still believed God called me to serve Him against all the odds.

The following Saturday Alex took me into town. 'Where are we going?'

'Just be patient, we are going to pick up something you need.'

He took me to a car salesroom. We went in; it was obvious that Alex and the salesman had met before. It turned out that Alex had been there the week before and bought a white Vauxhall Viva, for the princely sum of £150.

'What a lovely surprise.'

'It's yours, this will make life a bit easier for you, even for the weekly shopping,'

It was old, but adequate. I loved that wee car; it was a bit temperamental at times, but Alex was able to keep it on the road. He had served his time as a motor mechanic. Another good thing happened, I had applied for a grant, and it came through that week also; the money from that was to cover the cost of my books. The Selection School had turned me down, but the pointers were, carry on.

Trinity College was three years of hard work, but it was one of the greatest experiences of my life. All of us on the BD course were struggling, except for a few bright lads and Sheena Montgomerie, the only other female in the class of twenty six. We discovered we were the first class to study for this first BD degree. Our curiculum was Old Testament and Hebrew, New Testament and Greek, Systematic Theology, Ecclesiastical History, and Pastoral Theology. One Bible exam each year. Elocution, Psychology plus an essay of 2,000 words on a Saint of your own choice. I chose St Francis of Asissi. Let it be said at this point, we were the only class ever to do this particular course. The amount of study and work was reduced for the students coming after us.

We had an old Professor of Ecclesiastical History, who had been a missionary in China for a number of years. When we got a wee bit tired of the history lecture, one of the boys would ask a question about China, and the old Professor would respond. We learned a great deal about China, it was most interesting. The Professor would suddenly remember, history, history, we were then back to reality. Professor Barclay entering the lecture room, while moving to the podium would be fiddling with his hearing aid. As often as not he would say, 'I'll just turn this thing off, I've heard it all before.' He was straight and to the point, no words wasted at lecture time; your pen had to move fast, so had your brain. The one hour's lecture was over all too quickly. He would say, 'Put your Bibles away, get out your "Nestles".' No not "chocolate". Your "Nestles" was the Greek New Testament. Professor

Barclay preferred to teach from the Greek. He was known by all his students as Prof. Willie. I think he was aware of that and quietly enjoyed the knowledge. He was much respected by all his students, and was always available when a student needed help.

Professor Barclay told every student class this story. He had been ordained and inducted to a charge in Renfrew. He was visiting in his Parish one day. The old lady and the Rev. were having a very interesting conversation. The old buddy said, 'Could I be honest with you, minister?'

'Yes,' said the Rev., 'of course you can.'

'Well,' she said, 'how is it I can understand what you're talking about sitting here, but I cannot get the gist of what you're saying when you're in the pulpit?'

That conversation was to change Professor Barclay's life. The theological words were changed to ordinary language, so that everyone would understand. That's why he was such a wonderful teacher. The great communicator of the Gospel of Jesus Christ. He wanted to instill in his students the need to be down to earth. Of course he was the same on television, and his books have sold millions of copies, all over the world.

The other advice Professor Barclay gave sticks in my mind. When we were about to sit our degree exams at the end of our first divinity year, he came into the lecture room, walked to the podium, leaned over the desk, stared at us for a minute, and said, "Don't think you can sit these exams and pass if you have not done the work prescribed. Praying will not be a replacement for study, pray only to remain calm. Take one question at a time, forget the others, one question only, deal with it, then look for the next one.' A very wise man was Professor Barclay.

The Rev. Professor Murdo Ewan MacDonald, Pastoral Theology said, 'When, and if, you do become ministers, when you are preaching of a Sunday, if you don't strike oil in ten minutes, stop boring.'

We began our third year at University, our second at Trinity, in October 1969. It was to be an eventful year. This was make or break time. We were a very close-knit class; there was also a great deal of banter and fun. We did quite a lot of studying together. It helped greatly to share with one another, especially Systematic Theology. We were all aware of just how difficult the future exams were going to be. Even the cleverest ones of the class were a wee bit anxious.

My study pattern never changed. The days flew in, Christmas was on us before we knew it, and once January 1970 came, there was little time left before the degree exams were before us again. This time the burden was even greater than ever before. The pass mark for the BD degree was 60% for every subject. There were three exams of six hours each: Old Testament and Hebrew, New Testament and Greek, and Systematic Theology. The other two subjects, Pastoral Theology and Ecclesiastical History, were the usual three hours. It seemed like a mountain to climb. The exams were to be over a period of three weeks. The last subject and the one we thought was the most difficult, Old Testament and Hebrew, was to be tackled at the end of the third week. They certainly believed in keeping us on edge to the bitter end. On the night before this very important exam, I was just about beat. Dead in the water, as one would say. At 8 p.m. I'd had enough. I closed the books, went through to the living room and told Alex I would not be going in to sit the exam in the morning; I did not have a hope of passing, and anyway I could do a resit later on in the year. He was not amused.

'After all the work you have done, night and day you have studied, to give it all up now? Lets go for a walk.'

The usual pattern was followed, walkies with the big labrador. I knew what was coming, all the reasons for sitting the exam at the right time were put before me; I gave in and promised to go in the next day.

We were all outside the exam room, not very enthusiastic, but this was the last exam of the year. I think apprehension was the name of the game for all of us. The door opened, this was it. 'You may turn over the paper.' I could not believe my eyes. I could have answered any question on that paper, it was a dream paper for me. Ten questions, answer any five. I chose to do the Hebrew paper first, then the English. The three hours went like lightning, then we trooped out for some fresh air and some lunch. We had to be back for 2 p.m. I was desperate to get back to the exam room to begin again. Into the room, dead on 2 p.m. I was feeling a bit more at ease. I reckoned I'd done all right in the morning. 'Turn your paper over.' It was a disaster, there was not one question there I thought I could answer. Panic, what to do? Keep calm, Professor Barclay said, 'Just one question at a time.' That's exactly what I did. The exam was due to finish at 5 p.m., at 4 p.m. I had nothing more to add. I gathered my papers together and gave them to the invigilator, who was one of our lecturers.

He said, 'Effie, you still have one hour to go; if you go back to your seat now, I'll forget you ever left it.'

I replied, 'If I sat there for a whole day, I could not do any more.'

He accepted the papers, and I walked out the door, escape was essential. I could not go home too early. I wandered about for a while, then made my way home. I did not tell the family, it might have upset them; they would know soon enough when I failed.

The results would not be available till May, it was a long wait. Could I possibly have passed? then I thought, no chance, So I brought the books back out and tried to study, but it was no use, it had been a long winter and I was very tired.

The great day arrived; we had to be at the University at 2 p.m., that's when the results of all our hard studying were due to be presented. As usual they were late, and it was all of two hours before the officer came out to pin the results to the board. When I was able to get near enough to see, I discovered that my name was registered five times; in spite of all that had happened I had passed the lot in one go. No resits at all. There are no words in the English dictionary that could possibly explain how I felt. Maybe sheer bliss. There was no study on that night, and for many nights to come. The family were delighted. Alex said, 'I told you so, it's meant to happen, relax, get your breath back, you will prove the doubters wrong.' I never did tell Alex that I had left the OT exam early; there was no need.

The next thing I had to do was to find a minister who would accept me for an assistantship. The Rev. James Aitchison of Broomhill Church was looking for an assistant. I phoned him.

'I hear you are looking for an assistant, how would you like to take me, the name's Euphemia.'

There was silence at the other end of the phone, then the voice said, 'I'd need to ask my Kirk Session about that, I'll phone you.'

I thought, that's the end of that. But I was wrong, Rev. Jim phoned me at the end of the week to say that the Kirk Session had said yes, come and have coffee and we will talk about it. We met, and I was accepted by the Rev. Jim to be his assistant. He went home and told his wife and two daughters, 'We will be having an assistant at Broomhill, beginning Sunday first. She is five feet eight, a willowy blonde, 36–24–36.' There was consternation in the manse, till I walked into church on the Sunday, all of four feet ten inches in my stocking soles.

The next thing was the Selection School. Said the Pastoral Theology

Professor, 'Now is the time to return, you have passed all your exams.' Back I went, through all the rigmarole again, then had to wait another ten days … I was sitting in the library of Trinity College, preparing some work. Our librarian, who was a very gentle character, Dr Mechie, came to my desk and whispered in my ear, "Just to let you know, the Selection School have accepted you for the Parish Ministry. You will get official word soon. I thought it would be good for you to know now." I did get official word very soon after that. I then got a letter from the Committee on Education for the Ministry. The letter read, and I quote, "I am glad to be able to inform you that the Central Selection Board has agreed that you should be accepted as a candidate for the Ministry subject to your nomination by the Presbytery of Glasgow.' Another hurdle still to be got over.

I petitioned the Presbytery of Glasgow and was cited to appear before their Education for the Ministry Committee. It was a kind of awesome gathering. Many questions were asked of me. Then one older minister, the Rev. Dr John Kent, asked a very relevant question. He was sitting at the front of the committee, I was facing him. The question was, 'Effie, why did you decide to go back to the Selection School?'

I replied, 'Because I believed, and still do, that my call was greater than the Selection School, and I decided to keep knocking the door till they let me in.'

Dr Kent turned round and faced this august body of presbyters and said, 'Do you not think, gentlemen, it would be better to accept Effie now, to save her from the trouble of knocking our door again.'

They stamped their feet. I was advised that I was accepted. It was hard to contain my excitement. The convenor was still speaking,

'When you have completed your BD and graduated next year, you will be taken on trials for Licence, for the Parish Ministry of the Church of Scotland.'

It was music to my ears, I wanted to shout, 'Eureka!' but I managed to stop in time. There were many congratulations, I thanked the committee. I was aware that some of the committee were none too happy. It did not matter. I had an assistantship, was accepted to be a minister, had passed all my exams and was heading for my Final Year. Not bad for a potential failure.

Chapter Six

I enjoyed being at Broomhill Church, the Rev. Jim was quite a character. At one time he had played cricket for Scotland. I learned a great deal from Jim. Visiting was very important to him, and he passed the necessity for visiting on to me. He would say, 'People are very important, ministry is communication, not just in the pulpit.' I was given a list of members to visit. It was lovely to ring a door bell and get an invitation to enter someone's home. If I had taken cups of tea in every house I entered, plus the home baking, I would have been four feet square. Jim had warned me of the dangers and the congregation had been well trained. Usually the last visit was the time to accept the offer of a wee cup of tea.

While at Broomhill I entered my final year on 8 October 1970. Each student had to choose a subject to be studied at a higher level and had to ask the Professor of the subject chosen to be accepted by him to study for that year. I had received a second class certificate for Hebrew in my last exams, so decided to do Old Testament and Hebrew for my finals. Professor Mauchline was the man involved. I approached this austere, tall individual.

'Sir would you accept me to do my finals in Hebrew and Old Testament?'

'Certainly,' was the reply; that was all right till I heard I was the only one in the class who had contemplated that subject.

I went back to the Professor, and said to him, 'Because I seem to be the only one who wishes to do OT studies I don't mind if I have to choose some other subject.'

Professor Mauchline would have none of it. 'We will study together, we will probably learn something from each another.' These words from this erudite Professor helped to put me at ease. 'We will have three morning sessions per week, how will that suit you? 'If we get a bit behind we can come to some other arrangement.'

The other compulsory subjects for the final year were New Testament and Greek, plus Systematic Theology. We needed good pass marks on all our subjects to obtain that BD degree. It was quite a change to study in a class of one. To begin with I felt very strange sitting at a huge round table, Professor Mauchline sitting with his back to the window, and me with my back to the door. I enjoyed my OT studies especially the Book of Jeremiah, and when Jim asked me to preach, he said he was aware that Jeremiah had become a favourite of mine. Then there was Job, Ecclesiastes, etc, My time spent studying with Professor Mauchline turned out to be very valuable indeed. I celebrated communion at Broomhill Church sitting at the right of the Rev. Jim, and assisted in the dispensing of the Sacraments; it was a lovely experience. Advent and Christmas were also much appreciated. After the turn of the year, we were back to studying all the hours possible. Rev. Jim waived the visiting, he told me to concentrate on the books. We sat our finals in March, 1971. Time was moving on, Jim gave me a bit more visiting to do, he thought it better to keep my mind occupied while we waited for our results; he was right.

The day our results were to be posted on the notice board, again they were expected to be available at 2 p.m. It passed, 3 p.m. passed; it was after 4 p.m. when we spotted Professor Barclay crossing the quadrangle of the University, his gown, green with age and blowing in the wind. As he came towards me, he drew the gown round his body, and stopped long enough to tell me. He said, 'Don't worry, wee one, you have passed, I always knew you would.'

I waited for the results to go up, I wanted to see them there for myself in print. The BSc results were to be up on the same board. The officer came out with his bundles of papers, and pinned them to the board. I couldn't see a thing, so I scrambled through the group, almost on my hands and knees. I bounced up in front of the other students, and saw the name three times on the board with BD at each subject. I felt ten feet tall, my thoughts went back to my first selection school.

Alex and I had a very good minister friend, and wife. We had met many years before when we were involved with Seaside Mission work. When he became a minister, we remained friends and visited them in their first island charge. We always got on very well together. He had hospitality in our home when he came down to Glasgow. He was called to a church in Glasgow, and Alex helped in their new manse with carpet laying etc. The friendship remained solid until I went to the Selection School for the first time. He was one of the ministers on that board. After I had been rejected by the Selection School for the first time, Alex and I were invited to his manse for dinner. We had no car at that time, but I went by bus and Alex went straight from work. They seemed eager to see us. When I arrived at the manse only the wife was there; I presumed that the minister was out in his parish. I did sense a dryness from the wife, but assumed she was just a busy minister's wife. We had some small talk as she prepared the meal. Alex arrived, the meal was ready. To my surprise, the minister appeared from his study; he had not given me the courtesy of saying hello when I had arrived. Again there was some small talk at the dinner table, not the usual banter of friends. I was to find out very soon why we were asked for a meal.

The meal over, we went into the lounge. The minister said he had asked us over to try and put me off this stupid idea of becoming a minister. It was going against the will of God, and against the scriptures. The harangue went on for a long time; he was really very uptight about this. I reminded him that Alex had no car, and we would really need to get home.

'Don't worry about getting home, when I've convinced you of the error of your ways, I will run you home.'

Alex never said a word throughout the speech; I only asked the minister one question. 'Do you presume to know the mind and the will of God?'

This supposed man of God, said that if he had the opportunity no woman would ever get through a Selection School.

We rose to go, I had had enough, it was almost midnight. I turned and thanked his wife for a lovely meal, but said the after dinner speech had not changed my mind. It was then I discovered that his wife was in full agreement with her minister husband. Then this so called Christian minister said, 'We don't need to worry, anyway, you will never pass the exams.' We left in his car, there was silence on the way home, we arrived at 16 Lime St. We said goodbye, he drove off.

As we went into our home, Alex said, You know what you have to do, prove the man wrong.' That was the end of a beautiful friendship, they never contacted us again, not even when Alex died. But I was very happy. Remembering the words of Alex when he said, 'You know what you have to do, prove the man wrong.' Glad to say, I did just that.

I rushed home as fast as the traffic would allow. Mum was the first to know the results; she was in tears, she was at a loss for words, 'it's a wonderful day, I am so proud of you, do you mind if I phone so and so, and so and so, because I don't think they believed you could do it.'

The phone was red hot that night. Mothers are like that. Mum had been a great help in the last year of my studies; she used to hold the English Bible while I translated from the Hebrew script, and took great delight in correcting me when I was wrong. Faither was the next in the door. 'Well?' was the question.

'The BD is a reality, graduation will be in June.'

'Is there anything you need for that.'

'Yes,' I said, 'a gown for graduation.'

'I'll buy it for you, just go tomorrow and get it.' This I did and still have it today.

Alex was last to hear the good news. He said, 'I knew you would do it, looking back I can see the pattern and I've no doubt you will finish the course. Is there anything you need?'

'Yes,' and before I could answer, he said, 'A new dress for graduation.'

'How did you know?'

'I was thinking about it on the way home on the bus,' said the bold boy.

Our class graduated on Saturday 10 June 1971. My university hood was a gift from the good folk of Broomhill Church; it's a bit old now but I still wear it with pride. That day I received my University of Glasgow card No. 64868. Capped and knackered. What a feeling of elation. There was sadness too, my Dad was missing. He had died in 1958. Mum said to me that day, 'Your Dad would have been a very proud man today, but he will know,' I believed that myself.

Graduation over, Alex had arranged for me to have a photograph taken at a studio in Partick. Later on he said, 'Just keep the white dress on, we are going for a meal to celebrate.' The question was where. 'It's a secret.' It was a lovely surprise; Alex had booked a table at the Buchanan Arms Hotel in Drymen. Mum and Faither were delighted. It was a great joy to sit down at table knowing I could really relax. All the hard work was over, or so I thought.

I was leaving Broomhill Church in July. I felt very sad about that. The congregation had been very good to me, very supportive over the nine months I had been with them. I was wishing I could have stayed under the guidance of the Rev. Jim. It was not to be. Every potential candidate for the Ministry had to do what is called a probationary year with another minister. It's part of the training for the Ministry. Most of our year had already been placed in their various churches. What happened was that the Pastoral Theology Professor gave the student the name of a minister who was able to accept a probationer. The student had then to set up a meeting with the minister named. I got the name of my potential bishop, that's what we called our teacher. I made arrangements to meet with my bishop, and went to his manse. Let it be said, I knew the man; he had been a leader on one of the Seaside Mission teams Alex and I had served on. I arrived at his manse. 'Come in Effie,' he said, not unkindly. 'I can't take you as my probationer because I don't approve of women in the Ministry. It would not be fair to you, it would be better if you got someone who would have no hangups about the situation. I agreed, we had a cup of tea but at least he was honest and friendly.

Back to the Pastoral Theology Professor to tell him I was turned down. He gave me the name of another minister. I phoned, was invited for a cup of tea. He sounded quite interested on the phone, so I went with high hopes. We had our cup of tea and a wee chat. His church was beside the manse, he offered to let me see the church. I was sure this was it. He did say that he would have to speak to his Kirk Session about it. I left quite uplifted. He phoned two days later to say that the Kirk Session were not very positive; my age was against me, and I was a woman.

On the following Sunday I had to preach my Trials for Licence, which meant I had to go to a strange church and conduct the service. The minister of the church plus two elders would listen and decide whether or not the candidate was of suitable material. I was sent to St John's Renfield Church, off Great Western Road. The minister there was the Rev. James Simpson. I could not have been sent to a more caring individual. After the service, the Rev. James advised me that they would be puting in a good report to the Prebytery. He did not have to tell me there and then, but I was very grateful for the knowledge that I had passed the test.

That Sunday evening I was to be preaching in Broomhill Church. When I went into the vestry that evening, Rev. Jim said that a man had been on the phone about me that afternoon. It was the minister of Renfield St Stephen's Church in Bath St in Glasgow. 'Phone him when you get home tonight.'

My quick reply was, 'Not likely, I've been turned down twice already. If God wants me to be a minister, He will have a place for me. If this Mr Gillon wants me, he can come and get me.

Rev. Jim laughed, and we went into church. Jim conducted the service, the Sermon was mine. At the close of the service we made for the door. I was leading the way, but when the door was reached, Jim was no longer behind me. The congregation in their usual kindly manner shook hands and thanked me. I moved back into the church. Jim was speaking to another man, they were looking up at the lights, I thought, an electrician. I reached the two men. The visitor was certainly not an electrician, he was wearing a Trinity College tie. Rev. Jim said, 'This is the Rev. Campbell Gillon of Renfield St Stephen's Church, Bath St. I'll leave you two together.' Jim winked at me and left.

The Rev. Campbell Gillon turned to me and asked me if I would be interested in his church.

I said, 'I certainly would be.'

'If you are really interested, I would like to have you as our probationer this year.'

He waited for an answer. I just could not believe it. Trials for Licence in the morning and accepted, offered a place for my probationary year in the evening, what more could anyone want?

'Yes of course I will come to Renfield St Stephen's.' 'Right, we will meet tomorrow morning at the church offices at 10.30 a.m. and we will set it up.'

Then he thanked me for the sermon, and left. What an opportunity, just about the last student to be settled for the probationary year. That Sunday had been a very good day.

There were many in the ministry who were against the ordination of women. Yet I was richly blessed in the ministers who were my mentors all the way through University, through my training: men of vision, dedicated, ready to welcome a woman who had the fixed notion in her head that God had called her to full time service in the church. The Rev. Campbell Gillon was no exception. From the word go we certainly enjoyed working with each other, and he had a lot to teach me.

In June of that year 1971 we were licensed to preach the Gospel in Glasgow Cathedral. There were thirteen of us, twelve men and me. When students were licensed, the service was held within their own

Presbytery bounds. Only thirteen of our students were of the Presbytery of Glasgow. We all tried to attend each other's services. The Moderator of the Presbytery that year was the Rev. Jack Stewart, of Colston Milton Church, again a very caring individual. Each student was presented with a Bible of their own choice; the Moderator came down from the pulpit, and passed along the line of licentiates, presented each one with their Bible, laid his hand on each head, and gave a blessing and a special scripture sentence that was his choice. I was last in line; he chose for me these words from the Gospel of St John 11:28 Martha called her sister Mary and told her, "Jesus is here, and is asking for you." Well chosen words for the only woman to be licensed on that occasion. This very important step toward the ministry allowed us to wear a clerical collar. I had no intention of wearing a man's collar, I had my shirts made to measure and the collars were stiffened linen and attached to the shirts. They were quite expensive, but looked very smart.

The move from Broomhill was a bit sad, I'd felt very much at home there. Now I had to begin all over again making new friends. The probationary year began in August 1971. Renfield St Stephens Church was another lovely building, it was quite unusual. It had no gallery, but it did have a beautiful little chapel, there was also a marvellous suite of halls, which were used by church organisations and by many secular clubs. The bottom hall was quite large with a very well equipped stage. There was also a very good restaurant, well used each day, for morning coffees, lunch and afternoon teas.

The Presbytery of Glasgow also had their office and committee rooms within this suite of halls. The Rev. Campbell met with me at 10 a.m. on the Monday morning. He advised me that one of my duties was to have lunch each day, paid for by the Church. The idea was that folk who wanted a word with a minister would see me there day by day, and might unburden themselves. Many folk did come and speak to me; they were curious, they had never seen a woman minister before. There were few problems to solve, but I made many friends and I was learning the art of communication. The Rev. Campbell Gillon was very astute, and the lunches were very tasty.

After we had our chat in the office, the Rev. Campbell took me in to see the church. There was a huge golden eagle standing in the chancel – the lectern. Rev. Campbell said to me, 'You will read the lesson from there on Sundays, if you are not in the pulpit.' I thought he was joking, but his face was as straight as a poker. 'Try it,' he said.

I couldn't even see the Bible, let alone read it. In fact I could not see over the eagle, round the eagle or under the eagle, and there was no possibility of the congregation seeing me. There was no way I was going to read the lesson from there on a Sunday. Rev. Campbell left the church and returned with a box which was about a foot and a half high. The bold boy said, 'There you are, no problem.'

I responded immediately, 'Climb on, dreep off, no fear, the Congregation would laugh their heads off. If it's all the same to you, sir, I will read the lesson from my own Bible, standing beside the eagle, or not at all.'

I had called his bluff, he began to laugh. I joined in, that broke the tension. The Rev. Campbell said, 'Just trying you out to see if you had a sense of humour, you'll do.'

I was introduced to the congregation on the Sunday, and presented myself in the office on the Monday morning as directed. Says the Rev. Campbell. 'You will be preaching on Sunday morning.'

'Mr Gillon I take two weeks to prepare a sermon.'

The instant reply was, 'Listen, dear, Sunday comes up every week without fail. You will be in the pulpit every Sunday either in the morning or in the evening, you will get used to the discipline.'

That turned out to be the drill for the whole of the probationary year. I was very grateful for the opportunity given to me. Not every student was allowed into a pulpit as often as I was.

Rev. Campbell was off on holiday for six weeks, but he was very fair. I carried on with my pattern of services and the Rev. Campbell invited some very well known preachers to fill in. That again was a great learning experience for me. He was due back on a Friday morning, but on the Thursday, a family came into the office to make arrangements for a funeral service for the Saturday morning. The service was to take place in the house, the commital at Lambhill cemetery. I made all the arrangements, times etc. so that the Rev. Campbell could conduct the service on the Saturday morning. The lady concerned was an old member of the church aged eighty six years.

The Rev. Campbell came into the office on Friday morning. I told him about the funeral arrangements made for him.

'Not me,' he said, 'I am going to St Andrews University on Saturday morning to bring my daughters home for vacation, you do it yourself.'

'But Mr Gillon, I've never taken a funeral service before, I've never even been inside a cemetery before, let alone stand at a grave.' (Women did not go to cemeteries in those days.)

Rev. Campbell quickly replied, 'There is a first time for everything in the ministry. Take some notes, there's a book of Common Order, read it well, you will manage, because you have to.'

Come Saturday morning, it was pouring rain. I got myself to the house, a grey sandstone tenement, two stairs up, the far away door. As I made my way up the stairs, a man not much bigger than myself, who had obviously been drinking, said as I passed him, 'I don't like funerals, a jist needed a wee nip to gie me some courage.' To my way of thinking, it had been more than a wee nip, he was staggering about from side to side on the stairs.

The service in the house being over, we made our way to Lambhill cemetery. If you have ever been there you will know that the earth is red. By the time I reached the graveside, my feet were a bit damp, the shoes were covered in red mud, my coat was rather wet. It was a kind of nightmare experience as I went through the service, but I managed to keep calm, on the outside anyway. I shook hands with the family. I was about to make my way back to my car, when my wee friend of the tenement stairs threw his arms around me, and in his best Glasgow vernacular uttered the words, 'Yur the bestest wee minister we've hud the day, that wis jist great.' It was difficult to extricate myself from his drunken grip. One of the mourners rescued me from the situation. I felt as inebriated as my wee friend. I hoped I would never have that kind of experience again. I never have. The Rev. Campbell thought it was highly amusing.

Our year of 1971 were now advised to begin the task of finding a vacant charge. Some of the lads in our year were concerned about my chances of being called to a charge. My reply was always the same, 'If God wants me to be a minister, he will have a place for me.' But they insisted that no Church would call a woman, it was too soon to expect it, you will have to give it time Effie, maybe in a few years you will be accepted,

I had a very good minister friend, Rev. David Orrock of Lenzie Union Church. His wife had asked me to speak at their Womens' Guild. It was an afternoon meeting. I was invited to the manse for lunch. After we had eaten, David took me over to the window and directed my attention over the rooftops in front of us, across the valley to a church steeple. 'That's Campsie Trinity Church, and two miles along the road to the right lies Milton of Campsie Parish Church. It's a linked charge, it's vacant, it's just the place for you. I know the Interim Moderator, I could give him a ring for you. I believe your name's on it, Effie.

'David,' I quickly replied, 'I am not interested. I don't want to go to a country charge. I would like to remain in the Glasgow area, where I will be kept busy.' David said if I changed my mind to let him know.

I wrote quite a number of applications. When the mail for posting from Renfield Church was ready, I had to take it up to the Presbytery Office and they sent it out with their own. The secretary of the Presbytery Office said she would include my church applications with the other mail. I handed some of my letters to her. She then told me that they always had a list of vacant charges and she would let me know about them as they came up. 'In fact, here's one you could apply for now.'

'Where is it?' I asked.

'Campsie Trinity with Milton of Campsie, a good charge.'

'I have already heard about that one; you will notice if you read my mail that all my applications are for town charges, I don't want to go to the country.'

It would be about two months later when the secretary of the Presbytery advised me that a vacancy committee were coming to hear me preach on Sunday. 'Where are they from,' I asked. The secretary said she was not telling me, in case they did not turn up. On the Sunday morning, the Rev. Campbell told me that there was indeed a vacancy committee in the church. I conducted the service. We went to the door at the end of the service. This vacancy committee approached the Rev. Campbell. 'Could we have a word with your probationer?' Rev. Campbell detailed the Church Officer to take them to the vestry.'

'Where are they from,' I asked the Rev.

'Never you mind that, just follow them to the vestry.'

I went very slowly to the vestry. There were eight of them; they asked lots of questions. Eventually it was my turn to ask the questions. The first thing I wanted to know was where they came from, so that was the question. I could not believe my ears when the convenor of the vacancy committee replied, 'Campsie Trinity with Milton of Campsie.' Here it was again. They asked one more question, 'How would you like to be our minister,'

'No thank you,' replied the wee one, 'I am preaching for a town charge next Sunday.'

'Where are you preaching?'

'Airdrie.'

We shook hands and they left. Rev. Campbell could not believe I had said no, yet again.

'It's yours on a plate.'

'I am a Glasgow girl, the town is all I know.' I went home. I told Alex the story; we decided to go and have a look at the place. We were not too taken with it.

The next Sunday I set off for Airdrie to preach for this Glasgow church; I was really very interested in it. When the service was over, one man and two women of their vacancy committee came into the vestry. The man did the talking, telling me in no uncertain manner that women in the Ministry were not for him. He was the session clerk of his church and he was totally against the idea ... The two women were trying to apologise for the man's rudeness. 'Don't worry, I would rather hear the truth, I would never knowingly walk into that kind of atmosphere.' I thanked them for coming, and they left. Deflated once more, it seemed it was going to be a bit more difficult to find a charge. I'd written over three dozen letters by this time; most were not interested, some did not even reply. As I was about to put my coat on, the beadle of the church told me that there was another vacancy committee waiting to see me.

'Where are they from?'

'Don't know, will I let them in?'

'Might as well.' The hopes were raised again. There were nine of them. They sat down, the usual questions were asked, the answers given. They were a courteous bunch unlike the last three folk from Glasgow. When I got a word in, I asked the question, 'Where are you from.' Again, 'Campsie Trinity with Milton of Campsie.' Their speaker said, 'We agree with the other half of our vacancy committee, would you accept our invitation to be our minister?

A wee bit gob-smacked; I did not know what to say; this was the fourth time the name of this church was presented to me. One of the ladies asked if I would like to come out to see Lennoxtown and Milton. I couldn't very well say I'd already been and did not like it much. To placate them, I asked when they would like me to come. Today, about three p.m. Alex was not available that afternoon, so I said to Mum,

'Would you like a wee run to Milton of Campsie?' It really was for the company. 'Don't say a word when we get there I'll not be going to that parish.' We arrived at Milton Manse. The whole vacancy committee were waiting. We saw round the manse, a lovely house, eight rooms, with quite a lot of decorating to be done. Then to Milton Church. Campsie Trinity was next, then back to the manse.

One of the elders said to me, 'If there is anything in particular you want done in the manse, just let us know.'

I replied 'Sorry, whoever you get to be your minister, I hope you will be very happy with him.'

Mum and I drove off. Halfway home I turned to Mum and said, 'That's the place for me.'

Mother was astounded. 'You have been turning the place down over the past months.'

'Yes Mum, I know, but don't you understand, I've been blind; all through the last years of study I've been saying, If God wants me to be a minister, he will have a place for me. He has, it's Campsie Trinity with Milton of Campsie.' I had not applied for the charge, they had not asked for a CV, I was forty-eight years old, and I was a woman. God's call was real. What to do now? On reaching home I phoned David Orrock and told him of the situation. 'I told you so,' said David, 'put the phone down; I'll get back to you.' A few minutes later, David was back on the phone. 'There will be a vacancy committee meeting tomorrow evening, be in the house for ten o'clock.'

Monday night, exactly at ten o'clock the phone rang. 'This is the Interim Moderator of the vacancy committee of Lennoxtown and Milton of Campsie. Rev. Euphemia Irvine BD you have a unanimous call to the vacant charges of Campsie Trinity with Milton of Campsie. You have two days to make up your mind.'

I replied very quickly, 'I don't need two days, I know now, I want to come.'

'Fine,' said he, 'I can now set the wheels in motion.'

He certainly did, the *Glasgow Herald* newspaper were in our house at eleven o'clock that night. I was as usual dressed in old trousers and an old cardigan, I was given time to put on my clerical shirt and a jacket, and the camera man took the photograph from the waist up; it was a very good picture, which was eventually used on the Order of Service at my Ordination. There was no sleep that night. We were all too excited to think about sleep, but eventually we all went to bed.

The next morning I had to be in the office at Renfield Church. Rev. Campbell already knew, he had the *Glasgow Herald* waiting for me on the desk. The phone rang in the office; it was 121 George St Edinburgh, the headquarters of the Church of Scotland, to remind me that I was representing the Church. I replied that I was well aware of the situation and would be very careful. The TV were next to cope with, the news was on at six o'clock, it was a bit harassing. I did not enjoy all the fuss. Rev. Campbell said, 'get used to it, dear, this is just the beginning.' He was right of course. All I wanted now was to get settled in my Parish, but there was quite a road to travel yet. The very first thing on the agenda was to preach as sole nominee: to be accepted or rejected, that is another story. It was now down to the two congregations to make up their minds. The date for the preaching of The Word, was to take place on 7 May. All the arrangements were made, all I had to do was prepare a service, it took me about two weeks. The Rev. Campbell was highly amused. Remember, Sunday comes up every week without fail ...

Chapter Seven

I was called to preach sole nominee to the vacant charge of Campsie Trinity Lennoxtown, with Milton of Campsie. A linked charge. The background to the above charge was that, prior to this arrangement, Milton Church was a Mission Station under the juresdiction of Campsie High Parish Church, Lennoxtown. All decisions regarding Milton Mission Station were made by the Minister and Kirk Session of the High Church. Milton Church was served by assistant ministers, who were totally responsible to the High Kirk minister. Milton Church was raised to full status by Act of the General Assembly of the Church of Scotland on 26 May 1964. Milton of Campsie Parish Church was then linked with Campsie Trinity Church. The first minister of the linked charged was, Rev. T. Loudon Blair. He was ordained and inducted to the charge on 29 April 1965. He transferred to Dundee on 8 December 1971.

The invitation to preach as sole nominee was arranged for 7 May 1972. I was very apprehensive; it was one thing for the vacancy committee to extend a unanimous call, but the congregation had now to decide. I arrived at Campsie Trinity Church in good time, I wanted to have a look at the pulpit. Fortunately the book board was able to be lowered to suit me. The pulpit was like a ship's bridge, with a stairway on either side. It was a lovely church, very cosy, with a round shaped gallery, and a pipe organ. The nerves were jangling. I did get through the service and was glad to escape, knowing I had to go through it all again.

Milton of Campsie service was at 12 noon. It was quite a rush, but again I was in time to see the pulpit. There was no need to worry this time. The wee pulpit was against the back wall of the church, it was on a kind of platform about six inches above the level of the congregation, and it was right in the middle of the church. I was very close to the worshippers. I got started with the service. I reached the children's address. I had quite a big board with an illustration painted on it. I

The Manse.

leaned over to the left of the pulpit so that the children could see the drawing, then to the right, the door of the pulpit swung open and I fell full length on to the floor. There was complete silence, as I picked myself up. I said, 'You see I've fallen for you already.' The congregation exploded into laughter. I was told later that was why the call was sustained.

The call was indeed sustained, and the date for Ordination and Induction was arranged for 1 June 1972. For our family there were a great many decisions to be made. First of all, when would we be able to move to Milton of Campsie? The manse had to have some work done in it. On the other hand, I wanted into the manse as soon as possible, because I wanted Mum and Faither to be settled before I began my parish ministry.

At the end of the day, things did work out all right. We were able to move on 19 May. That gave us a breathing space. Slowly but surely, the manse began to feel like home. A house of eight rooms standing in its own grounds. We were able to use up the space, without any bother. Downstairs was a beautiful big lounge, a living cum dining room, and looking out into the back garden my study. Upstairs, four

62

bedrooms, all very comfortable. There was a very good sized kitchen, where we could have our meals, plus a scullery at the back door. It was a warm and comfortable house, and a very happy home for all of us. Of course, we had to sell our own home. It was sold privately within a week. The money received for the house bought carpets and new furniture for the manse. It also provided a new car for me Alex inherited the old banger for the time being. On leaving Renfield Church, the congregation gave me a cheque; that gift bought a desk and chair for my study.

On the Saturday morning after we arrived in the manse, I was organising my study, trying to put books onto shelves. There was a knock at the door, and two of the elders were on the doorstep with working overalls on. A truck was sitting at the gate.

'Mrs Irvine, would you like to come up to the church, there is something we want you to see.'

'Yes just give me time to change,' I was in an old pair of trousers and an even older pullover.

'Just come as you are, we are going up in the truck.'

I shouted to Mum that I would be back in a wee while and off I went. I climbed into this truck, between these two elders and they would not tell me what they were up too. We arrived at the church. One of the elders went round to the back, I discovered the church only opened from the inside, a good safety measure.

'We want to see if you like the improvements we have made in the church.' As I stood at the back of the church I could not believe my eyes; the wee pulpit was gone and a new platform had been built, making it look more like a chancel. In the left corner was a new pulpit. This lovely pulpit had been in a church that was now closed. These elders had shifted it to our wee church; they also brought some of the panelling, placing it along the back wall of the chancel. The amazing thing about it was, the pulpit and the panelling matched our existing communion table.

It was then I was told that on the day I preached sole nominee, the congregation could hear me but they could not see me, so they were determined to alter that situation. The next request was, 'Go up and try it.' I climbed the pulpit steps, they had done a wonderful job. The elders were very pleased with themselves; they had remembered that I was not very big and they had put a false floor in so the pulpit would not be too deep. As I stood there, very happy with the morning's events, one of the elders shouted from the back of the church, 'The false floor was put in for more than one purpose if you go over your preaching time on a Sunday, we have a lever, all we have to do is pull it, you will drop out of sight and sound.' We left the church laughing, I felt the signs were good, the wee church was looking well. These two elders were worth their weight in gold, Bill Barbour and Jim Jarvie. They were always very good friends. Sad to say both men died of heart attacks, Bill aged fifty one years, and Jim aged forty nine. I truly missed two very funny characters, very special elders.

Thursday 1 June arrived, I felt very cold all day, although the weather was warm and sunny. There were many friends coming to Campsie Trinity Church for this Ordination Service. People from Broomhill Church, and Renfield St Stephen's. The church was full. Mum was very weepy; she never thought this day would come, for her it was living a dream. Faither was in his element, the wee woman minister was his son's wife. Faither had been an elder for years, so he said he would just go into the church with the Presbytery, that would get him a front seat. I did not argue, if it made him happy, why not? Service was to begin at 7.30 p.m., I was at the church at 6.30 p.m. I was walking up and down the vestry, I could not sit down.

The Moderator of the Presbytery of Glasgow was the Rev. Stanley Mair. He came into the vestry, and said gently, 'Sit down Effie. This is a momentous night for you, and not only you, but for your family, and, don't forget, the Church of Scotland. You are the beginning of a new era. Tonight you will be ordained and inducted into the parish ministry. Its a hard road to travel, but with your background of determination I am sure you will make it work.' He went on to say that he felt honoured to be the one to ordain me, and would follow my ministry with interest and with prayer. One other word he said. 'When it comes to the laying on of hands, try to keep calm, you will find the weight on your head quite a burden, it's important that you do.'

We were called into the church hall where the Presbytery were waiting. The call was indeed sustained. I was taken into church to sit on the front seat with the Interim Moderator, Rev. Frank Haughton. The church was full. I was cold, very cold, I learned over the years it would always be like this for me, it was a nervous reaction. It was a very moving service. There was a lot said about being the first woman to be ordained into a parish. There was a lot of advice offered which was gladly accepted. I took my ordination vows to heart, and don't think I have ever broken them. Then came the laying on of hands, Rev. Stanley was right, I felt as though I was being pushed into the ground. Suddenly it was over. It was an emotional experience, I was shaking with excitement. I had made it after all, but would I be able to sustain my commitments made that night into every facet of the parish ministry?

Friday night on 2 June at 7.30 p.m., the welcome social took place. I had many good ministerial friends there, men who had supported me through the difficult periods of my studies: Rev. Ken Bethune, Rev. Jim Aitchison, Rev. Campbell Gillon, Rev. John Graham and Professor Mauchline of Trinity College. They all spoke on my behalf; it was so good I thought they were talking about someone else. New robes were presented, they were just lovely. I still wear them when I have the opportunity to preach. They have lasted well. It was then my turn to reply. I thanked the vacancy committee for the persuasive manner in which they pursued me, thanked the congregation for their trust in my abilities, and for the beautiful robes presented which I would be honoured to wear, I don't remember much else, but I did say I was aware of the history making of these two nights, adding that history was all right, but my objectives were a wee bit different, I was interested in the two congregations I now represented, and hoped that together we would make history.

Come the Saturday morning, I was feeling a wee bit jaded. I said to my Mum, 'I don't know where to begin.' The quick retort was, 'Try visiting them,' Mum was right again. Sunday morning 4 June, I was preached-in and introduced to each congregation by the Rev. John Graham. Remember him, he was the minister of Jordanvale Church in Whiteinch who leaned over the pulpit one communion Sunday morning saying, 'This is what Jesus Christ has done for you, what are you prepared to do for Him?' John Graham said to me that Sunday that God would claim me in His own time. I believe John Graham was right. In fact I know he was right ... I don't really remember what the Rev. John preached that Sunday morning, but I know it was all about service, about knowing your congregation as persons, encouraging your folks to be aware that they were the family of God. I was also made aware that I was not just the minister of those who had called me, but minister to the parishes of Milton and Lennoxtown.

I discovered that after ordination and preaching-in, the Presbytery leaves the new minister to get on with it. But on that Monday morning I had a phone call from another good friend. Rev. David Orrock called to say, 'Effie if you ever have any problem, no matter what it is, I'll always be here for you. 'To start with,' he said, 'you will be having your Kirk Session meetings very soon. If anyone brings up business that is not on the agenda, just advise them that the item will be discussed at the next meeting. That way you will get time to think about it and so will they. I used that advice all of my ministry.'

The first week as a minister was a wee bit harassing. Mother's words, 'Try visiting them,' kept coming into my mind. Where to begin? I wanted to rush out and get started, but thought the better of it. There had to be a pattern, it was so important not to get off on the wrong foot. I did not rush out that first Monday morning, I sat down in my study and planned out what I thought would be the right way to go.

I decided that Monday mornings would be spent in my study preparing for the following Sunday services. This I stuck to all of my ministry, except when circumstances changed the pattern of things. Hospital visiting would be done weekly. Sick visiting in the parish as far as possible once a week. The old folks, i.e., the house-bound, would get visited once in six weeks, and the congregational visiting done on a rota of elders' districts. Of course there were visits for baptisms and funeral arrangements. But I expected those wishing to be married would come and see me. Wednesday mornings would be taken up with the Primary Schools in Lennoxtown and Milton. Because it had been a June ordination, it gave me a breathing space. I decided not to begin the congregational visiting until September. Two parishes meant two Kirk Sessions; Milton had a Congregational Board, while Campsie Trinity had a Committee of Management. The minister was not the chairman of a Committee of Management, but I was immediately invited to break the rules and be their chairman, and I accepted.

There were two Woman's Guilds, two Young Women's groups. Two services on Sunday mornings. Trinity 10.30a.m., Milton 12 noon. Communion Sundays were a wee bit tiring. The times were: mornings the usual 10.30 a.m., then 12 noon, 3 p.m., 6.30 p.m., and 7.30 p.m., it was quite a day. On Monday afternoons there were three services in Birdston Hospital, the local geriatric home. Three wards, three services. It was a busy life indeed. The Boys Brigade were in Lennoxtown only.

Sunday 11 June 1972 was the most eventful day of all. I don't think I slept very well the night before. I was in my study very early, going over and over the order of service. It was really silly because there was no way I could change anything; it was too late. I made my way to Trinity Church, and was there too early as usual. The beadle, George, was surprised to see me. 'It's a good job I was early; the wife said you would be here on time, she was right, as usual.' That was my second meeting with George, who turned out to be a unique character. Mum and Faither decided that they would become members of Milton Church, because if they felt like it they could walk to church. If the weather was bad, Alex drove them to church. The congregation of Trinity numbered about 230 on the roll, but of course the attendance was far short of that. I was aware that some of those present would be there just to see how this woman minister would cope. The congregation were very attentive, all seemed well. The service over, I made my way to the door of the church to see 'my congregation out'. They were very kind, 'You did well' etc. I was aware I had to be at Milton for 12 noon. Time was of the essence. George came and rescued me shouting for all to hear, 'The lassie's to be at Milton.' I was very grateful and managed to escape. I just kept the robes on and sped along to Milton.

It was about five minutes before noon when I arrived at Milton Church. I began to panic. The session clerk cum beadle, Bob Gemmill, said, 'Whoa, take your time there's no hurry.' I understood his remark when I stood up in the pulpit. The congregational roll of Milton Church was about ninety. Including the choir, the congregation, the beadle and me, there were seventeen persons in the church, I had been able to count them during the first hymn. What a let down. Towards the end of the hymn, the door opened and a few more folk came in. During the prayer, I could hear movement in the church; when I looked up I was astonished to see the congregation had grown remarkably. I looked at my watch, it was leaving ten minutes after noon. The service over, I went to the door, and received again kind remarks, warm handshakes. I was cold, my hands were like ice, in the middle of summer. Down the aisle to the vestry, I collared the session clerk.

'What was happening out there?'

'Don't worry, the last minister was never here before 12.15 p.m. so some of the congregation just came late.'

That was quite a relief to know. There were more members on time the next week, but I did announce that the service would begin at 12 noon except in extenuating circumstances. As far as I can remember,

Milton of Campsie Church, communion.

the service was never late, I was very glad that on my first Sunday morning there was an explanation for the very empty church.

The last Sunday of June was the Sacrament of Holy Communion. For the very first time I would be dispensing the Sacrament. While training for the ministry, you are merely a spectator at communion; only an ordained minister was allowed to dispense the Sacrament. You can imagine the anxiety, while preparing for this very special act of worship. Three weeks a minister, facing this awesome task. Remember the communion service in Jordanvale Church all those years ago, the service that changed my life, and brought me to this day. Oh how I prayed for God's presence, I needed Him so much to get me through it. He was obviously with me because as I reached Trinity Church there was a calmness I could not explain but accepted that all would be well.

The elders of Trinity were all men; they were very smart in dark suits, white shirts, and black ties. The first part of the service was progressing normally, but the practicalities of dispensing the Sacrament weighed heavy on my mind. Sermon over, I moved to the Communion Table. The middle chair behind the table was mine. It was a bit large for my small frame, not very comfortable. I'm sure the elders sitting round that table would be pretty anxious themselves: how would this wee woman cope? I am sure they never thought of that when they called me to their church. No matter, this was one of the most important services offered by the church; there was a dignity to be maintained. We were reminding ourselves of the great personal sacrifice of Jesus Christ for all mankind. God's Son, Crucified and Risen, was the focal point of this Sacrament. The bread was broken, the elders shared, the wine was presented, again the elders shared; the Body and Blood of Christ, the symbols of our faith went out to the congregation. When all had been served, the elements of bread and wine were brought back to the table, then I accepted bread and wine. I had decided that I would always receive the elements when all of the congregation had been served.

The elders had served with great dignity, they never put a foot wrong; they were obviously very aware of the solemnity of the occasion, and were experienced in the procedure to be followed. The closing hymn was sung, the Benediction pronounced. The elders left the church carrying the elements to the vestry. I followed. On reaching the vestry, there were my elders waiting. One of them stepped forward, put his arm round my shoulder and said, "Thank you, we did not see you as a woman this morning, we only saw you as our very own minister." Those words gave me the feeling of belonging in the Name of Jesus; surely, my belief in having a call to serve was once more a reality, but wait, there are still four services to go, and I felt drained after just one.

From Campsie Trinity to Milton of Campsie, more or less, a repeat diet of worship. At the end of the service, the Session Clerk, Bob Gemmill, thanked me on behalf of the other elders, reiterating more or less what the elder at Trinity had said. Communion Sunday had been a long tiring day. We were not home until nearly 9 p.m. I was totally tired. Alex was waiting for me.

'Well done,' he said. 'Surely you can have no more doubts now, this really is your parish. David Orrock was right when he said, your name's on it.' It was enough.

Chapter Eight

The Kirk Session is the ruling body of the local Church. The minister is the Moderator. I was off to my first meeting with my elders, my Kirk Session. It was the last thing I wanted to do, but it had to be done. The meeting begins with devotions, then on to the business of the night. There was not much business, I was glad to hear. All thirteen elders were present, very affable, I sighed with relief as I asked the question, 'Any other business?' One of the elders cleared his throat. 'Moderator.' My heart sank. 'I would like to make a wee box for you' Jings, I thought, I've only been here three weeks, and they want to bury me already. The elder carried on. 'You see, I thought the Communion Table was a wee bit high for you on Sunday, the sleeves of your gown were just about touching the elements, a wee bit extra height would maybe help you.' The other elders agreed, so did I; the box was duly made – it was about eight inches high and definitely a great help.

The next kirk session meeting took place on the same week; this time Milton of Campsie was involved. All nine elders were present, we went through the same procedure, again there was very little business. I asked the important question. 'Any other business?' I got the same answer, and the box was presented, just about four inches high. It was obvious that these two kirk sessions were looking after the wee minister's welfare.

Holiday mood was upon the area of our parishes. The schools were on holiday, so were a lot of our members. I stuck to my original plans, and was glad I did. During the holiday period, I was finding out where my older folk were to be found. That was a great experience. One of my visits was to an old lady who was over ninety. It was a great thing to be a native of the area. To break the ice I said to her, 'You'll be a native here.'

'Not me, I've only been here seventy six years.' When does one become a native? The lovely answer was, 'When all the folk that were here when you came are dead, you're a native.' In other words, although she was ninety, there were others in the village who had lived in Milton before she had arrived.

During this reasonably quiet time, I prepared for services that would be coming up. Harvest, Remembrance, Advent, and Christmas. I also prepared the hymns for six months in advance. Sometimes these had to be changed, but it was amazing how well the system worked; my organists and my choirs appreciated it. June, July, and August went in very quickly. The schools began in August. I introduced myself to the head teachers and staff, and asked if I could come into the schools on Wednesday mornings. That was all right, Lennoxtown at 9.30 a.m., and Milton at 10.30 a.m. This arrangement seemed to suit everyone. When I went to Milton school I was introduced to the new head teacher, Mrs Matthew. We seemed to hit it off immediately. We had arrived in Milton more or less at the same time.

Before I moved to Milton, Bellway were in the process of building new houses. They had lots of ground, and they had carte blanche; they did not waste much time. It was a great opportunity for the Church. When the furniture vans began to appear, I took a note of where the new residents were sited, and I asked my congregation to do the same. I gave the newcomers about a week, then I moved in. It was amazing, the influx to Milton Church was wonderful. Not only that, a good number of them had come from other churches and some of the men were already ordained elders. New life was being poured into Milton Church. The Sunday School benefited, the Womens' Guild, the Young Mothers' group, and the membership of the church began to grow. Disjunction certificates were being handed in on a weekly basis. I was a very fortunate minister. One of our first tasks was to ordain and admit new elders. I say ordain because I did not want an imbalance in the Kirk Session. We set about ordaining new elders from the village membership first. When we had five new elders from the village then we admitted some of the already ordained elders. It worked, and that was the future pattern. There were, I think, three women elders on the Kirk Session when I arrived in Milton; we increased their number also.

I was also aware that because I lived in Milton of Campsie there was a chance that I would neglect Campsie Trinity. Every day, except hospital days, my car was driven to Lennoxtown, the old folks and the house-bound got the same consideration as Milton folk. When I started congregational visiting, I did week about and announced each week from the pulpit of each church where I would be.

I did begin the congregational visiting in the middle of September. One house I visited the man must have been over six feet. I was interested in getting to know where the men folk worked: that way, I hoped to involve them in the conversation, I asked this very tall gentleman where he was employed. He said he was a joiner and worked for a firm called Laidlaw's. 'That's funny, my Dad was a joiner, and he worked for Laidlaw's.'

'What was his name?'

'Brysland.' I replied.

He began to laugh, 'He wasn't very big, we called him wee Jimmy, and I was his apprentice. It worked out fine, I did the high jobs and wee Jimmy did the low jobs.' Then he said, 'I hope you're as good a minister as your Dad was a joiner.'

I couldn't get home quick enough to tell my Mum, she remembered the boy, because my Dad always talked about his boys and took a great interest in their progress.

I was driving out of the village one day, and one of my elders was coming into Milton. In the back of his car was his daughter, and her little cousin. Janice said to the wee girl, 'That's our minister away past, we have a lady minister.' There was silence. Janice tried again, 'That's our minister.' The wee one butted in, 'So what, you get women bus drivers.' Subject closed.

Congregational visiting threw up some characters. In Lennoxtown one night, I got to this house, rang the bell, the door opened, and the man of the house invited me in. He walked into the room, leaving me to shut the door. Then he shouted to the wife who was in the kitchen, 'It's the Prudential woman.' As she went to the writing desk, she stopped, looked round. 'This is the new minister, did you no see the collar?' and with some disdain, 'Men, they never get it right.'

Another night, this time in Milton, it was quite dark. There were three steps up to this door. I rang the bell and stood down a couple of steps. That meant I was looking up to the door. Again, the man of the house opened the door. He stepped back to a wee table, and handed me a bit of paper and some money. 'There you are, dear.'

I looked at the paper, it was the football coupon. I said to him, 'You can have the coupon back, I'll keep the money for the church, I'm the minister.'

'O hell, my wife will kill me, she's no in, but come on in, I'd like to talk to you for a minute.' We had more than a minute; he was very anxious that his wife would not be told of his swearing in front of the minister. Eventually I managed to convince him his secret would be safe with me, and was able to escape. Alex and I became very good friends, although he never came to Church. His wife was a faithful member, and like a lot of men that was all right with Alex. He was a keen angler, and when he went fishing, there would always be a wee parcel of brown trout, cleaned and gutted, left on the doorstep for the manse family.

Back in Lennoxtown, another character. I asked the husband where he worked. 'No much point, I'm a miner, you need to go down a pit before you would understand.' That's just what I did. One of my elders in Lennoxtown was able to arrange a visit for me at Stepp's Colliery. I arrived at the colliery, and two safety officers took me under their wing. They brought me a donkey jacket, miles too big, then I was presented with a helmet with a miner's lamp attached. Every time I bent down the helmet fell over my eyes. We went down in the cage so many hundred feet, then there was a wee train, which took us two miles to the coal face. When we got there, I was encouraged to make my way to crawl between the pit props. The safety officer said I'd do well as a miner because I was the right height for working at the coal face, the pit props were just about four feet high. Just to prove that I had actually gone down the pit, I was encouraged to bring a large lump of coal from the coal face. The return journey was even more exciting. The conveyor belt which brings the coal out from the coal face is also called the man rider. This was the way out for the miners. The conveyer belt moved forward continually. The safety officer said 'When I say jump ... jump' ... this I did, all went well; we arrived safely back at the cage and sped up to the pit head. It was a great experience, and I certainly understood a wee bit better what it would be like to be a miner. Once the helmet, lamp and donkey jacket were removed, I was asked if I would like to share in a pit head bath, I declined the offer. I went home, and Mum said, 'Have you had a look at yourself, you're covered in coal dust. Don't shake yourself, go into the scullery, and remove the top clothes gently. She brought a bath towel, and ran a bath for me. I went up the stairs, had a look at my face and had a good laugh. We had to scrub the bath, but the visit to the colliery was worth all the bother. I went back and had a long talk with the miner.

Wee Isa, of the Holy
coal and Baileys.

Many years later, I took that piece of coal to a friend of mine who lived in Bishopton. She had a coal fire. I wrapped the coal in tissue paper, and took it to my wee friend Isa, who had a marvellous sense of humour. She had a good going fire on. She unwrapped the coal, and began to laugh, 'Where did you get such a lovely big bit of coal?' I told her the story. 'Am I supposed to keep it?'

'No, put it on the fire, burn it.'

'How can I burn holy coal, I might even get holy smoke.' It did burn well and we both enjoyed the warmth of the coal, and our friendship.

Isa and I shared in a group holiday in Ireland. She asked me if there was a wee tipple I could enjoy it was decided that a wee Bailey's Irish Cream would fill the bill. Next day Isa led the way into a licensed grocer's. She said, 'This is my treat, I'll deal with it.'

The Irishman behind the counter was rather large, 'Yes Madam?' The wee character in front of him said, 'Do you have a bottle of Bailey's Irish Cream, please?' He placed on the counter the biggest bottle of Irish Cream I had ever seen. Isa said, 'Have you a smaller one please,' The next size was placed beside the first one, Isa said, 'Too big.' Yet another bottle of Bailey's joined the line-up. The man never spoke, Isa never smiled. I was giggling inside. Again the wee voice said, 'Too big.' As the Irishman turned to get yet another bottle, Isa said, 'I don't suppose you have a miniature.' The fellow never moved a muscle as he placed a miniature bottle next to the others. Isa's last words were, 'I'll have two of these please.' The man wrapped them, never said a word. I ran from the shop convulsed in laughter. It was like a comic sketch. The big man never spoke, Isa never smiled. That night I was encouraged to go to bed, while Isa poured the miniature Bailey's into thick mugs. We had a good laugh and a good sleep. Every time I am reminded of Isa, and that is very often, Bailey's Irish Cream comes to mind and the fun and friendship of that wonderful holiday.

My first meeting at the Presbytery of Glasgow opened my eyes a bit. Because Mum still had a sister living in Whiteinch, I had promised that I would take her there every Tuesday evening of presbytery. That meant she would be early, and after having tea, and a chat, Mum could go across the road to Jordanvale Women's Guild, and I would pick her up after the presbytery meeting. Of course that meant I would be early at presbytery. Thankfully, the Presbytery, provided teas etc., for ministers who, like me, had prior engagements. Presbytery meeting was constituted at 6.15 p.m. I went into Finnieston Church, and sat down where I thought I would be able to see without restriction. The Church was circular. I sat to the right of the chancel, on the front seat at the aisle. That meant I was looking into the middle of the church, but with a clear view of all that would take place during the business of presbytery. I was making an attempt to study the minutes and the agenda. I looked up, to see a tall nice looking minister, who said, 'That's my seat you are sitting on,' I was rather shocked but had no intentions of moving. I simply replied, 'Well, you will need to be here very early in future, because I mean to sit here every presbytery meeting.' He just walked away, and I did sit there every month till presbytery moved its abode.

I was appointed to the Business and Union & Readjustment committees. Never late for a meeting, I'd go in and sit down. The men would arrive, but never sat next to me, unless they had no alternative. For me it seemed tremendously funny. One day a Kirkintilloch minister, who was in our fraternal (a group of ministers from one area, who met once per month; each minister took a turn to host this group), Alex

Bobby Drummond

Robertson, looked round at the vacant seats beside me and said in a loud voice. 'I don't care who I sit beside, Effie, I'll just sit beside you.' That broke the ice; I was never again placed in that position. The situation was abundantly clear. There were a goodly number of ministers who were against the idea of women in the ministry. They had a right to their own opinion, but their opposition was irrelevant, the fact was that women were now accepted by the General Assembly, so I made up my mind that because nothing or nobody would be able to change the situation, I would just get on with my parish ministry and let the outcome speak for itself. Over the years and very slowly I did manage to break down a few barriers.

The visiting went on systematically. There was a wee house on the Main Street of Lennoxtown. There was an old couple lived there, Mr and Mrs Bobby Drummond. They were a joy to visit. The very first time I knocked on the door, I had to wait for a wee while before the door was opened, and wee Bobby said, 'You're just supposed to knock the door and come in.' 'I'll remember that in the future.' His reply was, 'That's right, and I see you've got your collar on, I don't like ministers who refuse to wear their badge of office.' I followed this wee character into the kitchen. He offered me a seat, and took off his bunnet; there was very little hair on the head. I said, 'If you feel your head cold just keep your bunnet on, that's OK.'

'Right,' he said, 'I'll just do that.' Sitting in the corner, in the shadows of the room, was Mrs Drummond, small with wispy grey hair and a lovely smile on her face. She did not move to get up, Bobby told me she wasn't great on her feet; again I said that was OK I became very fond of this old couple. He was about eighty-seven years and she I think about a year younger.

We were having a chat about the church. Bobby would be present every Sunday, if he could manage, and so it was. As time went by I found myself perfectly at ease at the fireside of these very homely folk. Bobby took a sweetie poke out of his pocket, he only took one sweetie out and handed it to me, it was unwrapped. I was about to put it in my pocket, when the old fellow asked me if I were not going to eat it. I looked at his face; there was a challenge, so I popped the sweetie into my mouth. He put the sweetie poke back in his pocket. It was my turn to look at Bobby. He smiled and said, 'She's no getting one, they're no guid for her teeth.'

Bobby Drummond kept his promise. Faithfully, he came to Church every Sunday. He sat in the gallery, on my left. Each Sunday I entered the pulpit, Bobby stood, he saluted me, I bowed to him, we both sat down. His son Maxwell was a bit upset about this and gave me permission to stop him. I told Maxwell, 'Forget it, he is a one of character, if he has it in his heart to salute me Sunday by Sunday, I will respond. Just leave it be.' One Sunday Bobby did not turn up. I went to see the reason on the Monday morning. He said in a very accusing voice, 'I wasn't there because I was locked out. I knocked and knocked the door and got no reply.'

Then the penny dropped for me. 'Bobby, did you not remember that the clock was changed on Saturday night, you were too early.'

'Ach, I'm too old to remember these things, they should just keep things simple.'

Came the day that Bobby wasn't very well; they took him into Stobhill Hospital. In I went to see him. The sister in charge was one of these old fashioned kind, starched apron and hat. I told her that I was there to see Mr Drummond. 'One of yours, we've had trouble with him already. I couldn't understand this until I reached the bed. There was Bobby, with bunnet plus tartan scarf. As I approached the bed, Bobby looked up, off came the bunnet, and it was placed beside his head on the pillow. The sister was beside herself; he would not take that cap off for the doctor. Bobby piped up, 'She's different, she's my minister.' The patient was not long in the hospital, he still wore that bunnet.

Milton Church, Guides and B.B. at the War Memorial.

There was a close next to the Drummond home. Bobby kept his coal in a shed down through this close into a kind of back court. I had gone in to see them one day. There was no sign of Bobby but Mrs D. was there in her corner. I asked her, 'Where's Bobby?'

'He's down sorting out the coal.'

'I'll just go down and give him a hand.'

'Wait a minute, have one of my sweeties.' She produced a scarf, unrolled it and a bashed box of Black Magic chocolates appeared; she held it out to me. I accepted a squashed chocolate, 'Fine,' she said, 'You can go down and help him now, he's not getting one of these chocolates.' I laughed, she was just getting her own back.

I went down through the close to the shed. 'I'll give you a hand with that bucket of coal.'

'Aye well it's no ready yet, seeing your here, you can give me a hand sorting it out.'

'Right, I'll just fill this bucket,' lifting some of the bigger bits of coal.

'That's no the right coal, it's the wee bits I've got ready, why do you think I broke them up, fill that bucket and take it up, then you can come back for the other pail.' I did what I was told. Many a time the minister carried up the coal. I must say the training was first class, I even got to break the sticks, and one day I got to poke the fire.

Remembrance Sunday was held in Trinity Church one year and Campsie High the next. In 1972 it was the turn of Campsie High. That meant that the minister of Trinity was responsible for the service, another first for me. After the service I was about to take the salute for the march past of the Boys Brigade, when I spied wee Bobby helping an old lady down the church steps. They obviously knew each other well. A right old chinwag was in progress. I asked someone who the old lady was. 'That's Lady Stirling of Glorat.' I had heard about her, but had never seen her. I thought, that's a caring old lady, I'd like to meet her. It was during the next week when I got the call to visit Glorat House. That meeting was to be the beginning of a great friendship with the Stirling family. I am still in touch with her daughter Marigold to this day. We will leave that story for another chapter.

I had been a few years in the ministry, when I was asked to take on an attachment for training. His name was Bill Stewart (his story will come up later) but for the moment, we will include him in the saga of Bobby. Bill was about to go out visiting in Lennoxtown. I was giving him a list. I said to him that when he went to Bobby Drummond's home, if Bobby needed coal up, he was to go for it, and Bobby would show him where it was; if he needed sticks broken, he could do that too, and if they needed a message he was to go for it. Bill said, 'They don't teach you this in Trinity College.'

'No,' I said, 'but this is the parish ministry.' Away he went with his list. When Bill was visiting, Mum always gave him his dinner. Bill was back home before me. Mum opened the door, and the wee fellow rushed into the manse shouting, 'I've passed, I've passed, I brought up the coal, broke the sticks, and went for a message.' That day Bill did not finish the visiting list, but I let him off.

Sad to say tragedy struck the Drummond family in November 1976. Bobby loved his electric blanket; he also took sleeping pills. His family were worried about this situation, but Bobby stuck to his guns, he would have the electric blanket right reason or none. The old couple had separate beds, As Bobby would say, it was better to be able to rassle around and make yourself comfortable. One morning, about 8 a.m., I got a call from the Police; there had been a fire at Bobby's home. The Police could not get the sons. Maxwell was a photographer, and he was away to take school photographs outside the Campsie area. The other son Tommy, who had his own butcher's shop, was at the meat market. The Police Officer took me into the house to identify the old couple. I still remember the terrible smell. Bobby was badly burned, wee Mrs Drummond was asphyxiated. The bodies could not be moved until they had been identified. I was glad they called me, but it took a long time to come to terms with the situation. The coffins of this remarkable couple were brought into church to lie side by side. It was a very difficult time for the family, and for the people of Lennoxtown and for the church. But at the end of the day, they had never been separated in life, and they would still be together with, as Bobby would say 'the Good Lord.' The wee house, the home of a very lovely old couple, was taken down. It was the right thing to do. The Main Street of Lennoxtown has never looked the same.

Chapter Nine

One day there was a knock at the manse door, I had just been in the parish for about a week. Standing there was a priest. He said he had come to welcome me into the parish. He came in and Mum made us a cup of tea. His name was Father McCulloch. The tea was produced. I introduced the Father to Mum; my goodness they became buddies immediately. It was as if they had known each other for years. When Mum finally left us together, we talked about sharing in the parish, Christian Aid, Remembrance, carol singing, etc. and that's how it was in Milton parish ever after. He had a very caring personality, and in the days to come I appreciated Father McCulloch very much. He asked me if I would object to him visiting my mother. He visited her regularly; very often it's easier to respond to another cleric. I was very grateful for his care and attention. Many a day I arrived home to hear that Father McCulloch had been in. Came the day our good friend the priest was moved to another parish. He arrived on the doorstep to say goodbye. Believe it or not my Mum was very upset. Said she, 'St Paul's have lost a very good priest, so have I.'

We started the minister's group in the autumn of 1972, the aim being to bring the eleven plus age group together. It was intended that the main meetings would be held on Sunday afternoons, so that we might study the Bible together, and we could be free to ask questions. Games nights were held in the manse each Wednesday evening; the young folk brought their own games and I provided others. I believed that we could not pray together unless we could play together and have some fun, that way we could get to know each other as human beings. At the same time I was very strict: if you did not attend on Sundays, don't bother to come on Wednesday, except of course, if illness was involved. No one was allowed to join unless they were at secondary school. In the summer time we took the children to as many places of interest as possible. But the place they liked best was the Irvine sports centre. There they could go swimming, ice-skating, bowls and eat. My helpers were my husband Alex, our session clerk Bob Gemmill, Tommy Cains, one of my very good elders, young Kenneth Gemmill, and all the parents who helped with their cars on every outing. No matter where we went we always had chips and whatever. The man in the Barrhead chip shop was never happy to see us; it took him ages to feed our lot.

We went to the Edinburgh Tattoo every year. The last Friday in August was always dry, and the folk in the parish said that if you were going to the Tattoo, go the same night as the minister's group, you will get a good dry evening. The minister's group was composed of children from both Lennoxtown and Milton.

We also took the youngsters to the cinema. There was one film they really wanted to see, *Chariots of Fire*, which was showing at the Colliseum on the other side of the river Clyde. We had about thirty children, their parents helped out with transport. We got to the cinema, and all trooped in. Our session clerk said to the man at the ticket office, 'I think we should get all the adults in for the same price as the children.' Being funny, the man with the tickets said, 'Are they all yours?' Bob said, 'Yes hers [that was me], and mine.' We got the cheap tickets.

One Sunday afternoon, we were discussing how difficult it was to get ourselves away on our outings. The minister's group was growing. I suggested to the group that they should pray for a minibus. There was quite a laugh about that, but I said I was serious and I would pray for that to happen. The following Saturday my two nephews were over at the manse. There were two village boys who knew my nephews. I phoned the McPherson boys, told them that Graham and Crawford were in the manse garden, and asked them over. The boys were playing football in the garden when the doorbell rang. A lady of the congregation was on the doorstep. 'Could I have a word with you, Mrs Irvine?' 'Certainly, come away in,'

I took Mrs Martin into the study, she was a wee bit shy. My husband sent me over to see if you would like a minibus. It's past its best, but his boss said if it was any use to your minister, she can have it for nothing.

I sat and looked at her for a second. The answer is, most definitely yes, but could you tell that story to two of my minister's group? I called the two McPherson boys in, 'boys, what did I ask you to pray for last Sunday?' No answer, I think they thought it a joke. 'Mrs Martin will you tell them what you have just told me.' She repeated the story. The boys were very quiet, this was something they had not taken seriously. In time they were to discuss the power of prayer in our minister's group. First of all, we took the bus along to the garage in Lennoxtown. We asked Jimmie McGregor if he would check it over to see if it was roadworthy. It was taxed and insured for us, it was ready for the road. We put a jam jar at the Church door and asked the congregation to put all their copper coins into the jar on a Sunday to pay for petrol.

The bus never cost the church a penny. It was used for our group, for the BB, and Alex took it out on a Sunday and did a minibus run for the elderly. I started what we called 'The Balmaha run', every Thursday. Mrs Babs Barbour and I picked up nine old folk, who did not get out very often, drove them to Balmaha, gave them a mug of tea, (flasks were donated by the Women's Guild), then they got a poky hat (ice-cream cone). Then back to Milton. They also fed the ducks; they did enjoy that. When Jimmie McGregor found out what we were using the bus for, he told me that he would service the mini-bus for nothing, and he would also tell us when it was too old. Who said prayer did not work?

The bus was well used. Archie Bell, our next door neighbour, had his own tarmacadam business, he laid a tarred base for the bus to sit on. That was a great help, because the wheels of the bus were playing havoc on the grass beside the garage. We were due to put the bus in for a service, and Jimmie from the garage phoned me. 'The bus is done, it would be too dangerous. I suggest you cut your losses, I will take everything that's able to be sold and give you the money.' We were actually saving for a second hand vehicle, because we knew that the bus was not going to last much longer. Jimmie got £450 for the spares, and we had saved about £600, it was in the bank. Alex, my session clerk Bob, his son Kenneth and I went into Argyle Street to a motor showroom which sold mini-buses. We saw a white Commer bus, we liked it and it was in very good condition. The owner of the showroom came out to see us. We explained what the bus was to be used for. I asked the price: £1200.

I said to him, 'We have £1,050.'

The gentleman looked at me, I said, 'You will get it cash when I am able to get to the bank.'

It seemed to take ages, then he turned round and said, 'OK, the bus is yours.'

Marvellous, we were over the moon, Wednesday saw me back there collecting the bus. Jimmie McGregor took the minibus and gave it a service, he said it was a very good buy.

Jimmie never ever let us down. he kept the bus on the road. The petrol jar was always full, not with copper coins, but with silver. We kept saving. The minister's group did a sponsored walk; they did eight miles of the West Highland Way. They raised £600, which was immediately banked for a future bus. The Commer was certainly a very good buy, it never let us down, but as we know, vehicles deteriorate quite quickly. Came the day when our garage man again said, 'The bus is done, I'll do what I did last time.' I don't remember what we got for the second van's spare parts, but we had £2,775 in hand. We got the offer of a very good vehicle through one of our elders, but it was to cost £4,175, out of the question. I announced on the Sunday that the Commer bus had to go. To have that new bus would cost us another £1,400, we would just keep on saving in the meantime. The following Saturday morning, I went to pick up the post. There was no post, but there was a grocer's white bag. I lifted it, and looked inside, it was full of £10 notes just like you get in the bank, held together with elastic bands. I went into my study and counted the money. There was exactly £1,400 in that wee bag and there was a note with it, which said, and I quote, because I still have that wee bit of paper today, and will always keep it. 'Dear Mrs Irvine, please apply this money to the mini-bus fund, no publicity required. This is given in Jesus Name, and is honestly come by.' I don't know to this day who put the grocers bag through the door. We had the cash we needed. I phoned the session clerk. A sleepy voice answered the phone; I knew by his voice I'd just wakened him. I told him the story, and the sleepy voice said something like, 'Aye, all right, I'll get back to you.' The phone went down, A few seconds later, the bold boy was back on the phone. 'Will you repeat what you said before.' I said we can go and get that bus.

Alex, Bob and I did just that. It was the best bus of all, a Thames, painted blue. We were thrilled to bits, and forever grateful to the person who made it possible. This bus was different, it was a lot younger than the other two, so we decided that we would put a sign on it in white and we got a sign-writer to do the job. On both sides of the bus in big letters, was printed MILTON OF CAMPSIE PARISH CHURCH.

There were two sisters who had lived in Milton of Campsie all their lives, Nelly and Martha. Martha was the one who had kept house for her parents. Now she kept house for Nelly. They were both spinsters. Nelly had been a fishmonger, but was retired. She had been out on the mini-bus a few times. I said to her one day, 'Do you not think Martha would like a trip on the bus?'

'Aye. She might go if you asked her.' A couple of days later I went in to see Martha. 'How would you like a wee run in the mini-bus to Balmaha?' She was not very keen, but I managed to get her to agree for just one time. On the Thursday of that week I picked up Nelly and Martha, for Balmaha. It was a great victory to get Martha on that bus or so I thought. We had our usual outing, they had their tea, ice-cream, a wee walk down to see the ducks, Martha never raised a smile. Back to Milton, as we stopped at the gate for Martha and Nelly, I got round to help Martha off the bus. I said to Martha, 'Did you enjoy that wee outing, dear?' She never batted an eye, as she said, quite pointedly, 'No.' Did you ever have the wind taken out your sails? It was a great lesson to learn, never press-gang anyone into doing what you want them to do.

About two days later, I met a married sister of Nelly and Martha. Betts said to me, 'That house in Scott Avenue is a war zone. Nelly is furious with Martha for daring to tell you that she did not enjoy the visit to Balmaha. I've tried to sort out the problem, but it's no use, Nelly is on the warpath, and Martha sits there like the sphinx.'

'I'll go in and see them.'

'Well, you had better be quick, it's getting serious.'

That afternoon, Scott Avenue was my first priority. I rang the bell, Nelly came to the door. 'I am glad to see you, maybe you can knock some sense into that Martha.'

'I'm not here to knock sense into anybody, I'm here to bring peace to this home, the way it used to be.'

Nelly began, 'She had ...'

I stopped her in mid flight.

'Nelly, you were always the one who said you liked to hear the truth, well, Martha did not want to go to Balmaha in the first place. I asked her to try it, she did not enjoy it, and she had every right to tell me, because I would have pestered her again and again. You like the bus run, Nelly, and it will always be there for you. I don't need any apology from Martha, we both need to apologise to her.'

Martha never said a word, but she was looking pretty miserable. They were both looking at me, waiting for the next move.

'Martha and Nelly, I'm not leaving this house till you make up, I must see this silly feud over before I go, and I am prepared to stay here till that happens,' and then I said, 'I'll phone home and say I'll be late; by the way have you a spare bed?'

That did it, Nelly got up; as she rose, Martha did the same, they met in the middle of the floor. It was a 'greeting meeting' but I left them saying sorry to each other. I was very glad it was all over, but I decided never ever to coax anyone to go on the bus run.

The minister's group was special to me, they helped to keep us young. For Alex and me, they were the family we never had. Edinburgh was one of their favourite venues; we visited the Castle, the Commonwealth Pool, the zoo. Other outings took us to a Safari Park, the Bear Park, Dumbarton Rock, Culzean Castle, the Police Tattoo, but of course the highlight was always the fish and chips at the end. The members of the group were encouraged always to think about the needs of others. They gave donations to Lennox Castle Hospital, Broomhill Hospital, the Royal Commonwealth Society for the Blind, Oxfam, Erskine Hospital, etc. Having the mini-bus made it easier for us as a group, but we still needed the cars, because the minister's group kept growing. The minibus was used by the other organisations of the church.

In May 1972, prior to my ordination, I went to the General Assembly. I was only there one day, but I did wear my clerical collar, I had been licensed the year before. I was on my way to the book room, going down a flight of stairs, and as I looked down, there was a minister coming up. We both had to stop. He looked up, and he said, 'Rev. Euphemia H. C. Irvine, you must come to the Holy Land with me next year.'

'When?'

'April, I'll put your name on the list, think about it, I'd like you to come.'

The minister involved was the Rev. James Currie. That invitation helped my ministry to develop and gave me a wider vision, and a greater knowledge of the scriptures and of people. I went home that night, and told Alex about the invitation to the Holy Land. Alex made me very happy; he said, 'A marvellous idea, but I'd like to come with you.' I was on the phone that night to the Rev. James to book not one place but two. That was the beginning of a great friendship which I treasure to this day.

The choir was very important to me, although I was never considered to be a singer, I loved singing. I also believed that the choir, singing an introit, set the mood for worship. It was also lovely to have an anthem on a Sunday morning. The organist *in situ* when I arrived in Milton was Mrs Johnston; we did get on well and she was a very dedicated personality. The organist in Campsie Trinity was a Mr Monteith, who was a very capable musician, and like Milton had a small but very good choir.

The Sunday Schools in both ends of the Parish were well attended; we had very faithful teachers. Trinity Church had its own small hall, which was quite a help. Milton had no hall of its own; the Sunday School met in the village hall, and when the SS began to grow we hired classrooms in the school.

The Women's Guilds, like the Sunday School, were both very active; the churches received a great deal of financial help from both Guilds. Without the help of a minister's wife, the guildswomen were able to organise their own syllabuses without any help from me. I was very grateful to these women for all they did for their churches.

Our Young Women's groups were the same; they looked after their own groups. It was great not to be involved, except when I was invited to speak. My husband Alex said from the very beginning, joking of course, that he would never agree to becoming the President of the Women's Guild.

The Boys Brigade was the First Campsie Company founded in 1927 and attached to Trinity Church. The boys in Milton who wanted to join a BB company went to Trinity Company. It meant that they had either to go by bus, or someone had to drive them there. It was only two miles, but it was a dark country road, and in the winter, the road could be quite lonely for youngsters. The village of Milton was growing; there were a lot of newcomers arriving who were already in BB Companies, and were now looking for that facility in Milton. I thought about this situation for some time and in 1975, with the help of my session clerk, Bob, we formed the Second Campsie Company of the Boys Brigade. We began with a Junior section first of all. While I was still minister of Milton Church, the senior section of the Boys Brigade was formed; it was a very successful enterprise. In due time there were boys working for their Queens Badges, and so many of them in the

Duke of Edinburgh Award Scheme. On 18 April 1982 Colours were dedicated and presented to the Second Campsie Company by the Langley and Wilson families, in memory of John Langley, one of our office bearers, and his aunt, Mrs Isa Wilson.

In Lennoxtown, tragedy struck too often. One Sunday, I had a word with a wee lad from one of our farms, he was a twin. Full of life, bright as a button. On the Monday I got a phone call to tell me that the wee fellow had died that morning in the dentist's chair. Another family were torn apart when there was an accident on a mini-bus outing. The bus turned over, and their eighteen-year-old daughter was thrown out and crushed under the bus. Trauma and disbelief within their family circles, and the parish. No minister or priest can ever cope with these situations in their own strength. It's then you realise how bereft one is without the power of the Holy Spirit in Christ Jesus. First you have to manage your own grief in the midst of tragedy, lay yourself open to the power of God, He and He alone can sustain both family and minister. The passing of time does not alleviate the suffering of grief, but allows us to accept the situation. Sanity is salvaged by the clear knowledge that God is love.

How was life for the manse family? They had accepted from day one that the congregations and parishes had to come first. I was a very fortunate minister. Faither was happy and contented; he was well fed as always, he had his own wee room, a television set, the bowling green, and the big dog to walk in the mornings. Mother was in her element, She was chief in the kitchen, She too had her own room, her own television, and her books. The big dog slept in her room. One night as I passed her bedroom door, I heard her say, 'No I am not putting out the light, until I am finished this chapter.' She was speaking to the dog. Lunch in the manse was 12 noon, dinner was 5 p.m., not to suit me, but to suit Alex, who still worked in Bridgeton. At these times the meal was on the table, for that was the old-fashioned way. Mum used to say, 'How do these folk know that you are home, every time you sit down to a meal the phone rings.'

I said, 'Because they know you are very strict with your daughter, I've got to do what I am told, and be in for my meals on time.' She just laughed.

Alex always said, jokingly, I think, 'I know my place, the congregations come first, Dougie the dog second, and I am last,' and so it was, but he was happy.

Faither took ill in 1975. He began to do silly things, out without a jacket, getting up in the middle of the night, half shaving himself, and going back to bed. It turned out to be dementia. We tried to keep our eyes on him, but he became quite cute. He would raid the fridge at night and take what he fancied to his room; he didn't eat it, just put it in his wardrobe. Eventually he was admitted to Bellsdyke Hospital in Larbert. He died in Stirling Royal Infirmary on Christmas morning 1977. Faither was eighty-three years when he died and had lived with us for twenty-six years. Sometimes he was an old rascal, but Alex and I would not have had the situation any other way. He was Alex's Dad and had no others to care for him. The Rev. David Orrock conducted the funeral service for us.

In 1976, it was first mooted that the linkage between Campsie Trinity and Milton Church should be dissolved and that Campsie High should be united with Trinity. This of course was a presbytery matter. There were many meetings and discussions with the kirk sessions of the Lennoxtown Charges. There had been new houses built in Lennoxtown, the firm was Comben; this meant that the parish of Lennoxtown was growing. Milton had Bellway and Barrett estates, both my charges were growing. I did not really have very much to do with it, I just attended the meetings in the interest of Campsie Church. Surprisingly enough, the Trinity folk seemed to like the idea. The Campsie High minister had been over forty years in his parish; they were also quite happy for the situation to be changed.

Over a period of time, I realised that I had been ordained to two charges, and that Milton Church should have a say in the development of this situation. No representative from Milton had been asked to attend any of these meetings. I contacted Rev. Andrew Herron, who agreed with me. A meeting was arranged, with a presbytery representative there, to ask the members of Milton Parish Church whether or not they were prepared to have me as their minister if the union in Lennoxtown took place. This meeting was constituted after a Morning Service. I waited in the vestry on tenterhooks: would they want me or would it be another rejection? After the meeting, one of my elders came into the vestry, put his arms round me and said, 'It's OK pet, we have decided to keep you; we know the devil we've got, we don't know the devil we might get.' What a relief. I then recognised that what was happening was the best for all concerned. I accepted the invitation to stay. I have never regretted that decision.

On an evening in May 1978, the General Assembly debated, accepted and passed, that the linkage between Campsie Trinity and Milton of Campsie should be dissolved and that Campsie High Church and Campsie Trinity should be united under the Ministry of Dr Morrison; further that Dr Morrison should retire in a year's time, and the vacant charge then call a new minister. Milton of Campsie Parish Church would become a full status Church in its own right, and the Rev. E.H.C. Irvine would be the minister of the new charge. There were a number of our elders and office bearers and members in the gallery of the General Assembly that night. We were very happy about the outcome and for me doubly so. The decision was to be implemented on 1 June 1978, which meant it was exactly six years since my ordination. A new era had begun for Milton of Campsie Parish Church. I did miss my folk in Campsie Trinity; we had shared a great deal, together. I had also managed to get the Trinity Kirk Session to accept two women elders.

Chapter Ten

Suddenly, I was the minister of one parish. The family were very happy about that, there would be more free time for me. That was the first mistake, because Milton of Campsie was beginning to grow, grow, grow. Certainly, there would be fewer meetings, but preparation work for Sundays did not diminish. We were very much hampered by the fact that we had no hall of our own. The Rev. Louden Blair had tried to start a hall fund when he was the minister at Milton, but it never got off the ground. The opportunity was quite different now. House building was still going on, our organisations were growing, we were now needing four classrooms in the school, for our Sunday School, plus the village hall. The Boys Brigade was growing, and there were other organisations in the village who also needed space. It was to be a few years before it was accepted that there was a need for expansion. Alex said, 'Patience, dear, it will happen, it's got to happen.'

In 1975, I got a phone call one morning. This voice said, 'My name is Bill Stewart, I am a student in Divinity at Trinity College. I have asked the Pastoral Theology Professor if I can do an attachment with you at Milton of Campsie.'

To be quite honest I did not want a student; at that time some of the divinity lads wore black polo necked jerseys, big wooden crosses round their necks plus long hair. I personally could do without the hassle. I told young Bill I did not want a long-haired layabout working for me. If any student went into the pulpit in Milton of Campsie, he would wear a suit and shirt with Trinity College tie, hair would be short back and sides. I was really trying to put the lad off. He was determined.

'When can I come and see you?'

I gave in. 'You can come and see me any morning, except Wednesday when I will be in the school.' I clean forgot all about the student; time was of the essence, even with one congregation.

Come the Monday morning of the following week, I was busy in my study, dressed as usual in an old pair of corduroy trousers, plus an even older jersey. The bell rang, I opened the door and there on the step was the smartest wee fellow you would ever meet. Blond hair, short back and sides haircut, suit, Trinity tie, white shirt. I knew immediately who he was, but he had no idea who I was. He said, 'I am here to see Mrs Irvine.' I put him into the study, because I realised he thought I was the house help.

I went upstairs to Mum's room, because I had a fit of the giggles. I told her the story. She said, 'Look at the sight you are, get changed.' There was no time for that, so down to the study I went, opened the door, walked round my desk and sat down. The boy was gob-smacked,

'Don't tell me your ...'

I stopped him. 'Yes, it's me.'

He went all indignant on me. 'You had the cheek to tell me how to dress.'

'Yes, but I was referring to dress wear for the pulpit.'

His eyes were dancing with mischief, and I thought, you'll do fine. He was not much bigger than me, to give him the benefit of the doubt, maybe all of 4 feet 11 inches.

'When do you want to come to Milton?'

The answer was, 'Now, if you will have me.'

'We will have a cup of tea, and a wee chat, I accept you as our attachment, and hope you won't regret coming here, there is a lot to do.' Mum knocked the door, the question was, 'Will you have a cup of tea, son, it's ready in the kitchen, or do you want me to carry it through?' The wee fellow was on his feet, we had our tea in the kitchen. Mother found out more about Bill in five minutes than I could have done in a month. She took a shine to him, and she never called him anything else but 'son'.

That day was the beginning of a great friendship. Bill Stewart was an excellent attachment. The congregation just loved him. He read the lesson every Sunday, and preached once a month. He was a good visitor when time allowed. Because he was still in training, I went kind of easy on him.

I was going on holiday for one week, but I had already booked pulpit supply, so Bill had to take a back seat that Sunday. When I returned, Nelly Ferrie, one of my members, asked me why I had 'got that fellow who could not hold a candle to our own wee boy'. We never had pulpit supply again while Bill was there.

Bill always had lunch with us after the morning service, and when he did do visiting he got his dinner. Mum just loved to have him share in these meals. After he had been with us about six months, I asked him why he had decided to come to Milton. He replied, 'I did not like women ministers, so thought I'd try one out.'

The meal that night was mince, and my retort was, 'Listen, son, the only reason you don't get this mince round your ears, is the fact that we have six plates that match.'

That story was told at his ordination by me, but he told the story of our first meeting, when he thought I was the charwoman in the manse.

Believe it or not, I had Bill Stewart for three years. When he was leaving, we were giving him a gift. He was asked what he would like. It was to be a preaching scarf, with the burning bush or some other design. I looked at him. I never wore a preaching scarf, because it would have been too long, and practically too difficult to alter. He was adamant, it had to be a preaching scarf. Remember, he was not much taller than me. We bought the scarf, the shortest one we could lay our hands on. The morning of the presentation, Bill tried the scarf on in the vestry. It was of course too long, but he said his sister would be able to take it up from the back of the neck. I suggested that we would just present the scarf in the church, then he could take it off. He would not have that happen, he was determined to wear it. Of course you know what happened. The fringes were polishing his shoes, he almost tripped going into church, and the congregation had a bit of a laugh; so did Bill. We missed our Bill tremendously. He did his probationary year in Stonelaw Church, Rutherglen, and in 1979 was Ordained and Inducted to Glasford with Strathaven East, where he is still the minister.

The pattern of my ministry never changed. Monday morning, preparation for the following Sunday. The diary and intentions were all in order, till the phone rang and there was a problem or a crisis to deal with, so Sunday services had to be well in order before the weekend. I managed to have our Board meetings and Kirk Session meetings on the same evening. Wednesday mornings, Milton school. I visited each class for a short period of time, but I spent an hour in Primary seven every week. This was the class who were preparing for secondary school. At the end of each year we had a voluntary Bible exam; no child had to do this, but their parents agreed with the principle, and it was very

Milton Church, Christmas.

surprising, how well they did. The first four with the highest marks got a book token. The rest got some small reward.

I taught Primary seven by showing them fifty slides of the Holy Land each Wednesday for six weeks. That made it easier for them and for me.

The school had a very wonderful head teacher, Mrs Matthew. She knew the name of every child in her school. Only Mrs Matthew could ever use the strap on any pupil, that was her rule, and I don't remember any child needing or ever receiving the belt while I was there. Joan Matthew and I became very good friends, Her husband was Dave, who was a pig farmer. Some of the classes in the school were taken to the farm to see the piglets when they were born, I was able to take my minister's group on occasions. Joan and Dave were members of Burns and Old Parish Church, Kilsyth. After two or three years, when we were approaching Christmas, Joan Matthew rang the manse and asked me to come up to the school. 'There's something I'd like you to do for me, and no one must ever know about it.' I was intrigued.

Joan said she was aware that there were some children in Craighead school whose mothers were not able to provide the school uniform, especially the pullovers. She was going to provide as many as she could. Joan would buy them, and my part in all this was to deliver them to the families in need. 'It's a lot to ask, but who would ask or question the minister as to where these jerseys would come from?' Of course I agreed, and year upon year I did the Christmas delivery to the children in need.

There was a lovely story about Joan and Dave. Dave was retired by this time, but they had remained in their farm home. Dave filled in his time by letting out stables for horses; he cleaned out the stables and fed the horses each day. One day Joan's car would not start, and Dave drove her to school. He had not shaved that morning and was in his working togs. They got to the school gates, and Dave came round to open the door for Joan. As she got out of the car, a wee five year old took her hand, looked at Joan then at Dave, and said, 'Is that your Daddy, Mrs Maffew?' Dave had to live with that one for some time.

Christmas was a great time at school. There was always a Nativity Play. The child of one of my elders, Andrew, had a part in one of these plays. The children as usual were all very excited, and Andrew was standing, very serious. I asked him what part he was playing. The quick answer was, 'I am a King, so are they,' pointing to the others, he's carrying the "Mirror" he's carrying the "Gold" and I'm carrying "Frankenstein", I met Andrew years later, when he was in his teens, he told me that the family never let him forget that Nativity Play.

Another five year old was playing the part of Mary. As she put the baby Jesus in the cradle, she said, 'Behave yourself, Jesus, I'm tired out.' She must have heard that one from her mother.

Joan Matthews retired. She was a very talented person, and painting was her hobby. She was in the Women's Institute, receiving first prizes year after year for baking and jam making. She won so many prizes at the Campsie Show so often, the only way they managed to stop her was by giving her the job of being Judge for the Show. She was a guide at the Glasgow Cathedral, and the Glasgow House in Garnethill. To be quite honest, I don't think there was anything she could not do.

Joan and Dave went on a cruise, just after she retired. She took ill on that trip, and came back to a time in hospital. Her health deteriorated very quickly. I was retired by this time, and so I was able to visit her mostly on Sunday afternoons. I had a letter from Joan one day, asking me to dinner; I was to choose which Sunday would be suitable. I telephoned, got Dave. Joan was in bed having a rest. Dave was upset that day. Just choose a date Effie, Joan has been preparing these meals for a month now. There will be a few friends who have been very good to Joan in her illness, and she wants to share a meal with them.' I gave Dave a date, and I did share in one of the most remarkable meals ever. There were ten guests on the day I went. A three course meal was presented, and it was beautiful. Joan was deteriorating very quickly, but although she was by now just a frame, she managed to cope. She ate little, but was satisfied with the effort she had made.

I still kept my visits going, usually arriving about three o'clock. One Sunday I arrived, and there was a person at the door I did not know, I asked to see Joan, Dave was out. The lady said, 'Joan is not well enough to receive visitors today.' I left in my car. I was not long back in Erskine when the phone rang. It was Dave, he was upset at the very idea I was not even admitted to the house. Dave had just come home, had gone in to see Joan. She asked him the time, he told her it was just after three, and Joan said, 'Where is Effie today? I must see her, its very important.'

I drove back to Auchenreoch. Joan was very low, sad to say the reason she wanted to see me was to make arrangements for her funeral. I gently told Joan I could not arrange her funeral service because I was not her parish minister.

She said to me, 'Hush, hush, I've already made arrangements with Alastair. He will be in the manse tomorrow morning, You know each other well.'

Rev. Alastair McLachlan, and I were in the same year at Trinity College. I had the privilege of preaching him into his second charge at Kilsyth. We were not strangers, but good friends; we both knew the situation so we did share in the service. Joan Matthew must have had some awareness that time was short, as she passed away on the Tuesday of that week. She was a remarkable woman. I knew her well, and it was an honour to pay tribute to her life. I was able to speak of her generosity of spirit, her hospitality and was able to break my promise about the school jerseys.

I still held to my original pastoral plan, to visit hospital once per week if necessary, but I don't ever remember not having someone in hospital. I had a very good member of my congregation, Mr Cooper. I went in to see him one day, late in the afternoon. He had had an operation that morning, and he was wrapped in tin foil, just like a chicken. I sat down at the bed, he seemed to be unconscious. I took his hand and said a prayer, and as I left the bed, I thought, Mr Cooper would not really know I was there. I went home with the idea that I would visit Mr Cooper again tomorrow; I did not think I could leave the visit till the next week. Late in the evening Mrs Cooper phoned to say that she had just come from the hospital and her husband was able to tell her that the minister had been and that we had a prayer together? Who says prayer does not work?

I always wore my clerical collar when visiting in the parish and especially in hospitals. It was better for the nursing staff if they knew who was walking into a ward. There was one episode I have never forgotten. On one of my weekly visits to Stobhill Hospital, two women were coming out of the hospital. One of them was obviously very upset, the other was trying to comfort her. As they drew level with me they stopped. The comforter said, 'You're a minister, can you help us. This is my sister, she has just had some very bad news. Her husband does not have long to live, he has cancer. They are both very upset, because they don't have a minister; they used to go to church, but stopped quite a while ago.'

'If I can help I will, let's go back into the ward.' They agreed and we all went to see the husband. We had prayer together, there were a lot of tears shed, but after a few minutes I was able to ask a few questions. The first was where did they live, and I was particularly happy to hear they came from Colston Milton in Springburn. The minister of Colston Milton Church was the man who had licensed me in Glasgow Cathedral, we knew each other well. The Rev. Jack Stewart I was sure would look after the needs of this family, who were living in his parish. I took the name and address of the couple and continued with my own visiting. When I got back to the manse I phoned Jack Stewart and told him the story, giving him the name and address. Rev. Jack phoned me later that night to say that he had visited the wife, and the husband in hospital, and he would look after them. Two weeks later he took the funeral service for the family. A few weeks afterwards the widow appeared at Colston Milton Church, and later on joined the church and became one of the Rev. Jack's very good members. The clerical collar, I believed, was my passport, it certainly worked on that day. I have never been afraid or ashamed to wear it.

Congregational visiting still went on, district by district; it was slow, but they knew I would come. By 1978, just before the linkage was dissolved I had visited both congregations once. That had taken me more or less four years. It was four years well spent; I knew most of my members names by heart.

The elderly and the house-bound were visited every six weeks, and they got to the stage they put the expected date of the next visit on the calendar.

There were also the visits for baptism, and funerals. The great thing about Milton of Campsie was that the parish folk, whether they attended the church or not, were mine, so their needs had to be met also. The parish only had two churches, St Pauls RC and mine, it was a compact area. After Father McCulloch was transferred, our new priest was Father Archibald. He was there all of my ministry, and we continued with the sharing principle.

The lady in St Paul's who played the organ took ill. Miss Annie McGarrigle was a real wee character. She had been one of Miss Moxon's professional dancers in her younger days, and had performed in some of the Glasgow theatres. Even when she was in her seventies, she did highland dancing for the old folks clubs. She was in Stobhill for an operation, and I visited her when doing my weekly visits there. She made a good recovery. When she was back on her feet again she visited me at the manse. She handed me an envelope, and inside was a five pound note. 'That's for your church, I appreciated your visits.' I said to her, 'Annie you've got your own church.'

'No, Mrs Irvine, I've got two churches now.' Every other month I got the envelope from Annie. A faithful wee woman, with a big heart.

Morton's Farm was a joy to visit, Iain and Margaret. The Shields was the name of the farm. It sat above the village on the fells of Campsie. My first contact was really while I was waiting to be ordained. I needed a walk and the Campsie hills looked very inviting. My big dog was very docile; he never needed a lead at all, and never left my side; labradors are like that. Up past the school and onto the farm road I did go. I kept walking, it was wonderful, a truly beautiful day. Being a townie, I was interested in the sheep and stopped to have a look. By this time I was halfway between the farm house and the school, so I had climbed up quite far. All of a sudden, there was what I would call a bellow, 'Get that so and so dog off my hills.' I was startled for the moment and then I hastily retreated. I was told later that the farmer went home and told his wife what had happened. His wife asked for a description of the person and the dog. Margaret had an idea that it was the new minister. Iain was nonplussed; he later explained to the townie that although I knew the dog would not touch the sheep, the sheep did not know that. Yet another lesson learned.

Ever after the episode on the Campsie hills, there was a welcome for me at Shields farm. There was always the smell of home baking in the farm kitchen. It was heated by an Aga cooker. I went up to the farm one dark night, it was the lambing season. The rain was teeming down. I had gone up to see Iain. He was not in, but Margaret said he would not be long, he was out looking for one of the lambs that had got separated from its mother. Iain appeared in the kitchen; he was absolutely soaking wet. There was a wee lamb hanging over his arm, a poor looking wee thing, I thought it was dead. Iain opened the oven door of the Aga and put the lamb inside, I couldn't believe it, surely he wasn't going to cook it, fur and all?

Iain began to laugh. 'Mrs Irvine, I'm not going to cook it; this wee lamb will be running about the kitchen in ten minutes, and if you just wait, I'll give you a bottle and you can feed it.' And so it was.

Many a time I got a phone call in the lambing season, to help feed the orphans. Since I retired, the third daughter of the Morton family was married. I was invited to the wedding, and asked to speak on behalf of the family. It was a wonderful reception, mostly farmers. I told the story of the dog on the hills. Iain got his own back, he told the story of the lamb in the oven. Both stories went down well with the farming community.

Chapter Eleven

We had a problem with the cleaning of the church. The lady who had been responsible for the church was quite unwell, and had to resign. The church had always been spick and span, and we knew it would be hard to get someone as good as Mrs Ross. We put an advert in the local paper, but there were no replies. The session clerk's son Kenneth came to me and asked if he and his friend could have the job. He was about seventeen. His Dad was not amused. I backed the boys. 'What have we got to lose, if they make a bad job of it, we just sack them. Let's give them a three months trial.' The trial lasted for the rest of my ministry. Kenneth was left with the job on his own, when the other young lad went to university. The church was a credit to Kenneth and his friend.

On 17 June 1979, 'Kirking' of Strathkelvin District Council, was held in the church. The lessons were read by Provost David Stark and A. W. Harrower. Milton folk were very happy about this, because the wee church had never been asked to host this occasion before.

When I arrived in Milton, in 1972, I did begin the congregational visiting. There was a couple called John and Barbara Ross. Barbara was in the church every Sunday, but John did not come. I went to see John. We had a nice chat, and I asked him if he would not consider coming to church with Barbara. I knew he was a member of the church before I arrived in Milton. It came out that he was not keen on women ministers. Over the months I persevered; we got on well together. I eventually challenged John, but the invitation was not accepted. One Sunday morning, with great joy, I saw John in church beside Barbara.

By this time I was taking my own groups to the Holy Land. and in 1977 there were a few of my own congregation going with me. I was amazed when Barbara booked, not just herself on the pilgrimage but John, who was eager to join with us. The tour went very well. John was a great help, there was a wealth of spirituality about John. He supported me on that tour, reading the Scriptures for me, and encouraging the group as much as possible. John became a very faithful member of Milton Church. He was a builder and stonemason to trade. When John retired, he came to me, and said that he had not all that much to offer the church, but wanted to give back to the Church all that he had received in fellowship, and in his pilgrimage to the Holy Land. He said there was only one thing he could offer. 'Your wee church is needing to be pointed, the cement between the stonework is beginning to become sand. I will repoint all of the church.' Every morning from about six o'clock, John Ross would be seen up the ladders, painstakinly pointing the wee church he loved. It took him all of six months. That's what I call devotion.

I was in Stobhill visiting one day, and standing outside the ward was one of my congregation.

'What are you doing here, Jean?'

'It's Bruce, he took ill at work, they think its appendicitis.'

I went into the ward to see him. He was not very good, had quite a lot of pain, but he was cheery enough, more concerned about Jean. That of course was typical of Bruce Robertson. Eventually it was discovered that Bruce had cancer, he was only thirty six. All the treatments which were available at that time were tried out on Bruce, but nothing stopped the progress of the cancer.

Bruce Robertson prepared himself for the inevitable; he also tried to prepare his family. While he was in hospital, on my usual visit Bruce had his will ready for me to sign. He seemed relieved that he had done this. Bruce did come home from hospital; he was just a shadow of his former self, but he still came to church. The phone rang one day in the manse, It was Bruce, he wanted to see me, so over I went.

Bruce said, 'We have something to tell you, Jean is expecting a baby. We want you to know it is not a mistake. We both decided that when I'm gone the baby will help Jean and the children to get on with life. We hope we will have your blessing.'

We did have our prayers together; Graeme and Heather were also told, there were no secrets within the family circle.

Time passed quickly for this unique family; they were all facing a harrowing experience, but there was never a word of complaint. Bruce continued to deteriorate. Young Graeme was to be a strong support for his mum Jean. The boy was only ten years old, but his Dad had told him what the future would bring. Graeme was to become the head of the family, to look after his wee sister Heather who was only eight, and of course there would be a new baby to cope with. It was a tall order for a wee lad, but Graeme made that promise to help Mum with the new baby.

Time came for this very special baby to be born. I think Bruce had reached the stage of hanging on to life, to see this baby, this very much wanted child, into the world. Bruce was no longer able to be on his feet. I got the phone call on the Saturday night to tell me that the baby was born, and I went into the hospital with a polaroid camera to take the baby's picture. She was named Fiona Gail. I hurried home with the snap of a beautiful baby girl. Bruce took the photo, kissed it and put it on his bedside table. He closed his eyes; he was content, all was well, we thought.

I was called out on the Sunday evening. The baby was not doing very well, and they planned to send the wee one to Yorkhill Hospital on the Monday morning, but thought it better, if I were willing, to have the baby baptized. Jean agreed, the baby was in an incubator. I baptized her, Fiona Gail Robertson, but we still hoped that she would be all right. It wasn't to be, the wee mite died just before five that morning. Jean pleaded with me to take her home. I tried to comfort her, she was crying sorely. Jean turned to me and said, 'This baby was to be special for me.' My quick reply was, 'You have Graeme and Heather, this wee Fiona is for Bruce.' Fortunately for all concerned, Jean accepted that explanation. I said to her that I would go home now and see Bruce. Jean's Mum was looking after the family at this time, and when I got to their house, Jean's Mum opened the door. She was in some state; she had been notified by the hospital that the baby had died, and Bruce had not opened his eyes since he received the snap of the baby. The doctor was due at any time. He arrived, went upstairs, but he was only gone a few minutes when he came back down to say that Bruce had died. There was only five hours between the passing of Fiona and that of Bruce.

The news spread rapidly round the village. It was a very sad time, how Jean Robertson coped I'll never know. The funeral arrangements had been made by Bruce: his coffin had to be in the church, as was his wish, and I had promised it would be so. Bruce had worked for the Automobile Association at Erskine, and there was a goodly number of his colleagues there on that day. Jean asked my husband Alex to carry the baby's coffin into church, and this he did. It's not often that a wee white coffin lies beside that of a parent. Daddy and Fiona were buried together at Logie Cemetery.

Just along the road there was the Davidson family. Twins had just been born, they were a wee bit frail and their older brother was only about two years old; he had been in hospital at the same time. When Ena Davidson got the twins and Euan home it was a bit of a handful. Jean Robertson went in to see Ena, and despite her own grief, offered to help Ena with the children. Her offer was accepted. The twins were called Alastair and Kenneth. They brought new life to Jean. To this day the Davidson family have included Jean Robertson in all their family celebrations. To the Davidson boys Jean would always be Aunt Jean. Young Graeme kept his promise to his Dad, and looked after his Mum and wee sister, he did not marry until he was twenty eight years old. Lorraine and Graeme now have a wee girl of their own. Heather is in her own flat in Glasgow. By the way, I conducted the wedding service for Graeme and Lorraine; the bridegroom asked me to do it in memory of his Dad. How could I refuse? I still keep in touch with Jean Robertson, I always admired and respected Jean and Bruce; their faith, throughout their testing times, shone like a beacon in a dark world.

There was always some fun on a Sunday morning in church. I tried to make the children's address as interesting as possible. There was a wee boy at Trinity Church who every Sunday would have a reply for me. No matter what I brought into church as a visual aid, either his granny had one, or his auntie had one. I thought I would sort him out one Sunday. I bought a six foot skeleton. I draped it over the pulpit and before I could say a word, the wee fellow shouted out, 'I saw one of these last week, and I ran away.' Talk about taking the wind out of your sails.

In Milton one Sunday when I had decided to have some time off, I'd got a minister to do pulpit supply. He happened to be a wee bit older. Young Grace, about five years old, was quite shocked when the minister entered the pulpit. She stood up and said to her Mum, 'Let's go, Mum, it's a man.' Mum had to take the child out, she was not going to have a man minister under any circumstances. That made my day.

We had a big Sunday School, and when it came to Christmas parties, we had to have three. The first one was at 1.30 p.m., the wee one's. I always got a present from Santa. Before the next party I would return the present to Santa. At the second party I got the present back. The same drill was used for the third party. On the Sunday morning, we were talking about presents. I opened the one I got from Santa three times. It was a handkerchief with the latter E on it. I asked the children what the E was for, and the smart answer was Wee Effie. 'So that's what you call me behind my back.' Another wee voice pipes up, 'my mammy says that too.'

I bought a huge oblong, piece of polystyrene. I wanted it to look like a huge cheque and I very carefully copied from my Bank of Scotland cheque book. 'Pay Jesus Christ from my account.' dated it and signed it, it looked great. It was put in the pulpit earlier so that the children would not see it. At the children's address I lifted up the cheque, and explained what promising to pay meant; it seemed to go all right. After the service was over, one of my elders came into the vestry. My Alison wants to know if that cheque's mistake was deliberate just to catch us out.

I said to Alex McFarlane, 'There's surely not a mistake on that cheque.' Said he, 'There certainly is, you have spelled Jesus wrongly.' He went into the pulpit and brought the cheque out, and sure enough, I had printed 'JESES'. By this time the church was empty, I said to Alex I would sort it for next Sunday. The following Sunday I brought out the cheque again, It was changed to the correct spelling in red. I said, 'do you know what it means when a cheque bounces?' The adults laughed and the children listened. Two children's addresses with one visual aid was quite good.

I well remember my first wedding service. The boy was walking up and down the vestry. I was doing the same on the other side. I said to him, 'You will need to excuse me, this is my first wedding service.' His quick reply, was, 'We are both in the same boat.'

Another bridegroom, he was out and in his pockets continually. I asked him if he had lost anything, 'no, its all right,' but this continual opening and buttoning of the jacket, and out and in the pockets was getting to me. I said again, 'Look, if you have lost anything, let's find it before you walk through that door.'

'I've lost my enthusiasm,' was the reply.

Bridegroom and best man came into the vestry carrying grey tile hats. The groom said, 'My future mother-in-law said that you would tell us how to carry these tile hats into church,' I could see problems ahead. I said to them, 'See that shelf up there, just put the hats up there.'

'But my future mother-in-law says "Start the way you mean to end, son".'

'The hats stay in the vestry, your future mother-in-law might be the boss out there, but I am the boss in here.' The hats stayed on the shelf.

There was a reception of a wedding in the village hall. Now don't ask me why, but the floor of the hall sloped from the main door, down to the exit. When you were playing badminton, if you were at the top of the hall you had a definite advantage. On the day of the wedding, a trestle table was at the bottom of the hall, and on the table was a three tiered bride's cake. It looked very appetising, I just loved bride's cake. The receiving party, the bride and groom and the rest of the retinue, were standing with their backs to the table. There was a little flower girl standing with her back to the table, right where the bride's cake rested. The little girl was swaying back and forward, and every time she moved backwards, she hit the table. I knew if I did not alert the bride's mother, the cake was going to go. I touched the bride's mother's shoulder, but I was too late, the top tier vanished under the table. There were the bride's mother and the minister, on our knees trying to stick this cake together again. Needless to say, I did not eat bride's cake that night, because that was the bit the waitresses served after the meal.

Yet another catastrophe at a wedding reception. The co-op purvey did not turn up. The bride was in tears, the bride's mother was in tears. Of course everyone thinks the minister has an answer for every predicament. The only answer I had was to have the speeches first, but the refreshments had not arrived either. However that's just what we did. It was the driest wedding reception I had ever attended.

The local undertaker phoned me one day. 'We have a parish funeral.' That is a funeral organised by social services. 'I will pick you up at three.'

'Will you bring me back?'

'Aye we only leave them one at a time up there.'

At Daldowie crematorium. I had the last funeral on a holiday Friday. Coming out of the building I said to the man in charge. 'How do you cope during a holiday week-end?' Without a smile on his funerial face he replied, 'It's all right, Mrs Irvine, we have a skeleton staff on.'

I baptised four sets of twins during my ministry, but there was also a set of triplets. Daddy was a policeman. I said to him that he would have to give me the right name for the right baby, because if he didn't I might make a mistake. His quick reply was, 'Mrs Irvine your guess will be as good as mine, I am on shifts, I don't know the difference between them.' I don't know to this day if I got it right or wrong, but Mummy never said a word.

There was another day, a wee lad about four was being baptised. I went through the service, and the child was very interested in all that was happening. I baptized him and as he stepped back his Daddy put his hand on his head. The wee fellow was quite hurt as he shouted at his Dad, 'Daddy, you've spoiled my wet.' It took a bit of pacifying, and he wanted it done all over again, but eventually he accepted that he was rightly baptized.

It was a harvest service, I had taken a Tupperware tumbler into the pulpit filled with water; I was going to speak about the value of water. I never got the chance; a very excited wee lad shouted up, 'My mammy had a tupperware party one night, she made a lot of money.' Nothing is secret as far as the young ones are concerned; his mother was not very pleased.

The Sunday School was healthy, we had a loyal staff. In 1977 one of our very dedicated elders, Tommy Cains, became the superintendent. He had a great influence on the children. He not only saw to it that they got a well balanced Bible study programme but he influenced the children to be concerned for those who were less fortunate than themselves. From 1977 to 1986, the Sunday School donated £1,354.73 to various charities, which was quite a sum of money. A Sunday School can only exist if if there are enough folk who are willing to be teachers. The dedication of Sunday School teachers over all the years in the Church of Scotland has sometimes been forgotten. We often fail to realise that the Christian faith and experience begins in the infants class in the SS. As a minister, I was always more than just grateful for the continuity of service offered by our SS staff. One of the most important parts of the church's life is to be found among the young. I've always believed, no young folk, no future.

Believe it or not, there are some children who do not like Sunday School. We managed to bridge that gap. We had a woman elder who sat at the back of the church each Sunday morning and marked the cards of the 'Young Worshippers League'. Mrs Edgar was very faithful to the task. When Sunday School attendance was recognised, and they were getting their awards, the 'Young Worshippers League' were also included in the prize list.

We also had a Youth Fellowship, who met in the manse on a Sunday evening. I tried to get them to stand on their own feet. It was rather difficult to maintain, because the young ones were maybe there a year, then off to university; the nearest halls of learning were in Glasgow, but it was amazing how many of our young folk went to Edinburgh. One of our group, Patrick, said he was going to Newcastle to study transport. I said to him, 'You surely don't need to go so far away to study buses etc.' He very kindly explained to the old minister that he was going to study the 'running' of transport. One was always learning.

Chapter Twelve

I did go to the Holy Land with the Rev. James Currie in April. It was the trip of a lifetime. We were there for fifteen days, and it passed all too quickly. To walk the streets of the old city of Jerusalem was something I could never forget. On these early visits, the narrow lanes were not tarred, you were walking on hard baked earth. The only transport was by donkey. All produce was piled on top of these small animals, and very often all you could see was a head, a tail and four spindly legs. Otherwise it was boys pushing barrows. You had to be fleet of foot, as the barrow boys and those with the donkeys, when they got the momentum of movement going they could not stop. The smells of the spices, fish and donkey dung were really something, though in a very short time one got used to it; the noise was the same. Moving through the Old City was fascinating, you were jostled by so many people, of different faiths and none.

On that first visit, Jerusalem was a place with treasured memories: we walked in the footsteps of Jesus, within the Old City walls. We had a marvellous leader in the Rev. James. It was obvious he was thirled to his Lord Jesus and the pilgrims who followed were to know the depth of his faith. James had only one idea in his mind and that was to teach and give his pilgrims the opportunity of going back home knowing and understanding the Scriptures better than ever before. Alex and I were thrilled to be part of the group.

Everyone on the group was given the opportunity to read from their Bible, and if you had a special passage all you had to do was tell James; he had an amazing memory for names and requests. Our first visit was to the Old City. We walked to the Ecce Homo Convent. Ecce Homo means 'Behold the Man', reminding us of the trial of Jesus before Pilate. It is traditionally believed that this place was the site of the Fortress of Antonia. Down under the floors, one can find a cistern, and above that, what is known as the 'Pavement' or 'Lithostratos'. Jesus was brought out from the Antonia Fortress to be questioned by the

Roman Governor. The original stones of the Pavement are there; the horses of the Roman soldiers were exercised on this pavement, and the slabs of stone are styrated, which was to prevent the horses' hooves from slipping. It was on The Pavement that Pilate asked the question of the crowd, '*Ecce Homo*' 'What will you have me do with the Man called Christ?' The answer was 'Crucify Him'. For the first three or four years of our visits, the Convent was cared for by the Sisters of Zion. Sister Agnes, who originated from Campbeltown, was the guide for us pilgrims. She had a rich Scottish voice and was a joy to listen to. On part of The Pavement are some markings obviously from the time of Jesus. The marks carved on the surface of the stones are recognised as a game played by the soldiers, known as the Game of the Kings. Sister Agnes believed that the soldiers of the Antonia played this game with Jesus. The soldiers would choose a prisoner, and they threw dice. If the prisoner was lucky he would be given a purple robe, another turn of the dice, the prisoner would be given a sceptre, next he would be crowned as a king, the next throw of the dice, determined whether the prisoner lived or died. I believe Sister Agnes was right. Being in the Holy Land brought us to a greater understanding of the life and times of our beloved Jesus.

James asked me if I would be willing to share in the prayers during the pilgrimage. I said yes. We were in the Room of the Last Supper, and someone had just completed the last of three readings. The voice of James broke into my reverie: 'Effie will now lead us in Prayer.' I did respond, but I asked the Rev. why he had not given me any warning, perhaps the night before. 'Always be prepared,' he said, 'read prayers are no use on a trip like this.' Another great lesson to learn.

Our pilgrimages were held in two parts. Jerusalem and Tiberias. To begin with we lived in the Panorama Hotel in Jerusalem. The owner of the Hotel was Joseph Aweidah, an Arab gentleman and I mean a gentleman. In Tiberias we lived in the Church of Scotland Hospice, which at one time was a Scottish hospital. Both the hotel and the hospice were very comfortable and very homely.

It was in the hospice that I first met Alistair McCabe. He was the warden of the place. There were lovely gardens, and it looked over the Sea of Galilee. The pilgrims were housed in three separate buildings. It was good accommodation, but no frills. We did not mind, to be there was a bonus. The dining room was part of the main, building and the standard of the meals was very good indeed. Those who cleaned and cooked were local girls. Tiberias is a Jewish town, so those who cared for us were Jewish. The stones of that area are made of black basalt; all the buildings of the hospice were built with the local stone and were greyish black.

We had a service of Holy Communion at six o'clock in the morning in the garden of the hospice. The sun had risen, the garden was bathed in sunlight, the birds were singing, we were wrapped in the peace of the place. That Communion Service has lived in my memory over all the years. The feeling of the nearness of the presence of Jesus was very, very real. The pattern of this first pilgrimage became the template for all that was to follow. Over all the years, we never departed from the pilgrim way.

These pilgrimages were organised by Inter Church Christian Travel. The man who had brought Inter Church into being was a great church man called Canon Peyton. He was a lovely character. He was very interested in the young man Alistair. About a year after I had met Alistair, Canon Peyton asked him to join the travel team at Inter Church. The Church of Scotland lost a very good warden but Inter Church Travel gained a dedicated individual. Alistair became Canon Peyton's right-hand man. All our groups were then booked through Alistair McCabe.

In 1974, both Alistair and the Canon were in the hospice in Tiberias when James and I arrived. They asked if they could have a word with me. Puzzled, I went to the office, I was asked if I would consider taking a group of my own in the next year, 1975; James said only if she comes with me in April. And so it was. The first of my own groups went out on July 1975, I had sixteen pilgrims. Alex went with me and looked after the tipping etc. It turned out to be quite successful. I went back with James nearly every year, but took my own groups in 1977, 1978, 1980, 1983, 1988, 1989, 1990, 1992, 1996, My own last group was organised for May 2000, but it has been cancelled twice, because of the trouble in the Middle East.

I worked with the Rev. James on sixteen visits, assisted Rev. Charlie McMillan twice, assisted Rev. Elizabeth Sutherland twice. I served on what was called Familiarisation Tours. These special tours were for ministers, who went for half price. The prime reason for doing this was to give ministers who had never been to the Holy Land the opportunity to learn to be leaders in the future. I assisted in these ventures six times. Rev. Ian Paton asked me on to his team one year.

When Doctor Eileen McIlroy and I visited the Holy Land together, Alistair McCabe got us missionary rates in Jerusalem and Tiberias. We travelled the Holy Land together, on Arab buses, and by taxi. We had a wonderful time. We were on the road early every morning and only returned to base when it was getting dark. The last pilgrimage was the Millenium trip, when the leader was Rev. Peter Hattersley, an English vicar. I had gone out with the idea that I was to work my passage, but learned later from Anne McCabe, Alistair's sister, that I was to sit back and enjoy it, this I did. In all I have visited the Holy Land thiry nine times, and hope to do my fortieth some time, before I get too old.

Alistair worked for Inter Church Travel until 1982. Canon Peyton was to retire at that time, he had trained Alistair well, and felt the firm would be all right with Alistair at the helm. Sad to say, that did not happen. Inter Church Travel brought in a businessman, who had never been in the travel business. Alistair and three other employees decided to leave, and Alistair started McCabe Travel. He has never looked back, because as always, Alistair believed very much in the personal touch. James and I switched to McCabe Travel and I have worked for them and with them ever since. It was 1983 really when Alistair got off the ground with his business. With hindsight I believe that Inter Church Travel did Alistair a favour. The grandparents of Alistair were missionaries in Kalimpong in India. George and Molly McCabe, Alistair's parents were also missionaries in Kalimpong in India. Alistair was born there and has an Indian passport. Dad George was a minister in Dalkeith Church and was a great help to his son, when McCabe travel was in its infancy.

Sadly George McCabe passed away a few years ago, Molly is still hale and hearty, and Anne McCabe, Alistair's sister, runs an office for McCabe travel in Manchester. There will be more information about this very wonderful family, because every new experience I had stemmed from the fact that McCabe travel gave me so many opportunities to travel with the firm.

There were plenty of funny experiences on our different tours. There were always the characters who were larger than life itself. The following memories couldn't possibly be in chronological order, nor do I remember on whose tour or which tour, but I was there.

The lowest number of persons James ever had on a Holy Land tour was sixty five. We had two buses. We were preparing for yet another trip. James phoned me to tell me that we were now booked for one hundred and six pilgrims. My answer to that was, we will be asked to drive the bus; his answer was, so what. On that trip there was a stool in each bus; you will know who sat on it in our bus. It was not very comfortable, in fact it was dangerous.

We had a Mrs Byrne with us one year, who was from Australia. The journey on that day was to Mount Tabor, the traditional site of the Transfiguration. When we come off the bus at the village of Dabouriya, we change to seven-seater taxis and are whisked to the top of the mount. On the journey up we traverse eighteen hairpin bends. The drivers are very skilful, but the first visit up that mountain makes you feel a wee bit light-headed. The rule for this part of the pilgrimage, so that everyone gets time to appreciate the architect's special gifts, is that those up in the first taxi are supposed to be first down again. When we reach the church which stands on the summit, we all enter together. The architect for this church was an Italian called Barlutzi. The church is built on three levels. It depicts the Transfiguration story. On the top level looking up, we see Jesus in mosaic, Moses and Elijah, plus Peter, James and John. We are standing on the middle level, then we look down and see the peacock windows which represent eternal life, quite beautiful. We usually have devotions there and then it's back in the taxis and off to Nazareth. But this day, when we got back to the buses, James realised he was one short. He said that the person missing would probably be on my bus. I had already counted mine and had the full complement, 'Count them again,' says he. I did, it was not one of mine. Time was being wasted, he hated to waste time. 'James, would you not be better to get one of the taxis and go back up the Mount?' Off he went; he had to hire the taxi, he was not best pleased. When he got to the top of Tabor, there was Mrs Byrne, very happily enjoying the peace and the beauty of the place without, as she said, all these other pilgrims. James was not a happy chappy that day, and I got strict instructions to really be last everywhere.

We were going down to Eilat for the day. Six in the morning saw us climb aboard the bus. We had never been there before, it was to be a journey of two hundred miles each way. This was a gift from Joseph Aweidah of the Panorama Hotel. Because I had not been before I had Joseph on my bus. About a hundred miles down the road we were travelling through the Negev desert. Joseph was pointing out various landmarks. He said these are acacia trees, you can see how they are bent and the branches are shaped by the wind. By this time I was

Own group, 1987.

needing very much to see a loo. I said to Joseph, 'Stop the bus, it's "acacia" – desperate need,' The bus was stopped, but a few miles along the road. When we got to Eilat, we went out in a flat bottomed boat with a glass hull, this way we could see the beautiful coloured coral and spectacularly coloured fish. Dr Eileen was sitting beside me. I said to her that the lady sitting across from us was throwing part of her picnic roll into the bottom of the boat. I asked the lady involved what she was doing. She replied, 'I am feeding the fish.' We tried to tell her that there was glass between us and the fish, but I am afraid she was not listening.

Rev. James Currie's own book is called *God's Con Man*. He certainly was. When there was a big number of persons on the tour it was impossible to have a large number of single rooms. James always said, 'Folk don't need single rooms on a pilgrimage, it's all about sharing.' Mind you, he never put them off with a sore heart. 'We will see about rooming lists when we get there,' you understand, and the poor souls went away quite happy, till we got to the first hotel. Standing there in the dining room about 1 a.m. they are all very tired, then the fun started, 'Och, Miss so and so, theres another young lady needing a companion, it would help me a great deal if some of you would share.'

The pleading would go on for some time, and eventually, everybody who wanted a single room had found some one to share with. 'You are marvellous people, I've never had such a caring group as you lot.' All went to bed quite happy. He did it every pilgrimage, and it never failed.

There was no smoking on the buses, James detested the smell. And it was the same with drink, he was so much against alcohol it was unbelievable. There was a day we were walking through the Old City. Passing the fruit quarter, one of the barrow traders, gave him a large handful of strawberries. I said to him, 'You are surely not going to eat them.'

'I can't hurt the lad's feelings.'

'The lad's not going to know, James, be careful, these strawberries have not been washed.' He was certainly enjoying them. I walked to the end of the group. I was annoyed with him. We were heading for the Church of the Holy Sepulchre. He was there before me, and when I got into the church the guide had already started on his story. I couldn't see James anywhere, then someone said, 'He's sitting down over there.' I knew that was trouble. When I went over, James was rather grey in colour, he was in a sweat. I said, 'Are you having a heart attack?'

'No, but I've got diarrhoea.'

We had to get him a taxi back to the hotel. We finished the visit without James. When I got back to the hotel, I dashed upstairs to see James. He was flat out. He had had a sore time of it. I took with me a miniature bottle of brandy; I always had one for symptoms of that ilk. I said, 'Sit up and take this teaspoonful of brandy.'

He looked up at me, and he said, 'I'll die first.'

That was it, I said, 'Well, just die, maybe this time you will have learned your lesson.' He was in his bed for two days. I called the strawberry barrows the diarrhoea factory and forbade any of my groups ever to touch them.

When we go to visit the Dome of the Rock, the most beautiful mosque in Israel, we are standing on Temple Mount. We always go inside the mosque, because it is built over Mt. Moriah, where Abraham was about to sacrifice his son Isaac. If you wish to enter a mosque you must remove your shoes. Someone is left outside to make sure that the shoes don't walk. On one of our visits, they seemed to take an awful long time in the mosque. I got a wee bit bored so I decided I'd mix up the shoes. It was great fun but James was not amused. He did see the funny side later on.

We were at the baptist bookshop one day, it was a good place to buy gifts to take home. The bus had not turned up to take us back to the hotel. One of our minister friends, Charlie McMillan, and his session clerk began to sing while we were waiting. They did a double act, and the Arabs were throwing money at them. They did enjoy the busking, so did we.

James always had a party on the last night of our pilgrimage. The pilgrims were supposed to entertain us, but James and I were also press-ganged into doing a party piece. My brother made a hardboard guitar for me. It was hinged in the middle and had the strings painted on. I carried it back and forward to the Holy Land each year. My song was, 'I wanna be a punk rocker'. My teeth were blacked out, I had teabag earings, big safety pins stuck on my cheeks, plus an old torn T-shirt and shorts, and bare feet. James was a riot with his rendering of Duncan McCrae's 'wee cock sparrow'. At least James could sing.

We had a lovely man with us from the highlands of Scotland. He was on my bus on our outing to Haifa. When we went up north we always took the opportunity to stop off for a quick dip in the Mediterranean Sea. You get five minutes to change into swimming gear, five minutes for the dip and another five to get dried and changed. Rev. James could do it in that time, so everybody else had to follow suit. Those who had made the effort were back on the bus. I began to count my people, but was amused by my friend from the Highlands, who had no teeth in, I tried to get him to behave, by saying 'Put your teeth in, I'm trying to count the passengers.' His reply was, 'It will be hard for me, I've left them in the Mediterranean.' His wife was furious with him; when he smiled all we could see was a mouthful of clear gums. His party piece was hilarious: he came into the lounge dressed as a fairy, no teeth, hairy legs. His wife was not amused, but we were. He, of course, was without teeth for the rest of the pilgrimage.

One of the lovely things that happened to me was on one of my own trips. I had a couple with me who were blind. Cathie had no sight at all, Stewart could just see shadows. I was prepared to take Cathie and Stewart to the Church of All Nations, at the Garden of Gethsemane on the Sunday morning. Mass was quite early, and there was plenty time for me to get the group to the Scottish Church of St Andrews. Canon Ronald Brownrigg came into the dining room for

Dome of the Rock, Jerusalem.

dinner. We were the only two leaders in the hotel; July was always quiet because of the heat. Ronald came over to my table to welcome me and my group. He said he had a favour to ask me. He had a gentleman who was a Presbyterian and wanted to go to the Scottish church on the Sunday morning. I said, 'That's no problem,' I explained my concern about Cathie and Stewart. Did he by any chance have a Catholic on his group?

'I can do better than that, I have a Priest on my group, I'll go and bring him over.' Cathie and Stewart were delighted.

Then I said, 'Where is this Presbyterian?'

The Canon had a smile on his face. His name is Gilbert McKenzie.

I followed the Canon to a table. Gilbert McKenzie was six feet five inches tall, and he was coal black. Gilbert came from Barbados. As he stood up, I said to him, 'Where did you get a name like that, with a face that colour?' I can still hear that swell of laughter rising from deep inside this enormous man. He was a very wonderful character. It turned out he was the Rev. Gilbert McKenzie. He came with our group quite often. A few months later, Gilbert arrived at my manse. He was going to France for some conference and had some time to spare. We had him for a whole weekend, he was very relaxed in our home. My mother thought he was the greatest human being she had ever met. Of course the home baking went down a treat and he loved his food. He promised if he was ever able he would come back but sorry to say he never made it back to us. We had a lovely letter of thanks.

In 1990, I had a group organised for my thirtieth visit. I was retired by this time. Some of my own congregation were going with me, plus the minister who had been called to Milton of Campsie, Diane Stewart. She had been an assistant to me after Bill Stewart, no relation. It had been discussed at the Kirk Session that they should recognise my thirtieth visit. One of my elders, Tom Cameron, suggested they should do something about the curtains in the chancel of the Church of St Andrew's in Jerusalem. Tom had served as an elder at a communion service, while on pilgrimage with me. He was aware that the curtains in the chancel were in disrepair. His suggestion was accepted, and the money was sent out by the church at Milton to the church in Jerusalem, and they had the curtains made there. Every time I go into St Andrew's Church I feel very proud of my wee church in Milton.

Rev. George McCabe and I shared in a few pilgrimages, He was another personality who lived his Christian life. Because he was born in India he had a lovely sounding voice; his preaching was superb. It was not easy to be a leader with a group of ministers. We had one with us who was a very keen photographer. We were at the Dead Sea. Having been there so often I didn't bother going into the water, but spent time taking pictures for other people. This minister went into the Dead Sea with his camera hanging round his neck. I shouted to him not to take it with him, but oh no, they always know better. One of the women decided to do the same, and as she waded into the water, she asked our friend the minister if he would take her photograph with her camera. Of course, he took her camera, forgetting for the minute his own camera hanging round his neck. He bent down to get the lady properly in the picture, and his own camera went below the water. It was too late to save it. By the time we got back to Jerusalem, the camera was a solid bit of metal. If folk would only be prepared to listen. I did write a letter to his Insurance Company, and he did get enough money to buy a new camera.

We will continue with The Holy land in the next chapter. There is still some mileage there yet.

Chapter Thirteen

We continue with our Holy Land memories. There were sad times as well as the usual happy days. We had only arrived in Jerusalem on the Thursday, and were making our way to the Church of Peter in Gallicantu, which means, the Church of the Cock Crowing. We had identical twins with us, whose names were George and John. I had just called them 'John George', because I could not tell them apart. They were dressed exactly the same, their luggage was the same. They had just retired from work, were bachelors, and had lived together all of their lives.

The church visit was over, and there was a flight of stairs to climb, about twenty steps. John and George were in front of me, and as they reached the road, one of them dropped to the floor. I went up the stairs two at a time. George said, 'It's John.' One of our faithful pilgrims, Ellen Pollock, who usually came with James, was the night sister in the Victoria Infirmary. She worked on John till the medics arrived but it was too late. John had died of a heart attack. James took the group back to the hotel. Unfortunately it was Friday, the start of the Jewish Shabbat: Nothing moves after twelve noon. We had no idea what hospital John had been taken to. George was getting anxious. James detailed Ellen, myself, and our guide Hamid, to find out where John was. Hamid had a car, which made things easier. We went round a few hospitals but no joy. Eventually Hamid remembered yet another hospital in new Jerusalem, and fortunately that was it. The only reason we were able to get information was that the doctor who had received John at the hospital was an Indian lady. She was still able to be on duty, even though it was Shabbat.

The doctor could not have issued a death certificate till she had seen someone who knew the circumstances of John's passing. George was able to advise the doctor that John had a heart problem, also the pills he was taking etc. While we were waiting I said to Ellen, 'Because these two men were identical twins, could George have the same condition as John?' Ellen said.

'That's right, we will need to find out, and we will need to have a word with the doctor.'

We were saved the problem of asking; the doctor was thinking along the same lines.

Burials take place as soon as possible in the Holy Land because of the heat. George was asked if he wanted John to be taken back to Edinburgh. The answer was no, John had always wanted to visit the Holy Land, and George thought it better that John's resting place should be there. He was buried in Tantur Christian cemetery. Joseph Aweidah, was a great help. He had the male staff of the Panorama Hotel and Hamid our guide to be the representives of the family of George and John. The Arab families do not have gravediggers, the male members of the family do this themselves. It was a great comfort to George and for all of us on this pilgrimage.

The question now arose as to what George would want to do: go home, or stay. He had the option, Alistair McCabe offered to get him a flight home. George said no, he would finish the pilgrimage, because he had been looked after by the group and his Arab friends just as well as he would have done at home. James placed George in the care of Ellen and myself. James said, 'One of you will be with George each day.' The group were wonderful, their support was first class, and gradually, George did not need any babysitting by either Ellen or me. John had had the threat of just such a heart attack before his journey. George was able to accept the situation, was happy in the company of the group. He was able to visit the cemetery before we left Jerusalem, and did make at least one visit back to Israel with James.

Always, the first Sunday of our tour we attended St Andrew's Church of Scotland in Jerusalem. The St Andrew's flag flies from the tower of this very lovely little church. From the church you look across the Kidron Valley to the old city walls of Jerusalem. When James and I went to Church on these Sundays we were asked to read the lesson. James usually read from the New Testament, and I got the Old Testament. Dr Craig had been the minister there for a few years; we were well acquainted with him. We never knew what the readings would be till we arrived.

That particular Sunday, my bus arrived first. Dr Craig was coming down the steps of the Church to meet us. He was about to hand me my reading, then changed his mind and said, 'I think you should read this today, James can do the Old Testament for a change.' When I got an opportunity to look at the paper, I knew immediately why he had changed the readings and given me the New Testament. It was the story of Zacchaeus, because it says in Luke's Gospel, Zacchaeus was little of stature. Dr Craig certainly had a sense of humour. He got his reward: the congregation did get a laugh, and so did I.

We had a pilgrim called Jim booked for one of our tours. His wife and a wee girl of about four were also coming. About a week before our departure, Jim fell and broke his leg, and was in plaster from hip to toes. He was dependent on crutches, but he was determined to make the tour. He certainly was a pilgrim; fortunately we had Dr Eileen with us on the trip. Before too long the lad's hands were blistered, he certainly was in agony. Some of the roads in Palestine are very rough. Dr Eileen went to the pharmacist and bought some antiseptic ointment. She also bought crepe bandages, and she not only bandaged Jims hands, as the blisters had burst before he had asked for help, she also bandaged the handles of the crutches. That did help Jim but the damage had been done. That young man never missed a day of our pilgrimage, he suffered much, and we learned a lot about courage from him. When it was all over, James asked him if it was worth it. Jim's answer was very direct: 'It was the most moving experience of my life. It's the greatest achievement in my Christian growth. I prayed every night to be sustained every day, and I was.' Speaks for itself, doesn't it. Faith and Prayer, together works miracles.

Nazareth, the place where Jesus grew up. Above the town on a hill is the Church of the Adolescent Christ, it reminds us of the Boy Jesus taking the Journey to Jerusalem. The money for the church was gifted by a French couple, and it was completed in 1924. What is thought to be the largest Christian Church in the Middle East is the Church of the Annunciation. It is the Parish Church of Nazareth. The large cupola or dome is the largest in the Holy Land, and is in the shape of a lily. We had paid our visit to the various places, and had our devotions, and after lunch we tried to give our group free range to wander through the bazaars. Dr Eileen and I were in the main street of Nazareth, when Peggy, wife of James, came to ask me if I was wearing breeks under my slacks, why? Seemingly a wee lady had an accident and two of our nurses were cleaning her up. James was involved as usual his idea was that if I had 'breeks on under my slacks', the

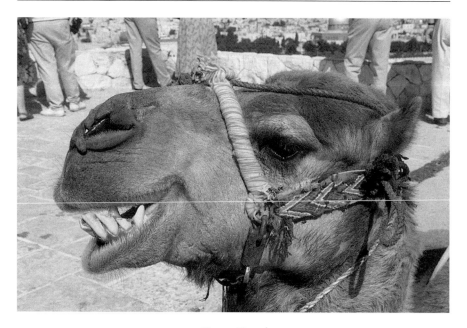

Happy Camel.

problem was solved. My answer, in quite a loud voice, was, 'I will not take my breeks off for any man, not even for James Currie.' Everybody fell about laughing. The outcome was better, the nurses bought two Arab headresses, and used them like nappies. Problem solved.

Saturday night in the manse at Milton. The family were with us, we were having a meal. The phone rang.

'Will you come to Stobhill hospital as soon as possible, there's been a very serious accident.' I can't put a date on this one. Of course, I went to the hospital in double quick time. I got the story from the staff and doctors. There had been an accident outside Lambhill cemetery between a car and a lorry that afternoon. Two men had been killed. A young woman in the car was very badly injured, and had just been moved to Canniesburn Hospital. I asked the name of the girl and said I would go to Canniesburn. That was not the whole story, they then informed me that the mother of the girl was in Stobhill, quite ill, and they needed someone to break the news to her about the accident. I did not recognise the names mentioned, but it turned out they were not very long in Milton. The mother's name was Mrs Milne, a frail wee lady. I was able to speak to her for a wee while, but obviously, she was not receiving the message, I left her in the capable hands of her nursess and went direct to Canniesburn Hospital. The girls name was Pat. She was unrecognisable, her face was enormous, and almost black with bruising. I did not think she would make it through the night. One of the men killed was her young husband, the other was her father, the husband of Mrs Milne. There was no way this scrap of humanity knew of my presence. I spoke to the nurses, who were to keep a twenty four hour vigil at that bed. I asked what were her chances. They told me that the bones in her face were badly broken, and they could not do anything until the swelling went down.

Over some weeks, I visited Pat at Canniesburn, and her Mum in Stobhill. No minister was ever mentioned. I think the family of the young man attended to his funeral arrangements, and Mrs Milne's family did the same for her husband. Very soon the doctors at Canniesburn were able to make a kind of steel helmet for Pat, and she was fed by a tube. The resilience of this young woman amazed me. One day I got a phone call from James Currie. He had been in Canniesburn visiting one of his own members. He was passing Pat's room, noticed how young she was and inquired what had happened. He learned the story, and also that the minister visiting was myself. One day I went in to see Pat and was informed that the 'scaffolding' holding her facial bones together, was to be removed the following week, if the x-rays were OK. The mother, Mrs Milne, would leave Stobhill at the same time.

I never knew Pat before her accident, so did not know how much damage had been done to her personality. They lived across the road from the manse, through a lane. Mrs Milne was poor physically, but was able to cope with the mood swings Pat was having, but they did get on with life.

One day I got a panic phone call from Mrs Milne, Pat said she was going to France on her own for a holiday. Her Mum did not think she was fit enough to do that. She was right, because Pat was having problems with memory, also with money; she never counted change, her mother had to do all that. It was too soon to be going alone anywhere, not even in Scotland. The difficult thing was, Pat had looked for her passport and had found it. Problems were raising their ugly heads.

My mother became very fond of Pat, and nearly every morning Mum would find her on the doorstep of the manse. Mum didn't mind. The young Pat and Mum would have a cup of tea, a wee bit of chat, then off she would go. Asking the same question, can I come back again. I was a bit worried about the intention of Pat and also her determination to follow this plan of a holiday abroad. I spoke to Alex about it. We were going to the Holy Land with James, on our usual April tour. I asked Alex if it were possible for us to take her to the Holy Land with us. It would be a big responsibility. Alex answer was, 'Why not, it might be the very thing, phone James.' Fortunately James was at home, most unusual. I reminded him of Pat, told him the story, then put the 64,000 dollar question. Could we take her with us to the Holy Land, if he had a place. 'I've just had a cancellation, someone's daughter is having a baby, just at the time of our departure. Pat can have that place,' the big man said, 'The group will help to look after her, you know how they are.' I had to let James know quickly because he always had a waiting list.

I ran across to Pat's home. I sat her down and said, 'Now concentrate on what I'm saying: How would you like to go to the Holy Land with Alex and me, on one of Mr Currie's pilgrimages.' She danced about the room, clapping her hands, I had to stop her, she was getting too excited. I told her it was about six weeks away, but the time would go in very quickly. I turned to Mrs Milne and asked her if it would be all right for us to take Pat. She was delighted. I don't think Mrs Milne had slept very well worrying about Pat's other plan. Back to the manse, James said that her name was already down and he would send me a booking form for her and I would help her to fill it in.

Come the morning of our departure for the Holy Land. We had to be at Glasgow Airport for 9.30 a.m. When we went to pick up Pat she was still at breakfast. We always had someone take us the airport, it was a good job it wasn't a taxi. We took her passport, her money, finished her packing, and we left for the airport with Pat finishing her toast. I don't think Pat had any idea where she was going. I said to Alex, it's like looking after a child. He said we would manage. When I really thought about it, I felt I was putting a lot of people on the spot, to help someone they did not even know.

On that tour, there was a very nice young man called Stewart. He was in the Civil Service, and was working in London. He seemed to take a shine to Pat. After we had been on the tour for a few days, Stewart came and asked me about Pat. I told him the story, then he said to me, 'Effie, you and Alex have plenty to do, I could look after Pat for you.'

'I don't mind in the least, but you will have to be responsible, for her money and make sure she does not lose it or give it away, and there is her passport.' That was it; Stewart, took the business of looking after Pat very seriously. She improved wonderfully well on that pilgrimage; day by day, Pat took on a quite different attitude. She seemed to be more responsible, was happy and very relaxed. Stewart was the medicine that Pat needed. I began to worry about what was going to happen when we returned to Scotland.

I need not have worried at all. God works in a mysterious way His wonders to perform. We were only home about a week, when Pat came over to the manse. Her eyes were sparkling. 'Stewart has asked me to marry him, he is coming up at Christmas time, but has no place to stay.'

Alex and I both said, 'He can stay here, just phone him back and tell him now.'

I stopped this rush into matrimony. Killjoy, but remember they had only met in April, Pat was a lot better, was able to manage much better with her money, shopping, etc. Her Mum said it was amazing. Certainly, Stewart was a bit older than Pat, to my mind that was all to the good. I had a wee talk with Pat on her own, but she was itching to make that phone call. We gave her the phone.

Stewart, was very serious about his intentions. He was a batchelor, and had never contemplated marriage before; it seemed to be the right thing to happen for both of them. Alex had a word with Stewart also and invited him to come and stay in the manse over Christmas, and they could make their decisions then.

Our Christmas visitor arrived. I phoned Pat to tell her Stewart was here. We left them in the lounge, to get to know each other again. After a few moments, Alex and I were asked to come into the room, they wanted to share something with us. Stewart had the engagement ring with him. They were engaged there and then, it was quite a night. When James Currie heard about it, he invited them over to Dunlop, and asked them if they would like to be married in the Church of St Andrew's in Jerusalem ... 'Oh yes!' was the reply.

The following April, Pat and Stewart were married in Jerusalem, They had three ministers in attendance, the minister of St Andrews: had to do the Marriage Service, to make it legal in Israel; James took part in the prayers; I did the readings; Alex acted as Father of the Bride, he even bought a new suit for the occasion. Dr Rhuna MacKay of the Nazareth Hospital was the bridesmaid, and an Irishman was the best man. The group were warned that they would be going to a wedding in Jerusalem. They all brought with them suitable attire for a wedding. Our Arab friends came up trumps again; they decorated the wedding car. It was a very good wedding reception, an unforgettable day. While we waited for the bride and groom to sign the register, James looked at me; our eyes met we were both in tears. James said, 'It's unbelievable that a scrap of humanity could look so beautiful a year later.'

A year later Pat and Stewart's first baby was born. There was only one thing to do. She was taken to the Church of St Andrew's in Jerusalem and was baptized there. Pat and Stewart moved to London, taking Mrs Milne with them. They did not like it there; they moved to Wimslow, did not like it there either. They then moved to Scotland, and settled in Scone, in Perthshire. They had four of a family, who must be all grown up by this time. I can honestly say, this was definitely a love match, there was no way any one of us could have said that Pat would have made it back to normality. Stewart saw Pat, and realised her need. He was the right man to offer enough love, to bring her back to newness of life.

Chapter Fourteen

I can still see the Rev. James stride through the Old City of Jerusalem, Bible in hand, camera round his neck, leading his pilgrim band, he never seemed tired, though he must have been, on many occasions. Those of us who travelled with him are never bereft of these lovely memories. The other is being on his bus, when I was learning the ropes. Laughter was the name of the game. Yes, we were pilgrims following in the footsteps of Jesus, but according to James, long faces were taboo.

James was a very patient man. He brought a couple with him one year. The husband let it be known that he wasn't really interested in the Holy Land. But his wife had been nagging him for years, so he decided that if he took her to the Holy Land she would get it out of her system. Mrs got a wee bit embarrassed at times because of hubbie's lack of interest on the tour.

Time passed and the scepticism began to get that bit less, our friend was obviously doing a bit of thinking. James never asked him once if he would like to participate. Patience is really a virtue, very difficult to maintain, but I saw it work out there in Israel. Our tour in Jerusalem was over, and we had moved up north to Galilee. We were at the Church of the Transfiguration. By this time everyone who wanted to read had had a turn. James was explaining the mosaics; when he had finished, he opened his Bible, and told us that he needed someone to volunteer to read the lesson. The so called unbeliever stepped forward. He was shaking visibly as he took the Bible from James. The big man put his hand on the reader's shoulder; he read the lesson beautifully. There were a few pilgrims with tears in their eyes. His wife completely broke down, but her eyes were shining, and you could see how proud she was of her man.

That man went back to Scotland a changed character. He went to church with his wife, then he joined proclaiming his faith before his own congregation. Patience, love, and the power of the Holy Spirit had won the day.

There was another very funny episode, though not funny for the lady involved. If you have read James Currie's biography, *God's Con Man*, you will have read this story before, but I tell it again because I was much involved in the facts. Dr Eileen McIlroy had come to the Holy land for the first time. Unfortunately, she came when a number of our group took a kind of flu. Dr Eileen found herself attending to a number of patients night and morning. One of the nights, we were both going back to our rooms, we were next door to one another. I asked her how the patients were and she said, 'They were all much better.' I said jokingly, 'Hope you don't have any night calls.' We both laughed and went to our rooms.

I was very tired, I was in bed in double quick time. About one o'clock in the morning I received a telephone call. I could not really understand it at first because, I discovered, it was the young Arab boy at the hotel desk. His English was not very good. 'Rev. Effie, you come quick, fast, lady in trouble, eye lost down sink.' I grabbed my dressing gown and went next door: the doctor was about to have her first night call. I knocked the door, no reply. I knocked louder, this apparition appeared. 'Get your bag, doctor, there's a lady has lost an eye down a sink, the young Arab boy phoned, I thought it better to involve you.' The two of us headed for the hotel desk. The boy who phoned was so laid back it wasn't true. We asked the room number, it was in the basement.

When we arrived, an almost hysterical women was trying to tell the story. Eileen calmed her down and I went to look at the sink. It turned out that when we had been at the Dead Sea that day, the lady had got some sand in the socket of her glass eye. When she had finally got to her bedroom, she decided to wash out the eye socket. She took the eye out to wash it, put the eye in the sink, and left it to soak for a few moments. What the lady did not know was that when you took the plug out of the sink in the Panorama Hotel, there was no drain, just a hole; when she was ready, she took the plug out, and to her horror the eye went down the hole with the water ...

Panic stations. The lady just wanted to go home, she had a spare eye at home, but nothing with her. Remember, I had worked in a plumber's office, and my plumbing qualifications were about to be tried out. I left Eileen to pacify the distraught woman, and I ran upstairs to the boy at the desk. It was now well after one o'clock, the hotel was very quiet. 'Yes, Rev. Effie, you find eye.' He did not understand

English very well, so had no idea what we were talking about. I tried acting the part. Standing there in my dressing gown and pyjamas, I felt a fool. I said, 'Sink, where you wash hands,' doing the actions, eye, pointing to my eye, down, pointing down, sink. I was getting a bit frustrated. Then I said, 'I need tools, S-bend under sink,' describing it, has to be removed. Tools, acting out hammer, screwdriver etc. Tools, tools, suddenly his face lit up, 'I get tools,' and he re-enacted all the charade that went before.

The boy was away for what seemed an eternity, it was possibly minutes, and believe it or not came back with a tool kit. Downstairs we went. I took him straight into the bathroom, opened the tool kit and there was a ratchet spanner. I tried to move the bolt at the bottom of the S-bend, but it was too tight for me. The lad got the message, but he was not very gentle, he was pulling the sink from the wall. I wasn't all that bothered about the sink, I just wanted to see that eye. Eventually, the cup of the S-bend was free. He held it up, to turn it upside down. I took it from him; inside it was thick with gunge, I think that's what saved the eye from going further. I tapped the thing on the floor, and suddenly the eye rolled out. The boy fell on his back, shouting, 'Eye down sink, eye down sink.' Eileen came into the bathroom and rescued the eye to sterilise it. The desk boy said he would go and make tea. He did, brought it back on a tray, then he charged us for it.

Dr Eileen gave the lady a sedative. We agreed not to tell her story while she was in the Holy Land, but we could tell it later anytime. She saw the funny side herself. That was not the end of the matter. Eileen and I were on the fourth floor; we went up in the lift, as we were coming out of the lift, I began to laugh. I was thinking of the antics of the desk boy and myself in the foyer of the hotel and in the bathroom. We both started to laugh, in fact we had a fit of the giggles. Along the corridor we went, unaware that it was about three o'clock in the morning.

The next day we went down to breakfast. I always had to sit at a different table every day, so that I would get to know the group. I sat at a table with three other women. Halfway through breakfast, one of the ladies said, 'Did you hear that terrible disturbance in our corridor last night about three in the morning?' I was about to say that was the minister and the doctor, but before I had time to utter a word, the ladies' companion said, 'It wasn't men, you know, it was women, and they were drunk.'

I said, 'Did you see them, did you open the door?'

'Oh no, drunk men are bad enough, but drunk women are worse, and we will be speaking to Rev. James about it after breakfast.'

Eileen and I got to the Rev. James first. With plaster falling of the wall, sink without S-bend, the lady and her companion got another room. I was speaking at a meeting in Busby many years later. I met our lady of the glass eye once more, and we had a laugh as we remembered her predicament.

When I was the assistant to James, he called me tail-end Charlie. He always said, 'If you are behind the wee yin you are lost.' On one of our walks I noticed that one of our group had some black and blue marks on her legs, they looked like bruises. I kept my eye on her, and became aware that she was having a struggle to keep up with the group. Dr Eileen was not with us on that tour, so I had a word with Ellen Pollock, our nurse, Ellen came back with me to the end of the group; she verified my suspicions, that there was something wrong. Ellen managed to get the lady to tell her the problem. She had a blood disorder, but she did not tell her doctor about her trip because she wanted very much to go. The result of that was that she did not get the pills she needed to see her through the pilgrimage, but thought she would be all right. Worse still she was not insured, because she thought nobody would insure her. She ended up in the Nazareth Hospital. Luckily for her, James had a very good friend who was a doctor in the missionary hospital there. Rhuna came down from Nazareth, and took the lady straight to the hospital. When we were ready for the return journey home, James went up to the hospital in the evening to see if we could take the lady with us. The doctor said that James could take her, but she would not survive the journey. In the morning we had to leave without her. The soul was in the hospital for a couple of months, but she did make it home ... We make mistakes very often but one mistake we should never make going abroad: never go without insurance.

On one tour, a lady determined that she would dodge me in the Old City. You see it was my job to keep folk from slipping into shops. We did give our pilgrims time off to shop, we even took them to shops that were safe to visit, so that they would not be paying higher prices than they should have. This lady had this wee adventure dressed in a white figure hugging dress, high heeled shoes a large black straw hat, and her handbag. Well she did dodge me, and it was the worst thing she could have done. The Arab boys know the strangers, and they are very amorous, she was a target at once. She was a very lucky lady that day, because an English group came on the scene and they rescued her. That dress, hat, shoes and handbag were never seen again on that tour, and she stuck to me like glue.

A husband and wife had left the group to go into a shop in the Old City. I knew where James was heading for, the Herod Gate, and to get to that gate we had to make a detour through part of the Arab quarter. I tried to get the couple to leave the shop; he said, 'Just leave us, we will be all right.' I left, and hot footed it after the group, but I did tell James that two had absconded. But it's a couple, they should be all right. We were in the middle of lunch, when our truants appeared a wee bit red faced. They had got lost, of course there was a little Arab boy with a lovely smile who recognised their problem. You are lost, I will show you the way. He did, and led them a good long way, taking more time, then the little hand held out for money. The gentleman in question, it turned out, was a member of the Police Force back home. James brought him over to my table and the culprit was on his knees to tail-end Charlie.

We had a lovely lady called Susan, who had been to the Holy Land with James many times. When the buses were stopped for comfort breaks, James told the group, just follow Susan, because she knew every toilet in Israel.

On one of our flights to Tel Aviv, the pilot appeared in the passenger cabin. He made himself at home, and was having a chat with the Rev. James. I was called over to meet the pilot; it was a very interesting conversation, then I realised that if the pilot was having this conversation, who was flying the plane? Stupid question. It was on auto-pilot, the answer did not help my nervous feeling, and I was glad to see the young man go back to the cockpit.

My camera was always my hobby, mostly slides. On one of our pilgrimages I had used twenty one films. I was busy putting the cassettes into their bags for posting in London. The little containers were of no use. I decided to ask a steward to put them in the rubbish bin. As he came towards my seat, he said, 'You seem to like photography.'

'Yes, could you get rid of these film holders for me, they are not much use for anything. '

'That's great, they will do for the pilot's heart pills.'

'What, you mean to tell me that the man in charge of this plane, with all these folk, is on heart pills.'

'Don't worry madam he's not taking them today, he's drunk today.' The penny dropped.

Returning once from Tel Aviv, one of my own groups had a hair-raising experience. I was doing my usual crosswords. I did notice that one of the engines was not coping very well. The cabin crew did not seem worried, so I thought it was imagination, then suddenly the pilot was speaking to us. 'Do not be worried, but I have decided to return to Tel Aviv. Try to relax, everything is under control. We are only one hour out of the airport, and they expect us back.'

I think that was the longest hour in my life. Our group were very anxious; it was difficult, but I knew I had to keep calm for their sakes. I continued to do my crossword, but I was not concentrating on anything but the sound of the engines. I was waiting for one to fall off. I was praying, literally, as if there was no tomorrow. We were asked to remain in our seats, but a few of my folk came up to have a word with me. I just said to them, pray. Then I went round the cabin with the agreement of the cabin crew, and had a wee word with as many as possible. Believe it or not, that settled me down, and helped me to keep calm. We did arrive in Tel Aviv, and were provided with dinner, which no one was ready for. We were told the plane had been flying on three engines instead of four. They said that the three engines would have taken us to London and back. The pilot made the decision to return to Tel Aviv. I was always very glad he did.

When we arrived in London, we still had to board another flight for Glasgow. It wasn't easy. On the plane, I was seated beside a young woman who was obviously a business commuter. I was wearing my collar and when we had lift off, she asked where we had been. We had quite a good conversation, but she said something that reminded me of the morning flight from Tel Aviv. I said to this young woman who thought that she needed nothing else in her life but her own ability to survive the rat race of society. 'You might not believe it at this very moment in time, but there will come a day when you will realise that there is a higher authority in this world.' I then related our experience of that morning telling her that pride often gets in the way of good sense. Our pilot, could have continued to London, but he was not happy with the engines on his plane, and despite assurances that the plane could have reached London. he returned to the airport at Tel Aviv. I admired that pilot; pride did not blurr his responsibility to his passengers. As we were preparing to land, my young friend said, 'I will be thinking about what you said, especially when I am flying back and forward to London.' I've often wondered if it made any difference to her life.

Chapter Fifteen

By 1979, a lot of work had been done in the church. We had a new stained glass window at the front and a cross and new blue velvet backdrop provided. All the windows on either side of the church were replaced. The vestry was panelled, and the church walls pointed. Where did the wee church get all the money for this work? Gifts from people, who wanted to see the church look its best. The craftsmen who were members of our church gave of their time and their talents on a voluntary basis. Meanwhile I was still thinking about a new hall.

We had reached the stage when the chancel of the church was too small, especially at our Communion Services. The Kirk Session continued to grow along with the congregation. Two pews were removed from the front, and the chancel was built out towards the congregation. The work had begun at the beginning of the week; it had to be finished by Friday, simply because I had a wedding on the Saturday. The work team, as usual, were the men of the kirk session and the office bearers. Come Friday there was still a lot to do. The workers were prepared to do overtime until the job was finished. They got the same wages for the overtime, tea and biscuits and a late pass from their wives.

I always tried to go into church when the men were at work – they said 'To make sure they did not slack off,' which was not quite true, but I was anxious about the Saturday wedding. The church was in a terrible mess, the organ and the communion table were up the aisle, some of the floorboards had still to be laid on the chancel and the new carpet was lying across the pews. The bride of the next day walked through the door with the flower arranger. There was absolute consternation on the poor girl's face. Everybody stopped work. 'I'm supposed to get married here tomorrow.'

Bob, the session clerk, shouted, 'Sure you've got the right church, we won't be finished till tomorrow.'

It was just as well this minister had decided to go in that night. It was about eight o'clock, I knew that the men were there till the job was finished and that Bob was joking but the bride did not even know the alterations were going on; the florist was not supposed to be there till Saturday morning.

I hustled the pair into the vestry, the bride was in tears. I gave her time to cry, then gently explained to her the circumstances, and that the men would be working all night if need be to have the church ready for her wedding. The florist agreed to arrange the flowers in the vestry and I would see the floral arrangements put in the church before I left. I would not leave the church till the place was spick and span, and everything in order. She calmed down and set to work in the vestry with the florist. When the flowers were set to their satisfaction, I took the bride and her friend back into church where our carpet layer had already started work. That seemed to satisfy our bride and off they went. By this time it was about ten o'clock. I didn't need to worry about Alex; he was helping with the renovations as usual. Alex left the church at midnight to walk the dog.

It was after 1 a.m., when the work was finished, then the clearing up had to be done. The organ, and communion table had all to be man-handled into our new chancel. The flower stands were brought into church; it was just beautiful. The chancel carpet was a rich red colour. We looked around, we were satisfied, our wee church was in splendid nick, fit for any wedding. A good few tired men got themselves off home. I had the session clerk to drop off. We got to his drop-off point, and as he got out of the car, he shouted, 'Goodnight darling,' the clown. The next day, the man who lived across the road from him said, 'Who was that lady you were with last night?' The quick reply was, 'That was no lady, that was my minister.'

Saturday turned out to be a fine day. The bride was beautiful and happy. On the Sunday our congregation were delighted with their new chancel, so were the wives of the men who made it possible. Another happy group were the choir, under the direction of Miss Caroline Hunter. She was a BMus. of Edinburgh University, and an LRAM a very talented girl. There was now more room for the choir, and when the organ was shifted to a position below the pulpit, Caroline could see her choir, and we, Caroline and I, could have some communication. On occasion if I did not think the singing was very good, I'd ask Caroline to play it again (Sam).

The organist's day job was as music teacher to about six schools. I was invited to see one of her musical productions in one of her schools,

'Joseph and his Amazing Technicolor Dreamcoat'. It was an excellent show and the children were a credit to her. We had a very good Junior Choir, who met in the manse every Tuesday after school. Caroline had her own key, which suited us both fine. Caroline was terrified of dogs, so I usually made sure that Golda my big labrador was locked in the kitchen on a Tuesday. I must have forgotten, and when Caroline came into the manse for the Junior Choir rehearsal, Golda was sitting in the hall, wagging her tail, it was great to have a visitor. Caroline did not know what to do, so she took courage in both hands, and said in a loud voice, 'Golda, into the kitchen at once,' The well trained big dog dropped her tail and walked into the kitchen, and a very shaken organist quickly closed the kitchen door. Not long after that Caroline was able to accept Golda into her presence, as long as I was there. Caroline remained our organist until I retired.

I haven't forgotten my invitation to visit Lady Stirling. I had to be at Glorat Estate for 3 p.m. I had not met any of the family, so I was a bit apprehensive. I had never met a real live Lady before, had never mixed in those kind of circles. It was about five minutes to go, I parked the car down the drive, and as I walked up towards Glorat House I was thinking how different it was from our room and kitchen in Whiteinch. Remembering what a struggle my Mum and Dad had to bring us up, memories came flooding back. I passed the wee pond, how lovely it looked, there were ducks on the pond, and up the hill there was another lovely house; I learned later it was called Stratford Cottage. I noticed the monkey puzzle tree, it was a lovely place and very peaceful. The Campsie Fells made a beautiful backdrop. I had reached the door, one minute to go. I rang the bell. Miss Betty Stirling answered the door, a big yellow labrador at her side. The ice was broken immediately, for did I not have a big yellow labrador at home. Miss Betty knew all about my big dog, she had been doing her homework.

Into the drawing room, and sitting at the window was Lady Stirling. She rose to her feet, took both my hands in hers, and with a welcoming smile she said, 'You are just a little shadow,' then I remembered that she was almost blind with glaucoma. There had been no need to worry about this meeting, Lady Stirling set me at ease right away.

'Betty tells me you are a Glaswegian, how do you find country life?'

We chatted on, and I was able to let Lady Stirling know the background of my life; she was very interested, and I was glad because it meant that I did not have to make any pretence of being other than myself. There was the silver tea-service, plus the little sandwiches. I was not to know that in time I would enjoy many a cup of tea at the fireside of the Stirling family.

At that time Lady Stirling was a member of the High Church, but of course, she had reached the stage when it was difficult for her to get to church. Miss Betty Stirling was a member of Lenzie Episcopal Church. But Glorat Estate was in my parish of Milton of Campsie. That was my first introduction to a very fine and loving family.

In 1979 we got a brochure from Inter Church Travel. There was to be what was listed as an adventure to Eastern Turkey. It was a new venture for Inter Church. Alex and I and two friends decided to go. Alistair McCabe was still working with Inter Church. There were to be thirteen persons on the group. The leader was to be a Father Brown, plus three nuns. About six weeks before we were due to set off, I had a phone call from Alistair. 'Effie, Father Brown is ill and can't lead this tour. The three nuns have backed out because he is not going. There will only be nine of you, two men and seven women; how would you like to lead this group? If you do, you will get a free passage.'

The Holy Land was one thing, but Eastern Turkey? My reply to Alastair was really no, but I did not like to let him down, so I made an excuse: 'I can't speak Turkish.'

'No problem, you will have an English speaking guide called Sumer Erdem, he is from Western Turkey and will meet you in Trabson. Effie, we need you. There is no one else, we want this trip to go ahead.' At the end of the day I agreed to take the group. I was crazy, you have no idea just how crazy.

We departed Heathrow on 24 July, and arrived in Istanbul. The Hotel was the Argun, which was very nice, with hot water, the last we were to see or feel till we returned to Kaisera. We had to be up at 5.30 a.m. to get to the airport for our flight to Trabson on the Black Sea. We did not in fact leave Istanbul till 8.20 a.m. The plane was a small, very small German plane, I think tied up with string? It was the survival of the fittest. The Turks did not know what it was to queue. The result was that all nine of us were swept aside, the seats on the plane were up for grabs and we were all at the back of the cabin. This great adventure did not start very well. Eventually we reached Trabson and we were told to fasten our seat belts. We were looking for the airport buildings, but there were none; the plane landed on a runway, then veered to the left on to a kind of dirt track. The luggage was dumped by the side of the plane; you were responsible for your own. We all brought our luggage up and grouped it together, and our guide appeared; he had no problem finding his group, as we were the only British folk there. He introduced himself: 'I am your guide, Sumer Erdem is my name, I am looking for your leader Effee,' with the stress on the two e's. Sumer was plump, short in stature, with lovely big brown eyes.

This man from Kusadasi in Western Turkey endeared himself to us as a group; he was a good guide, except, I discovered, he had never been to Eastern Turkey before. He led us up to a mini-bus that was to be our transport for the next two weeks. There were two young men waiting for us, Suleyman, and Nachi, both Kurdish. They were our drivers. They were both in their early twenties, but very capable drivers. We were in Trabson overnight, and toured the city in the morning. Ayia Sophia was built in the thirteenth century as a monastery church, but was converted to a mosque after 1461. Most Christian churches were converted to Islam.

On 26 July, we left Trabson for Erzurum. We stopped to visit Sumela monastery, dedicated to the Virgin Mary. This monastery was founded in the sixth century. We realised that Eastern Turkey or Anatolia was originally Christian. This building supposedly housed the icon of the Virgin Mary painted by St Luke. We arrived in Erzurum after a thirteen-hour journey in our mini-bus. This is where the fun began.

We were all very tired, and looked forward to our dinner and then to bed. The hotel San was to be our home for one night, which was just as well. The lights in the room were about 40 watt. There was no hot water, no soap, no towels, no toilet roll, no plugs in the wash hand basin, there was a bath which had not be cleaned for years. We washed with wet wipes. Our friend Bill McCallum came to my room and asked me to follow him to his room to see this wonderful mural on their bedroom wall. I'd never seen anything like this before. It was like a tree growing from the skirting board and spreading up and across the wall, and it was furry to touch. We discovered it was a type of fungi. It was a good job we were only to be there for one night.

By this time we were all a bit hungry. Sumer appeared, and I asked him where the dining room was. He said, 'No dining room in hotel, we have to go out to restuarant. Having seen the room, we thought it was better that we did not eat in the hotel. We entered this so called restuarant. There were no women present except us, only men. It turned out that women did not go to restuarants in Erzurum, only men; we were in an Islamic city. We noticed that there were a number of cats about the place, black ones, tabby ones, white ones, kittens. My friend Meta said to me, 'Don't you dare touch any of these cats, don't encourage them to come near the table.' We were served our meal, I ate little. The long table running parallel with ours was vacated, then we knew why the cats. They clambered on to the table and made short work of the left-overs. These cats had a purpose in life, no wonder they were fat. When we vacated our seats, we looked back and our table became the next dining table for cats.

We got back to the hotel and literally fell into bed. A cannon went off about 1 a.m., I jumped out of bed, shouting. 'We're being invaded!' Alex said, 'Don't be stupid, its the Ramadan gun.' I'd forgotten, then I felt the room moving under my feet. 'Alex the floor is moving!' It was, Alex found the light switch; the floor was a moving mass of cockroaches about two inches long, shiny black, scuttling about. I nearly had a fit. We had to empty our cases, to make sure we would not be carrying any of these dirty creatures with us. Our cases had to rest at the foot of our beds, I was OK, but Alex was 5 feet 11 inches tall. There wasn't much sleep that night.

It was nice to leave Erzurum and the hotel San; there was no real sanitation only irritation. We were supposed to stay in Agri for two nights. We had a ten hour journey over an unmade road, and when we reached Agri, we discovered that no one was to be allowed out of their homes till the next day. I had noticed the monument to Ataturk, the man who tried to bring Turkey into the twentieth century. I wanted a picture of that man, so I slipped out of the hotel, I told Alex I was just going round the corner to get the picture. Before I could blink, four soldiers were round me; they could not speak English, I could not speak Turkish. I pointed to my camera, held it up to my eye, and said 'Ataturk'. One of the soldiers spoke French, I couldn't, but he got the message, he conversed with the others and I was marched round the corner to get my picture. Despite my shaking limbs I did get quite a good picture.

Our next stop was a place called Dogubeyzit. We passed Mount Ararat, where the Noah's Ark had rested. It lies on a flat plain like an upturned pudding bowl, topped with ice, for it is a glacier. Maybe one day the archaeologists will find that boat. We arrived in this town which is about fifty miles from Iran. There were tanks everywhere. It was like a town from the American Western movies. Wooden shacks, dirt roads, all we needed were the cowboys. Sumer said to me that the boys had to go and fill the bus with petrol, he on the other hand was going to buy raki (his tipple) and cigarettes. My group were in the Post Office, buying postcards and stamps. I was sitting outside on the wooden steps of this ramshackle building. All of a sudden I realised that the boys had been away with the bus for over half an hour, and there was no sign of Sumer. It was a very hot day, but I began to shiver. Everything we owned was in that bus, what if they had scarpered with the lot? I sat glued to my step; there was no point in my trying to find them, the place was a seething mass of people, barrows, bikes, the lot for about three quarters of an hour: my group did not seem to be perturbed, so I decided not to say a word until they got worried. Two of my ladies came out of the Post Office. I rose from the step, they would have to be told, and I'd need to find someone who spoke English. I just had my foot on the next step, when one of the ladies said, quite matter of fact, 'Just in time, there's Sumer.' The Glasgow vernacular sprang to mind. Keep the heid, Effie, and I did. 'Where have you been, Sumer?'

'I had to wait in the queue for the cigarettes, the soldiers have to be served first.'

'Where are the boys?'

'They too have to wait in a queue, petrol very scarce, they will come.' It was over an hour before the bus came back, and by that time I was sick, but it seemed that I was the only one who was worried. It's better not to be a leader.

When I was preparing to go on this adventure, I bought with the help of my doctor, £20 worth of Lomital tablets, Dr Harrison advised it for "the runs". It was very wise counsel, because my lot were having some of these daily. I was particularly bad myself. It was a very trying situation. Sumer said to me 'Effee, you are very unhealthy people, you have zee leetle white pills every day, we [meaning the boys and himself], are very healthy, we do not need zee leetle white pills.' We were on our way to Lake Van, I had wanted to have a communion service, Sumer nearly had a fit.

'You cannot have this service, it is Christian, not allowed. I will let you have your service, we go to Lake Van, we take a leetle boat to leetle island called Akdamer, there you have service.' We had to go to this small uninhabited island to have our communion service. We saw the ruins of an Armenian Church, It was a beautiful day, the lake was very calm, we felt the better of our service. It was a pity it had to be done in secret.

Now we were on our way to Diyarbakir, 255 miles we had to face. When we stopped for lunch, there was no way I could eat, I had some bits of dry biscuits, I knew I would need to stay on my feet, but nausea was getting to me, I did not want to worry Alex. The Demir Hotel, was quite good. There was some tepid water, good clean beds, and the food looked good but I could not stand the smell, so went to bed. Had a good sleep except for the visitations to the loo. In the morning I felt a wee bit better, and went down to the dining room. Sumer was sitting with his head in his hands, I slapped him on the back, wished him good morning, he looked up, his big brown eyes were very sad, 'Effee, do you have zee leetle white pills, Sumer has zee runs.' I had to laugh, I gave him two Lomital and said he was not to eat at lunch time. Come lunchtime, he was eating as usual.

I said, 'Sumer, you are not supposed to eat when you have these pills.'

The quick answer was, 'If I do not eat, I have nothing to run with.' No reply was of any value.

We walked the walls of old Diyarbakir, were taken to see a mosque, and did not get in because it was Ramadan. We were then taken to see a Syrian RC Church. We had to go up a lane to this church, there was a huge double door. We had to ring a bell. A little wooden door set in the top panel was opened, we were invited in, three locks were opened, and we were in quite a big compound. A family of six lived within the walls of this church. There was a congregation of fifteen persons. They were persecuted when the moslems felt like it. We were taken into the church. the Bible was in Aramaic, the language of Jesus, the covers of the Bible were in gold. One of the men read from the Bible for us, and we had prayer in English and in Aramaic. This was the first time I or my group had met with a persecuted minority. It was very difficult to understand. When we left the church there were some small children following us back to the bus, word must have got round that we had been in the church, and it was Ramadan. Bigger youths joined, the retinue. I sensed trouble. The drivers and Sumer got between us and our followers, but the boys had to get the bus opened and we could only get on the bus two at a time. Sumer hustled the group on, as we boarded the bus our fears became a reality little stones were being thrown at us, Sumer was angry, he tried to reason with them, at the same time pushing the group on the bus. With Sumer I was last on, then the big stones were thrown, the back of the bus was a little dented but none of us were hurt, just a wee bit apprehensive.

Our next stop was Adiyaman. We were to visit the statues of Nemrut Dagi. On a Mountain (Dagi) over 7000 feet high. The monument was built by Mithhradtes Callinicus and his son Antiochus. In memory of Alexander the Great. These statues represented Zeus, Ahura, Apollo, Helius, and Hermies. The seated bodies were about 40 feet high, the heads 15 feet in height, they had been removed from the statues, and stood in an independent row.

We had to be in bed early, because we had to be ready to move at 1 a.m. in the morning. We did not get much sleep because the cockcroaches in the hotel were even bigger than the ones we had seen in Erzurum, so we tried to sleep with the light on. It did not work, we were called to surface at 12.30 a.m., climbed aboard a jeep at 1 a.m. and set off up this mountain (Dagi). It was very dark, we arrived at a tea-house, which was sitting on the edge of a cliff. At 2.40 a.m. we were regaled with some Turkish tea, seated on divans. At about 3 a.m. we left the tea-house, and climbed on to the backs of mules for the next stage of our climb. I was not feeling very great, and when we reached a particular ridge, with a sheer drop on one side, I prayed fervently, that if the mule slipped, my demise would be quick.

We arrived at the top of Nemrut Dagi about 5.30 a.m. It was still dark. We waited till the sun rose over the mountains. It was an awe inspiring sight. The sun was like a golden orange, frosted with sugar all round the edge. We turned to look back at the heads of the statues standing in a row, their colour had turned to gold in the glow of the sunlight, how wonderful God's creation is. We had been girning about our lack of sleep, our early rise, and the climb, but these grouses melted into the background of time. The mountain top experience fulfilled all our expectations and more. Too soon we had to make our descent from Nemrut Dagi; it had just been a glimpse into another world. The mule seemed safer on the way down the mountain, maybe it was because I was more relaxed, and the animal sensed the atmosphere. Sure-footed, the mule descended, right to the door of the tea-house, and to breakfast. With all the will in the world, I could not eat it. From there to the Jeep; we arrived back at the hotel about 10 a.m., fell into bed, the cockcroaches could have a free rein, we slept till 3 p.m. What a truly, wonderful, wonderful day. We did praise our God in Christ, that night.

We went through Cappadocia to Kaysera. The hotel was first class, from there back to Istanbul. I don't remember much more of the return journey, what I did not know was that I was suffering from dysentery. I did get home on the Wednesday 8 August, thought I would be all right, and prepared for the Sunday service. I did take the service on the Sunday, baptizing twins. Then on Monday I just collapsed. Dr Harrison was astounded, but how was I to know I had dysentery, and that it was a notifiable disease? Doctor asked me if I had taken the service on the Sunday. When I told him I had shaken hands with everyone at the door, and had baptized two babies he near had an apoplectic fit. The results were, the health authority had to be notified, The twins had to be visited, and I was in quarantine for ten weeks. A doctor came out from Ruchill Hospital to take me in, but the hygiene in the manse satisfied him and I was allowed to stay at home. Alex was off work for four weeks just to be on the safe side. The adventure was no holiday. We had travelled 2500 miles in our mini bus. At the end of the day, I would not have missed it for anything. I learned a lot of lessons on that trip, first and foremost how fortunate that we could worship our God at home without fear.

Chapter Sixteen

Ten weeks of quarantine was difficult to live with, as time passed and my health improved. I set to work preparing for the weeks ahead. I was not back to the parish till October, when it was like beginning all over again; the congregation were very understanding. At least I was, by then, feeling quite well and everything was going well at home.

Getting back into the routine was hard, but very soon I felt I was back into the swing of things. The visiting was up and running again, the organisations were active and in good heart. The Sunday Schools were also well into their sessions work. Those responsible for the various youth groups had really done a very good job, and a burden was instantly removed when I realised the work had not stopped, nor was anything neglected.

I think my older folk were the ones who had really missed their minister, but we soon made up for that but the funny thing was, there were very few funerals or crises while I was ill. Pulpit supply was up to scratch, in fact I became convinced that they could have managed fine without me.

The Lennoxtown Church, Milton Church and Cadder Church were in the habit of climbing the Campsie Fells on Easter Sunday mornings. The minister of Cadder Church carried a very large Cross to the top of the fells, and there we would have a Service as the sun rose. We would leave Milton about 5 a.m. to make sure we were there on time. Sometimes, it was a reasonably good morning, other times it would be a bit dismal. In 1980 was the best sunrise ever; the morning was so clear, we could see the runway of Glasgow Airport. What a wonderful Easter Service we had. I have a photograph of that Sunday morning, we never did have that experience again ...

There was a phone call from Miss Betty Stirling saying that her mother wanted to see me. Lady Stirling was waiting for me. She was concerned about my health. I thought that was it, she was now about ninety-five years old. But there was another important matter to sort out. I had said earlier in this book that the two churches in Lennoxtown were to be united, and Dr Morrison, the minister of Campsie High, would be the minister of the united charge for its first year, then he would retire, to enable both churches to call a new minister. Lady Stirling felt she was too old to begin with a new minister; she asked me if I would consider taking her into my congregation as one of my members. She was well known by the folk of Milton, and it was she who had started the Women's Guild in Milton. There was no problem providing she asked for her disjunction certificate before the new minister was in situ. This meant that there would be a visit to Glorat Estate every four to six weeks as time allowed. She was now one of my old buddies.

Miss Stirling also knew that I was trying to get the idea of a new hall into the minds of the congregation. On the day she called me to Glorat, she referred to the hall situation. 'There are a few pieces of ground I could let you have, providing you get planning permission.' Miss Betty did offer me two sites, but both were turned down by the local authority in Bishopbriggs. Eventually Barratts built some houses on Glorat ground, gas and electricity were now provided and one of the first sites offered by Miss Betty was available. I drew up some very rough plans and took them into Bishopbriggs. Lo and behold the planning committee told me to make it official. Now all we had to do was to get the General Assembly to give us some money.

In 1980 I was a commisioner at the General Assembly of the Church of Scotland. I had two of my elders with me. The kirk session and congregational board were now supporting the building of a hall. It was now essential, if the work and witness of Christ Jesus were to keep going on. It was costing the church quite a lot of money to hire the village hall and the school. The report of the church extension committee was being presented by the Rev. Duncan McPhee. I alerted my two elders that I would be on my feet when he had finished. Mr McPhee finished his report; it was now question time. I waved my papers to draw the attention of the Moderator. I was successful, and invited to speak. I had been a minister eight years now, but this was a first go at speaking at the General Assembly. I was just a wee bit excited. The Moderator was The Very Rev. Robin Barbour. As I explained the situation in Milton of Campsie, the Moderator reminded me that I was there to ask a question. I replied that I was aware of that, but had to qualify the question first. He allowed me the privilege of speaking on. Then I asked the question. 'Will the Church Extension Committee help Milton of Campsie Parish Church to build a hall?' Mr McPhee, sitting behind me, only said one word. 'Yes.' I was over the moon, and my two elders were very excited; we would be able to take good news back to our church.

Some people are never happy unless they are putting a damper on things. I left the Assembly Hall, needing a wee cup of tea after all that excitement. There was another minister in the corridor, heading for the tea-room. He stopped and said to me, 'You did not need to waste the Assembly's time asking that question, you could have made an appointment to speak privately to Mr McPhee.'

I replied, 'No fear, I had 1500 witnesses in there, it would be very difficult for the Church Extension Committee to dodge this one.'

He was not very pleased, I was.

We were all very happy in the parish and congregation of Milton. We had a piece of ground, we had planning permission, now we waited for officialdom. I went to see Miss Betty, and give her the good news. She had already set the wheels in motion, and her lawyer had drawn up the papers to be signed. Legally the ground had to be paid for. Miss Betty told me she was selling her piece of land to me for one shilling. I paid it at once, and the ground was ours. Next we had to get three tenders for the building of the hall. These had to be presented to the Church Extension Committee. Once we had done that, the plans had to be drawn up. Miss Betty had added a rider to the plans: it was that the hall should be pebble dash on the outside to match the new houses. I asked for another rider to be put in, that the roof should be an apex type. That was added. Now we had to be patient for things to happen. It was not easy.

1980 was a very busy year. I did my usual Holy Land tours, and Alex and I went to Egypt, for the first time. Up the Nile on a boat: it was a wonderful holiday, we did enjoy it. Alex had usually one week's holiday in February, one in November. We sometimes went to Crieff Hydro, or did a tour of Scotland, and sometimes we just stayed home in the manse, which was the best holiday ever. When we stayed home the congregation were always very good and never called me unless it was absolutely necessary.

Alex was still the quiet man, but was always busy for the church. He drove the mini-bus when required, looked after a very big garden, made sure my car was always cleaned inside and out, he was a very reliable elder, and sang in the choir. It was a wonderful situation for me, he was well liked and in his own quiet way made his mark. If the phone went after 12 midnight, I always answered it; if someone needed help, no matter the time, I went. There were always some clothes left in the spare room every night. If I had to go, I just tiptoed to the spare room and got dressed. and left the manse. There was a back light at the garage, so there was no problem. The big labrador usually went with me. There was one night when I had forgotten something and had to go back into the bedroom. The voice from the bed said, 'you're losing your touch, you used to be out in five minutes, tonight it's about seven.' I said, 'I never knew you heard me.' It turned out that Alex always knew, and never slept till I was back safe and sound. He would never have tried to stop me but he did worry about me being out during the night. Thankfully it did not happen too often.

1980 was also the year of the Oberammergau Passion Play. My Mum decided she would like to go, and off she went with the Rev. James, for the very first time to Austria and Germany. She came back full of the marvellous experience she had, and said that she was now prepared to go to the Holy Land with me. It was not to be. We had workmen in the house, two very nice young men, who we knew well. They were there to examine the central heating system and had to be under the floor. There was a hatch in the pantry which had to be lifted to let the men down to where the fault was, with a drop of about three feet. I told Mum not to go into the pantry till I got back; I said I'd be back about 12 noon. The dog was always fed at 12 o'clock. Mum forgot about the men under the floor, and the fact that there was no floor in the pantry. She went through, and fell down through the hole, hitting her foot on an old toolbox on the way down, splitting her head down the back into the bargain. I was five minutes late, and when I arrived in, these two young men were just bringing Mum up from below the floor. What a mess she was in. One of the lads phoned for the doctor, while the other one was trying to stop the bleeding. Mum was in shock. She had broken her foot, and had damaged the back of her head; they had no idea as to the extent, but she was kept in Stobhill Hospital. That was the beginning of the end for a very active old lady. She was never the same again.

Mum was a terrible miss, remember she was our very good cook. I had to begin to learn all over again. But more than that, she was my sounding board, and my greatest critic. I always got the truth from her, she always helped me to keep my feet on the ground. We did get Mum out of the hospital, and we were able to take her to my brother Douglas and sister-in-law Sheila's house for Christmas. That really was the last day she was out. She took a stroke just after Christmas in 1981, and was out and in hospital thereafter.

In the meantime the background work for the building of our hall continued, The planning approval was given by Strathkelvin District Council. The builders chosen were Gilchrist and Lynn of Airdrie, and the architect was Mr J.S. Inglis of King, Main and Ellison.

The total cost of the hall was to be £160,000, of which the Church Extension Committee had agreed to give a grant of £112,500, and a loan of £47,500 repayable at 8 per cent interest over a seven year period. This burden of debt frightened the life out of me, and I'm sure it was the same for all the congregation.

We had a very good treasurer, Mr Ian McCalman, who was a bank manager. He guided us through our commitment of repaying our debt. A cheque would be sent monthly to the Church Extension Committee; our treasurer's good advice was to pay the interest on the loan at the same time. We also had a very good architect on our Kirk Session, Mr Roger McGowan, who liaised with Mr Inglis all the way through our building programme. He was also responsible for keeping our Congregational Board and the Kirk Session informed of all the progress made monthly. The wonderful thing about the situation was the great enthusiasm throughout the congregation. It was worked out that the cost of the hall for every family of the congregation would amount to £300. We made a very good start even before the site had been cleared because many families gave their £300 immediately. Others took monthly or weekly envelopes, and the OAP were a great means of support. Many of them could not afford to pay so much, but they saved their pennies and halfpennies, and we received that all during the project. We were most grateful for the widow's mite.

Mother had a few more little strokes. She was now unable to walk, and was taken into Stobhill Hospital again. It seemed that these little strokes had affected her mind, she could speak very well, but she thought I was just about ten years old. Very sad to watch, but she was happy in her own small world. Eventually Mum was moved to Foresthall Hospital in Springburn, which was only eight miles away, so was quite easy for me to visit. She was well cared for there, and was very contented.

Stirling Hall. Milton of Campsie.

I managed to visit every day, just for about ten minutes afternoon and evening. She always asked why Grannie had not been in to see her. My hair was combed every visit I made, and I was always being sent for messages (shopping). One day I went in. In rather a hurry, I said I had a job to do, but would be back in the evening.

'A job,' she said, 'You with a job.'

I pointed to the clerical collar and said foolishly, 'Remember, Mum, I'm a minister.'

She began to laugh, and shouted up the ward, 'Did you hear that, she's a minister now, she's got delusions of grandeur.'

I never mentioned the word minister again, she had well and truly forgotten. I felt very sad. It was more difficult for Douglas and Sheila to visit, because they had to travel from Erskine, but they were over as often as possible.

We always had someone in the manse to help keep the place clean and tidy. Mum had always loved the company twice a week. Sad to say the girl I had coming in had to give it up, so into the bargain of losing a cook, I had also lost my very good housekeeper. One Sunday morning, Marigold Langley, Lady Stirling's youngest daughter spoke to me at the church door after the service.

'I'd like a word with you.' I asked her to wait for me in the vestry.
'No,' she said, 'I'll come and see you in the manse in the morning, about eleven.'

I said that would be all right, I was curious, Marigold was a lovely lady, married to Ted, who was a potter, and had his own little kiln and pottery business. Monday morning and Marigold was on the doorstep at eleven. She came in and we had a cup of tea. I asked her what was worrying her, and the answer was, 'You. I know you have lost your home help and your mother is in hospital. I will come and work for you twice a week, I can also feed the dog.' Then she told me what the cost would be. Talk about being practical.

I laughed and said to Marigold, 'What will your mother say when I tell her I have a new charry in the manse, and it's your daughter.'

'Mummy loves the idea. I've already told her.'

And so it was, the daughter of Lady Stirling came to help in the manse, it was a wonderful arrangement, and we became very good friends. We still keep in touch.

Sadly, my mother died on 20 August 1981; she was eighty-two years old. It was a sad blow. I had promised my Mum I would be the one to conduct her funeral service. This I did in our wee church, a wee church that my Mum had grown to love. She had made many friends there, and the church was well filled on that day. Sitting in the church was the Rev. James Currie, who was prepared to take Mum's service in the church, if I could not manage. But I was able to keep my promise, made a long time ago. Who knew Elizabeth Brysland better than her daughter? I was grateful to the Rev. James, who conducted the service at the crematorium. James knew my Mum quite well; he had taken her to Oberammergau, and had visited her when she was in the hospital. Another chapter in my life had been closed.

Towards the end of 1981 the ground was being prepared for the foundations of our new hall. The steel framework was slowly being put in place. On 23 January 1982 the Moderator of the General Assembly, the Very Rev. Andrew Doig DD, laid the foundation stone for the new hall. It was a bleak day, grey and misty, with snow on the Campsie Hills. It was a day of great rejoicing in our village, but we were well aware of the hard work that lay ahead. St Paul's folk were at the same time building a new church, as their little church was just too small. Their Priest, Father Archibald, and I were kind of in the same boat, and we wondered which building would be finished first.

St Paul's won by a short head. It's a lovely church and it was a pleasure to be at the opening of the Catholic community's new church. The children of Milton School were not really aware that the new building was a church, so we took the the whole school down there, and Father Archibald and I had a special service for them. That was a great day; the children sang their hearts out, and so did the grown ups.

The congregation and the people of the village responded and supported the many fund-raising events. The Milton Valley social committee ran barn dances and supper dances; the St Paul's people shared in running these events and we shared the money between the two Churches. The Morton family allowed their farm buildings to be used for these occasions, and they were very successful. There were a tremendous number of private donations, and sometimes we did not know where they came from. The building of the hall progressed at a pace. I was down at the site every day; the workmen called me the 'gaffer' and presented me with a helmet. It had printed on the front GL, being the initials of the building firm. I told the workers it meant 'God is Love'. They laughed but I stuck to it, in fact it became a Children's address.

The hall was beginning to look as if it would be ours very soon. I wanted it to be opened in the September of 1982. There were doubts about that but I stuck to my guns. I did not see us paying for halls come September, when we should have our own one ready. I don't know what they expected, but the president of the Young Women's group phoned me to ask if the hall projector would be available for one of their speakers who would be showing slides in their next session. It seemed that some of our folk thought the hall would be handed over fully equipped. Come the Sunday I made an announcement, that when the hall became a reality, we would only have bare walls and nothing else. I said we did not even have a toilet roll. That did it, I received so many toilet rolls we did not know where to store them. Not only that, we had sweeping brushes handed in, pails, basins, and washing up liquid. It was a marvellous time, every one was waiting for this hall to be opened.

We had one very big problem: we had no chairs. How can you open a hall without chairs? One of my congregation came to visit me one day. He worked with Black and White Whisky. 'Mrs Irvine, our firm are renewing the chairs in our works canteen, would you take the old chairs, they are in quite good condition.'

I jumped at the opportunity. 'I sure will, can they hold on to them till the hall is cleaned up. It will only be for about a week.'

'There's only one problem Mrs Irvine, the chairs will be delivered in a Black and White Whisky lorry.'

I laughed and said, 'Just get the chairs here; this time last week, we had no chairs. We will contact your firm and thank them in anticipation.'

The chairs were first class, and lasted us for quite a number of years. Tables were gifted by the Boys Brigade.

The Stirling Hall, named after the Stirling family, was opened by Miss Betty Stirling on 18 September 1982. The Moderator of the Presbytery of Glasgow, the Rev. Angus Stewart, MA, BD, SJM, conducted the service. Interests of Presbytery were conveyed by the Rev. Alex Cunningham, MA, BD, Clerk to the Presbytery of Glasgow. We were up and running. We were all very proud of our very own Stirling Hall. Bob Gemmill our Session Clerk said, 'We canny allow folk into the Stirling Hall, they might waste it.' Despite the fact that the Stirling Hall has been well used over the years it still looks in very good condition. I can't get used to the idea that the building has been there for over twenty years now. It was a dream realised, but we still had to pay for it . . .

Chapter Seventeen

The Stirling Hall was an immediate success. It was in use every night in the week, and every organisation rated it a very happy place to be. We had one big hall, with a stage. There was a badminton court. There was a small hall for Kirk Session meetings, and Board meetings and very good kitchen accommodation. The modern toilet facilities were particularly good. The entrance hall was modest but adequate. The windows of the hall were high up, so that the youth groups could have their games without having to worry about breaking windows. Every one was happy with the finished article.

The first time I went up to Glorat Estate after Marigold became my home help I was a wee bit apprehensive. I wondered what I was going to say to Lady Stirling about Marigold working for me in the manse. I need not have worried, the Old Lady sorted it out. 'I'm very relieved that Marigold is looking after the house for you; you will be able to depend on her, she is honest and reliable.' That was it, my mind was at ease immediately.

Lady Stirling died on 14 January 1983; she would have been a hundred years in the September, I was very sorry she did not make it. Her remains lie in the vault in Glorat Estate. I had lost a very good friend. Her life was one of giving and sharing. I learned a great deal from my visits to this elderly lady, who was a Lady in every sense of the word. She interested me greatly in India, her husband Sir George had a distinguished military career, and received a DSO in 1900 and a CBE in 1919. They were married in 1902, and had two sons and three daughters. The eldest son Charles died in a yachting accident in 1938, his body was never found, a tragic loss to the family. The younger son Mungo, who was a Captain in the Black Watch died in action in the Middle East in December 1941 and is buried in Heliopolis in Egypt. In the early part of their married life Sir George and Lady Stirling were posted to India, and it was wonderful for me to hear about life there. In fact she gave me a great yearning to see the Indian continent, and some years later I did just that.

There was another connection between us. We both shared a love for the Holy Land. There is a plaque on the wall of the Church of St Andrew's in Jerusalem for her son Mungo Stirling. But there was another connection. Lady Stirling's sister was trained as a nurse in Guy's Hospital in London. She and a friend had decided to become missionaries in China. They stopped off in the Holy Land and realised there was a great deal of work to be done in the missionary field there, so China was forgotten. These two women became Russian Orthodox nuns, took the names of Martha and Mary, and settled down in the convent belonging to the Church of Mary Magdalene. They taught in a little school in Bethany. They were very highly thought of by the Arab community. When the Russian revolution took place in 1917, the Russian Church, its monks and its nuns were left destitute. Lady Stirling was one of their supporters, and sent money out regularly. They lived on a shoestring budget. The British Government helped during the time of the Mandate. When Lady Stirling found out about my journeys to the Holy Land, I became the go-between, taking money out to the Russian Orthodox Church. Unfortunately for me, Lady Stirling's sister Mother Martha had died earlier on. I never met her. But I did become friends with Mother Barbara who was the Abbess of the Convent, and had escaped from Russia during the time of the revolution. When I met her, she was over ninety years old, but still had a very active mind The nun who looked after Mother Barbara had always to describe me. 'It is the little Scottish woman,' as her sight was very poor, then Sister Elana would say, 'Mother it is English today,' because this frail old lady could speak in Russian, Arabic, Hebrew, and English.

The last time I saw Mother Barbara, she was confined to bed. It was at Easter time, and we had a lovely talk, then she presented me with six wax Easter Eggs, made by the nuns, depicting Jesus ascending to God from the empty Tomb. I still have mine; the others went to the Stirling family. By the time I was back in the Holy Land, Mother Barbara had reached the end of the road. Up above the Convent at Gethsemane is their cemetery. There are three burial places, Mother Martha, Mother Barbara, and Mother Mary, in that order. They were a trio who served their Lord faithfully in that part of the world. The local folk have never forgotten them, especially our Arab guide, Hamid, who had been taught by Mother Martha in the little school at Bethany.

On Sunday 6 February 1983 I was honoured to be asked to conduct the Memorial Service for Lady Stirling in the Church of the Holy Rude in Stirling. I offered to stand aside, if the Stirling family wished to have another minister. From Miss Betty came the answer, "Mummy would not approve of that." The choir of Milton Church were asked to participate, and they responded whole-heartedly. On that day we were celebrating a life well lived. In 1922 Lady Stirling was the County Commisioner for the Girl Guide movement for Stirlingshire. She was President of the Campsie District Nursing Association, owing to her devotion, and through the efforts of the Nursing Association a bungalow was purchased for the district nurse to live in, in Campsie. When the NHS took over, the house was handed over, and for a long time was still used to house a district nurse. Lady Stirling was the local organiser for the Earl Haig Poppy Appeal 1926 saw her appointed as a JP and she became President of the Stirlingshire Branch of the British Red Cross Society and was co-opted to serve on the Stirlingshire Education Authority. It is not difficult to imagine why Lady Stirling was honoured and awarded the OBE in 1926. During the Second World War, Glorat house was offered by Sir George and Lady Stirling to serve as an Auxiliary Hospital. Lady Stirling became Commandant of the Hospital, and during the War Years, over 1300 service-men spent their time of convalescence in Glorat House at the foot of the Campsie Hills. The life story of this very wonderful lady was a joy to read. Her life was based on faith, her faith in her Lord and Saviour Jesus Christ. She said to me one day, 'My faith has sustained me throughout my life, I learned at my mother's knee, a little text, "God is Love"; I live secure in that knowledge.'

In 1946, Lady Stirling was again honoured, she was awarded a CBE for her work with the Scottish Red Cross. She began writing her memoirs when she was eighty-one years, and completed them when she was ninety years old. So the day of her Memorial Service was indeed a celebration of a life of service, totally committed to helping others.

There was one man she was always interested in, and he was usually the first person she asked about on my visits to her. This man's story gives us an insight into the other side of the coin of life. My friend will be called Robert, he gave up the rat-race of society and was living in an old broken down hut on the banks of the River Glazert. He had come from a very comfortable home, as far as I knew he had been to University, he was a very fine artist. Of course that hut was in my parish, which meant he was one of mine. His mother visited him, and his sister, and I'm sure they would always try to get him to give up his way of life. Because he used a paraffin heater, his clothes smelled of paraffin; he was also quite dirty in appearance, and his beard was also black. But to me he was a gentleman. I used to visit him in his hut, and enjoyed a jam jar with tea in it. My big dog and Robert got on very well, except that after Robert stopped clapping Golda, she was as black as him.

One Sunday morning, it had been snowing quite heavily, I was ready to set out for church. The phone rang; it was Bob Gemmill, my Session Clerk. His living room window looked down to the field beside the Glazert. He was very excited, the news was, 'Robert's hut is on fire, and I don't know where he is, he could be inside it, I've sent for the Fire Brigade.' I said I'd be up. As I got to the field the firemen arrived, and thank God so did Robert, he had been to the farm for his milk. Poor soul, all that was left were ashes; this gentleman had nothing but the clothes he stood up in. I offered him a room in the manse immediately, but the answer was no thank you. I offered him the garage, the answer was still no. The snow was about a foot deep, what were we to do? Bob and I decided to ask him what he wanted to do, his request was for a tent. Bob got started on the phone. I had to leave to take the church service, but said I would be back when I could. By the time I got back to the field, Bob had arranged for a tent to be brought from a friend's house. It was a good sturdy one; with an inside liner and had a zip inside and outside. I was about to clear the snow away from where they were going to pitch the tent, but Robert stopped me and said to leave the snow, it would be good, and would heat the bottom of the tent.

By about 3 o'clock that afternoon the tent was up, Robert was quite happy. It had got round the village by this time that our friend had lost all his possessions, such as they were. The village responded to his needs; one lady brought a lilo, and some blankets. By evening he had as many necessities as he could cope with. I was anxious about food. Another woman said she would provide Robert with one hot meal a day till something was organised. Another brought a camping gas cooker, and a tin kettle. We made him as comfortable as we could in a cold wintry day. Before I left the camp site, I took Robert aside and asked him if I should contact his sister, so that she could take him home for a few days. The answer was no, because Milton of Campsie was his home, and if he left the site the farmer might not let him back.

On the Monday morning, I checked Robert's situation. He was quite happy in his tent, no complaints. Again I offered our garage plus meals, but he would not leave the field. I went back home. Alex had said on the Sunday evening, 'Why don't you phone round some of these caravan sites and ask them if they have an old broken down caravan that was past its best?' I began the phone calls on the Monday morning, but nobody was interested in the plight of this poor soul. I gave up and went out to do some visits. There was an elderly couple I decided to call on, who were quite upset about Robert, I was telling them about the caravan idea, and that nobody wanted to know. Mr was very quiet, then he turned to me.

'I know where there is a caravan that is no longer in use, my son-in-law's brother, he has this one lying at the farm. I'll phone him now.'

He came back into the room with the news that the caravan was mine for £50. I said, 'I'll take it.' I did not have the fifty pounds at that moment; but that was the least of my worries. That was on the Monday, I got in touch with some of my elders, because this was a big caravan, and it would have to be moved in two parts, so it had to be halved, and then put together again. I spoke to my next door neighbour, who was in the tarmacadam business; he had a tractor, and knew the farm. Archie Bell said if the elders would split the caravan in two he would bring one half of Robert's new home to the field on the Saturday. I was over the moon. I ran into the manse to do a few phone calls, and found an envelope behind the door. I opened it, there was a £10 note inside, and a note said, 'Hope this can help Robert.' Little did they know, I only needed £40 now to pay for the caravan; of course, the gift was anonymous.

Tuesday morning I went down to see Robert. He was still having a hot meal, each day, and was quite comfortable, I asked him if he would like to live in a caravan, where his hut had been, I don't think he could believe it. I told him the first part would be on the site by Saturday, would he manage till then? His face lit up, he was very very happy. I went back to the manse, there was an envelope behind the door, yes, another £10, yes, another anonymous note, this was for Robert. Wednesday produced the same story, another £10. I now had £30, only needed another twenty. On the Thursday I went back to the manse and looked behind the door, but there was no envelope. I was in the study, when the phone rang, It was the farmer who owned the caravan. 'I'll let you have that caravan for £30, Mrs Irvine.' I went straight along the road and paid the £30. The caravan was mine … Who says there is no God? Who says Prayer does not work???

The Saturday was a dry clear day. About ten of our elders set to work. Archie Bell with plenty of help brought the one half of the caravan to the field; they laid some railway sleepers down first, then sunk the wheels of the caravan into the ground. It took the men most of the day. Robert made tea for them with the tin kettle, Bob Gemmill's wife gave us some mugs. That night the tent came down and Robert slept in his new home. The following Saturday, the same routine, the men of the church worked very hard, and Robert was amazed. These men became his friends. We knew that Robert would not change his way of living, we would not have tried to do that anyway; we respected his privacy and made it quite clear that no-one would encroach on the privacy he held most dear. Come the Sunday morning, I could not believe my eyes. There was Robert sitting in the back seat, against the wall. I was thrilled to bits. After the Service I went to the door, came back into church and there was Robert waiting for me. He thanked me and the church men for all they had done, then he asked me if I would object to him being in church on Sundays; he would just sit at the back in the corner. Then he asked if he would have to join. I told him he did not have to, he could be an adherent, which made him a member of our church family, but if he ever felt he wanted to join, he was only to ask. He never missed a Sunday. He never joined, and the back seat was just as black as him, so was the wall. It did not matter, that seat was his; no-one would have been allowed to sit there, Bob Gemmill saw to that.

I visited Robert in his caravan; it did get a bit tatty and dirty with the usual paraffin stove, but we became very good friends. The church family always made sure that Robert had all he needed in the way of warm clothes for the winter. Over all the years, Robert never asked us for anything. He never asked for money ever. He cultivated a wee plot of ground beside the River Glazert and when harvest time came round he brought some of his produce to the festival. Then he began to turn up to our social evenings, and the men who helped him with the caravan, were happy to see him amongst us. His sister still came to see Robert and could not believe all that had been done for him by the good folk of Milton of Campsie.

The week before Lady Stirling's Memorial Service. I explained to our congregation the arrangements made for the following Sunday afternoon, at the Church of the Holy Rude. Those who were hoping to go to Lady Stirling's Memorial Service, were to give their names to one of our elders, and those who had space in their cars were to see me. After the Service, Robert came to me and said, 'Mrs Irvine, I would like to attend Lady Stirling's Memorial Service. I had a great deal of respect for her, although I never met her, could I put my name down to go.'

I was kind of rocked back on my heels. Robert really did smell of paraffin. I could not ask anyone else to take him, so said, 'That will be all right Robert, you can come with me.'

I picked Robert up for the Memorial Service. He was his usual self, scented with the paraffin, and not too clean; his mittens were full of holes. He just looked like a tramp, but he was our Robert. If we had tried to change him, he would have gone back to being a recluse, and that would have been very sad. We drew up outside the church of the Holy Rude. It was a lovely day, and there were quite a number of people standing outside the church, but they were not of my congregation, and they had no idea that this wee woman with the tramp was the minister. I went to the back of the car for my robes, and opened the boot, Robert, ever the gentleman, lifted the case out for me, and followed me to the door of the church. There the beadle was waiting for me. He went to take the case from Robert, who just said, 'Please lead the way.' The beadle, I could see, was about to say something, but thought it better just to let the matter rest, and guided us through the church to the vestry, Robert went into the vestry, opened my case, gently took the robes out and laid them across a bench. Then he turned to me and said, 'I will attend to you at the end of the service Mrs Irvine.' The beadle was astounded, but it flashed through my mind, that Lady Stirling would have enjoyed that wee cameo of real life. Robert was as good as his word; he came back to the vestry, carried my case to the car, I'm sure there would be many questions asked that day about the companion of the minister of Milton of Campsie.

One day I went down to visit Robert who, seemed very pleased to see me. He had been into Glasgow to get something very special for his minister. It was a very lovely statuette, made of white china, about nine inches high. Two nuns were holding a book between them. It was a beautiful gift to receive. He had bought it for no particular reason, except he hoped that I would like it. I certainly did, and still have it today. It constantly reminds me of one very special gentleman, who deserved a great deal better out of life, but was content to live in this world, but on his terms.

I came in from the church door one Sunday. I did not think that Robert looked particularly well. His colour was poor, and he seemed to have got a bit thinner. I asked him if he was feeling all right, and it came out that he had been very sick during the week, he could not keep his food down.

'Have you got a doctor you can contact?'

'No I've never needed one,' he said.

'Maybe it would be a good idea if you got one now.'

He did not like the idea so I did not push the matter. I did not see Robert on the Monday. On the Tuesday morning, Willie Turner the farmer phoned me to say that Robert had not turned up for his milk. Down I went to the caravan, There was no sign of life, I did something I had never done before, I knocked, turned the handle of the door, and walked into this very private home. Robert was lying very still.

I said, 'It's the minister.'

He struggled to sit up, he was just bones. I took the bull by the horns, and said, 'You need a doctor.'

He stopped me, 'No, please not just yet.'

The place was a shambles, but I made him some tea; he never ate anything,

Then I said, 'I will be back in the afternoon, and if there is no change in your condition, I will get a doctor.' I left.

My mind was not on my work that day. Late in the afternoon I went back to the caravan. One look was enough; I intend getting a doctor. Robert said, 'No doctor will come here, anyway it does not matter.'

That evening I had a Presbytery Committee meeting in Glasgow. I phoned our very good Councillor, Charles Kennedy, he was one of St Paul's congregation but knew Robert very well, Charles was the type of councillor, who bent over backwards for the people of the village.

'Charles, Robert is very ill, he needs a doctor, but is not on any doctor's list, I'm going to Presbytery tonight, I should be back about 9.30 p.m., could you try and get a doctor who will visit this very sick man in a hovel of a place. It's dirty, so is he, but he is a human being, and we are all responsible for him.'

The answer was, 'Leave it to me, I'll get to work on that one.'

I was home at 9.20 p.m., phoned Charles. 'Doctor Henderson who lives in the bungalow across the road from the manse will do the necessary, just phone him.'

The doctor across was not my doctor, he was in the Lennoxtown practice. I phoned him.

'This is the minister across the road, I believe you have agreed to visit Robert, I think he is very ill. What time tomorrow?'

'Why wait till tomorrow, are you afraid of the dark?'

'I'm afraid of nothing, but we will have to climb a five barred gate, and we will need a torch.'

'I'll see you in five minutes,' says the doctor.' That is why a minister and a doctor were seen together, scrambling over a five barred gate into a field about eleven o'clock one dark night in Milton of Campsie.

We had to hammer at the caravan door, but the doctor decided just to open it. The patient was just too ill to be bothered objecting. Our doctor was wonderful with this very determined patient. Robert was well and truly examined. I held the torch, the rats were running about, but glad to say our doctor never batted an eye. The outcome was that Robert needed hospital treatment as soon as possible. Our doctor explained to Robert, and said he would get on to the hospital, first thing in the morning, and he would arrange for an ambulance, and bring a letter round to the caravan in the morning for the doctor in the hospital.

Robert was having no ambulance. Said he, 'I'll only go to the hospital if my minister takes me, I am not going in an ambulance.'

There was no alternative. The doctor phoned into Stobhill Hospital in the morning; I was to have Robert there for nine o'clock, with the letter. He was to be kept in for tests. The hospital staff did the unthinkable, they put Robert into a bath. When he was in bed I went in to see him settled, I did not know him. His beard was pure white, so was his hair. The strange thing was he accepted all the care and attention quite happily. I think he realised just how ill he was.

The outcome was what we all expected, Robert had cancer. We notified his sister, who came up and gutted the caravan, put in a new mattress, blankets etc. and made the place livable once more. His sister was heartbroken that Robert would not take any help, but she certainly cared very deeply about him. He did get home to his caravan. The congregation rallied round, with pyjamas and a warm dressing gown which Robert thought was grand; food was prepared for him but he was not able to enjoy it. For a few weeks I had been taking him into hospital on a Friday for check-ups, an operation was not feasible. The last Friday I took Robert to hospital, the sister of the ward said that we would not be getting him back again, the cancer was spreading rapidly. Robert passed away peacefully that Sunday.

Robert's funeral service was held in the Church. The people of Milton of Campsie, made sure that our friend had a service that told of their caring concern for the man who endeared himself to the villagers. Every seat was used, even Robert's seat was filled.

Chapter Eighteen

On 3 March 1983, I had a committee meeting for the Presbytery at Renfield Church Centre in the afternoon. Unfortunately, my car was on the top storey of the car-park in Bath Street. After the meeting, I was a bit late, so I ran across the road to the car-park, and walked up all the stairs. When I got to the car, I was having some chest pains. I sat in the car for a wee while and the pains disappeared. There were no more pains so I never said anything to Alex when he came home. I was not very hungry, but that was not unusual for me. That evening I had two baptisms to see about, and had to pay a visit to the Junior Brigade.

I left the manse at 7 p.m., my usual time for evening visiting. I usually spent about half an hour in each home, baptism took a wee bit longer. Having reached my first home, we were well on our way with the arrangements for the baby's day in church, when suddenly the pains came back. I tried not to move too much, and did not hold the wee one. I was longer than usual in that home, but the pain eased away again and I moved on to the next home. The same thing happened again, but I completed the arrangements, left the house and made my way to the church hall, where we were going to be making a programme for the Junior Brigade display. They had a cup of tea ready for me but I never drank it. I was beginning to feel nauseated, so excused myself, telling the team I was very tired; they could prepare for the display without me, and hand me in a copy. Bob Gemmill, Officer in Charge, asked if there was anything wrong. I said I was all right, but needed to be home. Most unlike me. Bob knew that, but did not want to push me. I went off home to bed.

I never said a word to Alex; he was taping music, so I said I'd just go up to bed. The pains went away again. I fell asleep, but wakened about 2 a.m. it was worse than ever. Trying to lie very still did help a wee bit. These pains came and went most of the night. Alex's alarm went off at 6 a.m. I knew if he went to work I would be on my own, and I was beginning to get a wee bit worried. As Alex got up, I said to him that I did not feel very well, and told him about the pains. He phoned the doctor. It turned out I was having a heart attack. The ambulance was there in double quick time. At that time ambulances were stationed locally, and I knew the two men attendants who turned up. They fairly raced to Stobhill. Oxygen was needed, the attendant said. 'It's all right, Mrs Irvine, we will get you there, don't worry.' I was past worrying. They gave me an injection; I was in cloud nine, the pain was gone. Right away I was put on a heart monitor.

When Alex came into the ward I said to him, 'If I die now, the congregation will remember me as the woman who got them into debt for the Church Hall.'

Alex said, 'There's no danger of your dying, I think you have a lot of damage to do yet; anyway we need you, I need you most of all.'

I was in Stobhill for a week. They needed the beds and the heart doctor came to see me. He said, 'Can I trust you to do exactly as you are told? I think you would get on just as well at home. You have had what we call a stress heart attack, there is no scarring on the heart, but it is a warning.

I promised. My sister-in-law Sheila came over from Erskine to look after me for a week. The doctor came in to see me, and said, 'Who is the wee lady who opened the door, I would like to speak to her.' Sheila came through, and he asked her if she was going to be staying.

She said 'Yes, for a week.'

'Right, she has not to lift anything heavier than a cup of tea, I'll be back next week.'

Our sister-in-law from Australia was coming home the following week; she volunteered to stay in the manse for the next week, Then Alex took two weeks of his holidays.

The rest was beginning to take effect, I thought I could get back to work. When the doctor came back in the second week, he said I could go for a walk. I thought, great, I can take the dog for a walk. Then the doctor said, 'Do you see that gate out there, walk there and back three times a day.' The first time I reached the gate, I was glad to get off my feet, but each day I got stronger. After the first month I looked forward to being back in the pulpit, that was a laugh. I was off three months, but I did do as I was told, and bit by bit I did recover.

In April 1983, the Ways and Means Committee of the Church started a coffee morning which went from strength to strength. It was a Mrs

Jean Gilmour who proposed that they should try it. There were no tearooms in Milton, and it certainly took off, it's still going strong in 2002. Their secret was the home baking. Mrs Miller was the quartermaster. She and her husband went to the cash and carry and bought all the ingredients for those who were prepared to do a weekly baking. The minister knew not to visit in any of these homes on a Monday. They collected their ingredients, then set to work baking all day on Mondays. They presented their home baking on Tuesday morning. There were no biscuits on the premises, and into the bargain there was plenty of home baking for sale.

They also had a white elephant stall which sold some very good articles. Children's school clothes were a great idea; we are all aware how quickly children grow out of their school uniforms. At one time the coffee morning was earning £300 per week, which went a long way to help paying off the hall debt. If you were not there on a Tuesday at 10 a.m. the home baking was finished, I used to order mine. Mrs Lindsay made birthday cakes and sold them; that money also went to boost the funds. If I or anyone else was having visitors, all we had to do was phone Mrs Miller, and she would deliver some home baking to your home. She was a dab-hand with the apple tarts and fruit cakes. The coffee morning was also a great help to me. I did not bother about tea, but I was able to go round the tables, and if anyone needed a wee chat in private, I used the small hall. Believe it or not we got quite a number of new members through the coffee morning.

One of the new streets was named after me when the Bellway estate was finished; it's called Irvine Gardens. In 1983 five elders received long service certificates for thirty years faithfulness. One of them was Alex. I did not get to the Holy Land with James in 1983 but was booked to go as a leader in the July; I did manage to do that. I was also booked to go to India for the first time. I was not working on this tour, so was looking forward to it in November of that year.

Alex was with me on our July visit to the Holy Land. He looked after the money and the tipping, and we had a wonderful pilgrimage. Everything was fine, and I was looking forward to being in India for the first time. Alex was not booked to go, because we couldn't afford two fares. But Alex insisted that I should go. About the middle of October, when Alex was on nightshift, he had developed a very bad cough. He did smoke, always had done; often I had tried to get him to stop it, but he just could not do it. The cough got worse, I said if you don't go to the doctor I will bring him in one morning. He made an appointment to see the doctor on the following Monday morning. He said he would go straight from work, and would also see about a new exhaust for his car. He did not come in till 2 p.m.

I said, 'Where have you been, I thought you were going to fix the exhaust at home.'

Alex's reply shocked me, 'I was sent from the surgery to Ruchill Hospital, the chest hospital, for an X-ray; they will send me word.'

Two days later we got a phone call from the surgery; the doctor wanted to have a word with Alex. We went together, much against the will of Alex. Unfortunately our own Doctor Harrison was on holiday, and it was a woman, young, who was filling in as locum.

She said, 'Mr Irvine, you have a tumour which is inoperable, it is on the bronchus, the tube between the two lungs, and there is nothing we can do. You can go back to work, and when you get pain we will give you something to help. Is there anything I can do for you now.' I was absolutely furious. I know it's better that the patient knows the score, but there must be a better way of breaking the news.

Alex did go back to work. We got a letter from Ruchill Hospital: the chest specialist wanted to see Alex. It was the end of October. I wanted to cancel the Indian trip, we were due out in November. Alex and I went to Ruchill to see this specialist. He told us more or less what we had already been told, but he wanted to take Alex into Ruchill in November, to try chemotherapy. He hoped this would slow the tumour down. Alex told this doctor of the trip to India, and he advised me to go.

While you are in India we will have Alex in here. It will take three weeks for these tests.

Alex said, 'If you don't go to India, I will not go into the hospital, that is final.'

I went to see Dr Harrison, I knew I would get the truth from him. He told me he could not give me any good news: go to India, if it will keep Alex happy. He told me that Alex had at the most two years, and the chances of him being able to go anywhere was minimal.

It seemed so unfair: Alex went into hospital, I went to India. It was a hard decision to make. Marigold Langley was with me; she was also very sad about Alex's problem. Of course I phoned the hospital more than once. Alex said he was being well looked after, and had plenty of visitors, but the tour for me was a bit of a nightmare. I could not

Wee man with blanket.

sleep. Alex's face was there before me most of the time. The thing that took our circumstances away from my mind for a wee while was the abject poverty of India. Children begging in the streets were so malnourished, it didn't seem possible that people could be born on the streets, live on the streets and die on the streets. Nobody seemed to care; the caste system was blatently obvious. What could people like us do about it?

We were living in the Kinishka Hotel, very posh, marble floors, beautiful decor. On our first morning I went outside with my camera, I wandered round the corner, there sitting on what we would call "his hunkers", was a wee thin grey haired soul with a plastic cup of coffee in his hand. He was wrapped in a grey blanket. The coffee stall owner said he gave him that plastic cup of coffee every morning, and the blanket covering him was the only thing he owned. I took a photo of the wee man, then I asked the young man if he would stand or sit beside the wee fellow and I would take another picture. The answer was no, because the man wrapped in the grey blanket was an untouchable, and the coffee stall owner would lose most of his customers if he were seen too close to his untouchable customer. I went back to the

Outcastes in India, man with turban.

hotel upset about the awful lack of care there was for the many folk who were destitute. George McCabe had a brother Andrew, who was the manager of the James Harvey Memorial School in North East India. George said that our church could adopt a boy and educate him; that would be a help for just one child. I said I would think about it when we got home.

I was glad to get home, and so was Alex. He went back to work, and it was like living in a dream world. I had asked Alex if he were going to keep his problem a secret. His answer was that if anyone asked him what was wrong he would just tell them. It made it easier for both of us; we could discuss things together. My husband was a very brave and considerate man, and all that bothered him was that I was all right.

On 17 January 1984, Alex came in from work in the evening. He came in the back door, and said, 'No dinner, I'm going to bed, phone Dr Harrison, tell him I have gone to bed, I won't be up again, and I don't want an apprentice doctor.'

Alex was remembering the young locum doctor. Dr Harrison was over in twenty minutes. He went straight upstairs and told Alex that he would be the only doctor who would attend, and I was to get him night or day on his home phone, and his wife Jessie would relay the message to him wherever he was.

The chemotherapy certainly did not work. Dr Harrison contacted the hospice beside Stobhill Hospital and Dr Welsh came out to see Alex, said he would admit Alex to the hospice when the time came, that time was not far away. There were times when Alex could not breathe and he needed oxygen. I just had to call the hospice and they sent out an ambulance. The oxygen did help, but Alex was in and out of the hospice very often. I had moved Alex into what had been my mother's room; it was big and airy, with an oriel window, and seemed to be more easily aired than our bedroom. The bathroom was next door. He still insisted on getting up. One of my elders, Jimmie Young, who worked in Woodielee Hospital, volunteered to come into the manse and give him a bath. That was great because Alex was five feet eleven and too heavy for me to manage. I was still working in the parish, but I left the door of the manse open so that his fellow elders could pop in and see he was OK.

I was given little morphine tablets, to help Alex when the pain got really bad, but I was warned to be careful not to overdose him. One day he took a turn for the worse. I phoned Dr Harrison; he immediately phoned the ambulance and Alex was taken back to the hospice. Dr Harrison warned me that I would have to ease up or I might have another heart problem. I phoned presbytery and asked for leave of absence. I only asked for a month and said I would play it by ear. Pulpit supply was organised. Alex did not know I'd taken leave of absence. He thought I had taken holidays. This time the hospice seemed to work wonders: Alex looked particularly well. You began to live in hope that the powers that be have made a mistake, and the patient has turned the corner. That's how I felt that week.

On the Monday Dr Welsh said, 'If there is a time to take Alex home again its now, we will send him home on Wednesday.'

I said, 'Why not tomorrow, I have his room all ready, I've even got a wee television set for him, with a remote control.'

One of my elders; Bob Stevenson, volunteered to go in for Alex, 'You have a cup of tea ready for him, it's better if you are here waiting for him.'

Alex walked into the manse carrying his own case. I couldn't believe it, he looked great, very thin, but better than he had looked for ages.

His bed was ready but he said he would like to stay downstairs for a while. I had bought one of these padded garden chairs for him, because his bones were sticking through. He loved that chair, it brought him quite a lot of ease. Late afternoon he decided to go to bed.

The wee television was much appreciated. He did use it that night, but the next day he was too tired to be bothered with it. He did eat some small meals. On the Thursday, he said to me, 'I know you've been off work, but I'll be all right, I want you to be in the pulpit on Sunday.' He would not take no for an answer. I promised. I made arrangements with the session clerk. On the Friday night two of my elders came in to see Alex; the husband Tom was an engineer like Alex. They did enjoy their chat, so much that Marion and I left them together to go and make the supper. They left about 9.30 p.m. Alex was very tired. I gave him some of his tablets, but kept the sleeping pill for later; it was better to keep that pill till the last minute. I managed to help him up to the bathroom, and got him into clean pyjamas. He lay down and said, 'That's great.' It was now about 11 p.m., I gave in and gave him the sleeping pill, and crawled into bed.

I was wakened about four o'clock. Alex was gasping for breath, I phoned the ambulance; they were there very quickly, and he was given oxygen all the way to the hospice. They are wonderful people who work in those very sad situations; they had Alex breathing a bit better within five minutes, an injection of some kind did the trick. I had alerted my next door neighbour, Moira Bell, who came into the hospice to take me home. The sister in the ward said he was quite stable. He was not very good on the Saturday, but reminded me of my promise to be in the Pulpit on the Sunday. Believe it or not it was the last place I wanted to be.

However a promise was a promise; it would give me the opportunity to thank the congregation for all their support and kindness over the previous months. I informed them that Alex was back in the hospice. I went to the door that morning as usual, and felt that Alex was right as always, it was somehow right to be in the pulpit this morning and thank all these very wonderful people.

I went into the hospice in the afternoon, and the first question was, 'Well, were you in your own pulpit this morning?'

I replied, 'Yes, are you satisfied? You got your own way as usual.'

Alex laughed, 'That's a good one coming from you.' He was still smiling.

The windows of the room were wide open to give him air. I left, the dog had to be walked and fed; it was one of the chores that helped me to cope, walking the dog is a peaceful exercise ... I was back in the hospice at seven, I sat for a while, Alex did not know I was there, he was deeply sedated. The Sister said to me, 'Go home, Mrs Irvine, phone in about ten and we will let you know if we think you should be here.

I did phone at ten, Alex was very comfortable. I prepared for bed. The phone went at ten thirty. 'Come in now, Alex is having difficulty in breathing.' I had left the car in the drive so was on my way quite quickly, I had not taken time to inform anyone. I was minutes too late. I was devastated. Alex died on Sunday 13 May, the Sunday he had insisted that I be in my own pulpit. All the time he had was six months from when he took ill, a man who had never been off work as long as I had known him. The chest specialist told him, smoking has caused your illness. Alex stopped immediately, but it was too late,

The night staff in the hospice would not allow me to drive home by myself. They phoned Douglas and Sheila, who came over to the hospice. I drove home with Sheila, and Douglas went home. Sheila stayed to help with the funeral arrangements. She phoned Rev. James Currie who knew Alex very well, for Alex had been in the Holy Land with James a few times, and James had visited Alex very often during his illness. There was no other minister who knew my Alex as well as James. He came over from Dunlop immediately and agreed to conduct the funeral service in the church. Alex was cremated at Daldowie Crematorium. There were thirteen ministers at the funeral of the quiet man. He was a man of great faith, and if it had not been for my Alex, I would never have made the grade. He was my mainstay all the way through my training and beyond. How was I going to manage without him?

To face life alone was going to be very difficult, Alex tended to spoil me, I never had to worry about anything, all financial concerns I left to him. I only looked after the food, Alex even dealt with furnishings, decor, and if I liked something, I'd take him to see it, and then waited for the results. If he liked what he saw, it appeared very soon after. He was a faithful man in all things, but there was also a stubborn streak, and if he dug his heels in, forget it dear. When we had any arguments, he let me rave away, then he'd say, 'Is that it, wee yin, do you think we could get back to normal now.' I could have bashed him on many an occasion. Always very calm, never in a hurry, tremendous patience, he had to have to live with me. I could not see life without him.

I bought a box of crisps and a box of Mars bars. That was the main diet for about six weeks. I was saved by the good auspices of my congregation, inviting me for dinners. When I learned about Marks & Spencers dinners for one, I was home and dry. I was back to work within two weeks. I had two Sundays off, and was glad to be back to the discipline of study. Alex was right when he pushed me into my own pulpit the Sunday he died, it had given me the opportunity to thank the congregation for all their kindness to Alex, and for the support I received during his illness. I did not have to do that when I went back to work. It had already been done. In the weeks after Alex died, the congregation and the people of the parish ministered to me, their practical care and concern was second to none. I have never forgotten them for their wise counsel and spontaneous love.

The day I returned to my pulpit, as I stood up to begin my service, I noticed just how many were in a similar situation. There were many widows, some trying to bring up children without their menfolk. It kind of threw me, but also said to me, get on with it, you are very fortunate. To see them there made me think. If I can't cope with my grief, how can I preach God's love to them? That was the turning point for me. Slowly but surely, I did get back to full time service. Don't get me wrong, Alex is never far away from my thoughts, and I have always believed that the personality of our loved ones never leaves us.

Dr Eileen McIlroy came up from York for Alex's funeral service and stayed on for a few days. She said I must have a break, but I was not in the mood. The Passion Play at Oberammergau was celebrating its 350th anniversary. James Currie had a group going out at the end of June. Eileen phoned James from the manse, and booked for the two of us. I really wasn't interested, but at the end of the day, it was a great help. While we were in Oberammergau Eileen suggested we go off to Israel late in the year, not with a group, just the two of us. She said she would make all the arrangements. Eileen phoned me from York to tell me that we would be going to the Holy Land in late November. Alistair McCabe got us missionary rates in the Church of Scotland Hospices in Jerusalem and Tiberias. We did have a wonderful time, travelling about in Arab buses and taxis.

On Christmas Day I was in Erskine with Douglas and Sheila and their family. I was not looking forward to New Year, but was invited to Glorat House, the Stirling family invited me to share in their New Year's Day dinner; that invitation came every year until I retired. I was very grateful for all the lovely kind invitations I received when I was on my own. I was certainly looked after by good friends. Lady Stirling's wee text: 'God Is Love', is very true.

Chapter Nineteen

During the ups and downs of 1984, the question about adopting a child in the School in North India was discussed by our Kirk Session. It was decided that we could do this, if various organisations took part in the project. The Womens' Guild agreed, the Boys Brigade, the Sunday School, and the Young Women's Group. I was very happy about that, and contacted George McCabe, who said he would let Andrew know. Very soon we had word back from the James Harvey Memorial School with the good news that our boy's name was Hari Krishan Sharma from Nepal. Hari was then nine years old; his health was not very good, he was undernourished, and in need of medical care. He had been born on 4 April 1975 in the Hindu Religion, as all Nepalese are. His father and mother worked on the land in Nepal; it seemed that they scratched a living, and had very little income. Hari had two brothers and a sister. Our Church in Milton of Campsie became very interested in the wee boy from Nepal.

In 1985 the interior of our Church was repainted over all, and two ceiling panels replaced. While that was being done, we worshipped in our Stirling Hall. The church furniture, the Communion Table and chairs, etc. were taken to the Stirling Hall, and we felt quite at home there. All our organisations continued to grow, and so did the congregation. We were always able to meet our financial responsibilities, and keep the hall fund going at the same time. There were no real problems facing us in the Church. The Fabric Committee of the Church inspected the manse and decided that the large front room needed to be papered and painted. The Congregational Board agreed, and so one day two of the elders came to the manse with the usual books of wallpaper for me to choose. I had never chosen wallpaper before, Alex had always looked after that, so I said to the elders, 'You choose.' They looked at me, amazed. I said, 'I've never done that before I'm not going to start now.'

One of the elders asked me if I would mind if his wife chose the paper, the answer was, of course not. The wife was phoned and over she came; her choice was very good indeed, and so the manse front room was redecorated.

The congregational visiting continued. Hospital visiting was vitally important, as was the care of the elderly. The minibus was still on the road and the Balmaha run continued in the summer months. For me, loneliness was the name of the game, so work was my salvation. The big dog Golda was a great comfort, always at my side. Walking her allowed me the fresh air I needed, and helped to keep me fit. Of course, the school was visited weekly, children help to keep your feet firmly on the ground. The family came out as often as they could. Graham and Crawford were growing into young men, and of course there were now girl friends on the go. Graham, the elder of the two boys, joined the Air Force in 1977, so we did not see much of him, but he was quite good at writing to his old auntie, and visiting when he was on leave ...

I was coming home from a presbytery meeting one Tuesday evening. The meetings of presbytery were held in Govan, which meant I had to travel via the Whiteinch Tunnel and along Clydeside Expressway. I was approaching the Finnieston turn-off, when I noticed a car in front. It had its hazard lights flashing. I began to slow down, but unfortunately for me, the man driving a van behind me did not slow down, and he hit me, doing about fifty miles per hour. My car was whipped across the road onto the Finnieston turn-off. The back end of the car was shattered, glass was everywhere, in my pockets, hair, even in my shoes, but I was unharmed. I did not have a scratch, but the car was totally out of commission. The doors of the car could not be opened, except by a crowbar. The police arrived, the story was told. The minister was breathalysed. I was wearing my clerical collar, there was no doubt about who I was. The policemen were full of apologies, but I wasn't bothered. The driver of the van and the minister were both sober, but the fellow was had up for dangerous driving; when I slowed down so should he have, but he didn't.

Because my car had to be towed away, I was taken to Finnieston Police Station. They asked me who they could phone, and I gave them Bob Gemmill's name, my session clerk. They made tea for me and we had quite an entertaining evening. Eventually Bob appeared, the Sergeant, at the desk said to Bob Gemmill. We had to arrest her she was drunk in charge of a car.

Bob's quick reply was, 'I am fed up bailing her out every Friday, we'll try and get her to the AA (Alcoholics Anonymous) meetings.'

As usual come April 1985, I was going to the Holy Land with the Rev. James, so even on holiday I was working. There was always something very special for me about the land of Jesus. My Bible became an open book. The company was always good. There were only sixty-six persons on that trip, which was enough; it meant there was more room on the buses, and not so many heads to count.

My very special visit was always the Church of the Transfiguration, and the second was the service we always had, sitting in the boat on the Sea of Galilee with the engines stopped. We were now using the Pilgrims Palace Hotel in Jerusalem which was an Arab Hotel; this hotel looked across a busy road to the Old City walls of Jerusalem. You just had to cross the road and the Damascus Gate was just along the road to the right. The Old City was like a magnet to me, any free time I had, I was off to explore the Old City: no bag, just a camera, hands in pockets, it was a dream come true. That Old City still means the same to me; Jesus walked among men 2000 years ago, I and thousands of pilgrims have walked that same road.

When we went up north on our second week, we lived in the Ron Beach hotel. This is a Jewish hotel which literally sat on the shore of the Sea of Galilee. If we were going across the lake, the boat would call at the hotel to pick us up. We could watch the sun rise early in the morning, if we were up on time. One day on one of my own group visits, we had just returned from one of our tours. We were all relaxing beside the Sea of Galilee. The Ron Beach facilities were great; we could have ice cream, drinks, tea or coffee sitting there, and some of the group were in swimming. Suddenly, the Golan Heights became shrouded in mist. It was as though a curtain was being drawn across a stage; the sun was blotted out, the wind rose, the Sea of Galilee was churned up like a whirlpool, then the hailstones came battering down. We ran to get our cameras, we had to get a picture of this phenomenon. Chairs and tables were thrown about. What a marvellous experience, for we remembered the story of Jesus.' He was asleep on a pillow at the back of the boat, a storm arose, the disciples were afraid. It's a wonderful story. 'Jesus stilled the storm' and all was well, you see it's difficult to imagine a storm on the Sea of Galilee, it's usually so calm. The lake was back to its usual within about ten minutes; the only way one would have known about the storm was the evidence of chairs and tables lying about the garden.

Our congregation honoured their commitment to the wee boy Hari, in his school in East India. We had remembered his Christmas, and his birthday in the April of 1985. McCabe travel had arranged for another tour to India and Nepal for November. That was my opportunity to meet Hari. I put my name on the list. Hari was brought to New Delhi to meet me; he was just a wee shaver, but a very good looking young man, with impeccable manners. I had brought out with me a grey sweatshirt with Scotland written across it; the wee boy was thrilled to bits, he had to wear it immediately, even though the sun was very hot. One of the school teachers was responsible for Hari, so the child was able to join our group for a few days. I got the chance to get to know him a wee bit better. In fact it was hard to leave him when we travelled north by plane to Nepal. That meeting with Hari made our commitment as a church more personal for me. I made up my mind that I would be back in India as soon as possible.

The first visit to India had been a bit of a nightmare for me, all I really did take in was the poverty of the place. I had been too caught up in my own problems, but this second visit was altogether different. I was able to relax and enjoy the people and the places. My camera was working overtime. New Delhi is a beautiful city, its tree lined avenues give it a look of spaciousness, but are filled with traffic. From New Delhi to Old Delhi, is really a transformation from a very modern city to a labyrinth of narrow lanes and streets, mosques, temples, monuments and the usual bazaars jumbled together in a kaleidescope of colour. Our hotel in Delhi was first class, spacious. The entrance was floored in marble, and the bedrooms were luxury status. After touring the back streets of Old Delhi, we felt rather guilty about our accommodation.

We went to Agra by train to see the Taj Mahal. This building fascinated me. I think it's the most beautiful edifice I have ever seen. Its story is one of profound love. Nur Jehan was the second wife of Emperor Shah Jahan. She married him in 1612 at the age of twenty one. She changed her name to Mumtaz Mahal; she was known for her generosity of spirit and her great wisdom. Her husband admired and respected her, but loved her above all others. She had given him thirteen children and died with the fourteenth at the age of thirty nine years. When she died Shah Jahan was numb with grief. He laid aside his imperial robes and wore white cotton clothes. He vowed to build a memorial that would surpass anything the world had ever seen in beauty. The Taj Mahal lies

Taj Mahal.

on the banks of the Jumna River and can be seen from the Agra Fort. It was built by a Persian, Ustad Isa, and he built well.

This jewel of India took seventeen years to build. The first glimpse of the Taj Mahal for the visitor is through the red sandstone gate which in itself is a magnificent building. The gate leads you in to a walled garden, where there is a rectangular pool which directs your eyes to this fabulous mausoleum, which is built on two bases, one of sandstone and one of marble. The whole building is inlaid with precious stones. The Taj Mahal was built primarily for the wife of Shah Jahan, but when the Shah died, his son had his father buried next to Mumtaz Mahal, his beloved wife. It is said that the cost of building the Taj Mahal today would cost in the region of $70,000,000, but who would dream of trying; there is only room for one such building in the world, that's why it is unique.

The other side of the coin is to be found at Varanasi, at one time called Benares. No one knows how old Varanasi is; some say it goes back to 500 BC. Others say it is the oldest continually lived in city in the world. There are over two thousand shrines in Varanasi; it is said that it is just one big shrine, Siva is the God worshipped on the steps

Mount Everest.

leading down to the River Ganges. Early dawn is the time to be there, as the multitudes of people make their way to the Ganges, to immerse themselves in what is said to be the most polluted river in the world, and there they worship Siva. It's a silent multitude of worshipping men and women and children, a spectacle, as the sun's rays throw up a rainbow of colours. We walked down the steps to the river. Boats for hire are plentiful, and our group were crammed aboard a rather large boat, with one man rowing. This man fascinated me, because he had hairs growing out of his ears in profusion. I did get a picture. A little rowing boat drew alongside ours, with two children huddled together, a boy and a girl. They were begging for money. They did quite well from our boat, but what a sad thing to see. I did take a slide picture. When the slides of that trip to India were developed, one of the children was out of focus. Usually any slide or picture which is out of focus I throw out. Not this one; it was truly out of focus, but when I show that slide, I draw folk's attention to the fact that the slide is right, it shows us that the lives of that wee boy and girl were decidedly out of focus, like many thousands of children throughout our world. To me it's a condemnation of worldly society, it certainly made me think.

We went back to Nepal on this tour. I was very glad about that. One of the reasons, my friends maintained, was because the Nepalese are mostly small folk like me. Nepal was a closed country until 1951. It lies at the foot of the Himalayas. The backdrop to this country is the snow covered mountains. The highest mountain in the world, Everest, over 29,000 feet, is just magnificent; no wonder people want to climb it. On a clear day with the blue, blue sky, it's a sight one never forgets.

One of our tours in Nepal was to take a flight along the Himalayas. The plane provided for the flight looked as if it were held together with string and chewing gum, but it was another adventure. The seats on the plane were numbered; that was important, because once in the air, when your number was called, you were allowed to join the pilot in the cockpit, and take a photograph of Everest. The flight was wonderful. We were flying close to this fabulous mountain, I was itching to get into the pilot's cabin. My number was called, I ran up the aisle, and into the cockpit. I felt as if I could touch the icing on the cake. The slides I took that day are some of the best I've ever had, and the wee plane and the pilot were first class. That outing is a never to be forgotten experience.

There was more excitement to come. Some of the group were asked if we would like to do a one day trek in the foothills of the Himalayas. My name was one of the first down. The folk who were not interested were to have a bus tour, and we would all meet for dinner at a hotel in the hills. If I remember rightly there were about eleven of us who wanted the trek. We had of course a Sherpa with us, a Nepalese guide. We started off well. A young Nepalese boy was carrying lunch for us in a huge basket; as usual it was held by a strap round his forehead, the basket then sat on his shoulders.

We had our lunch facing the snow covered mountains. It was just beautiful and so peaceful. We met many villagers. George McCabe was able to converse with them because he spoke Hindi. We were all very happy and relaxed.

Our Sherpa guide seemed in a bit of a hurry, the space between his small group of three, the fast walkers, and us began to expand. Gradually the group was being broken up, which was very wrong. Another lady and I were next, there were just the two of us. I did not know the lady before but we got to know each other very quickly. Her name was Janet and she came from Balloch. She was seventy-five years old,

James in kilt, India.

but was very fit. Behind us were another six, and three of them were men, including George McCabe. Janet and I found ourselves down at the bottom of the hills in to a paddy field. By this time the Sherpa was long gone with three of our people. I realised we were well and truly lost. It was getting dark. How do you tell a lady of seventy-five, we are lost, dear, in a paddy field somewhere in the foothills in Nepal?

I turned to Janet. 'I think we are lost, the Sherpa is gone, there should be another six here, but we seem to be on our own. I think we should just wait till someone comes for us.'

Janets reply was, 'I can't think about being lost at the moment, I need the toilet, then I can be lost.'

We sat down in the paddy field together, then when we had made ourselves comfortable, we had a bit of a laugh, and we both said together, now we can be lost. We began to shout. It seemed a long time, and we were getting a wee bit hoarse, when we heard a reply, we kept shouting, and suddenly there appeared the other three women. By this time it was getting cold. The moon was large and clear, the stars were shining. One of the women wanted us to keep walking.

I said, 'We must stay where we are, the Sherpa will have to come back for us, and there are still the three men missing. I think we should huddle together to keep warm, and let's sing, it might help to guide the men down.'

That's what we did. After some time the men appeared. They were in some state; one of the men had taken ill, and he was on the point of collapsing, he was quite a tall man. George McCabe was small; poor George, he had walked all the way down the hills with this very heavy man's hands on his shoulders, the other man was holding the sick man up by the belt round his waist. George and the other man were exhausted. I was pleased to hear that our singing had guided the trio down the hills. Even though the singing was rubbish, the sound had carried in the silence of the night. It was pleasing to think we had done the right thing by staying where we were.

We waited for what seemed like hours, then we saw lights flashing in the distance. It was the men from a village with wood burning torches. We had been reported missing and the head man of a village volunteered to send out a search party. It took them a while to reach us but we were very relieved to see this motley crew arrive. We were all very cold, but not for long; we had three miles to go before we reached our destination. We had to wade through a stream, climb over I don't know what, through trees and bushes, but the village men were wonderful. I was a wee bit anxious about Janet, and I asked her if she was all right. 'I'm fine,' she said, 'don't worry about me, I walk miles every day with my greyhound.'

Eventually we did reach the place for dinner, none of us were hungry, we just kind of picked at the food. We still had to climb aboard a bus to get back to our hotel.

Tired was not the word to use, knackered is better. I was very lucky, I was sharing with Dr Eileen, and after she saw every one else all right, she came to our room, ran a bath for me, got me a hot drink, and saw me into bed. I was asleep in minutes, but Eileen could not sleep, for worrying about what might have been.

Rev. James was with us on that trip, and so was Molly, wife of George. They were beside themselves with worry, we were about five hours late. The Sherpa was in deep trouble, but I don't know what happened to him. The three persons who had gone off with him were just as much to blame, they were a bit shamefaced. It should always be the rule that a guide should only go as fast as the slowest member of the group. The man who had taken ill was suffering from exhaustion, but the rest of us were none the worse of the experience. We learned the next day that the Nepal authorities had been alerted and were on the point of sending out a team of Gurkhas. I was very sorry we missed the Gurkhas.

We were taken to see, the house of the Living Goddess, the Royal Kumari. The Living Goddess is chosen from a selection of girls, four or five years old. They must belong to the Sakya clan of goldsmiths and tinsmiths. The Kumari's body must be flawless. The final phase of the selection process is a terrifying ordeal in the hall of the temple; men masked as demons try to scare the girls, and buffalo heads are placed around them in the darkness. The girl who remains calm throughout this ordeal is chosen to be the Living Goddess. Once the child has passed all the tests and the astrologers are satisfied that her horoscope is in harmony with the King's, she is settled in the Bahal (Temple). This Temple becomes her home until she reaches puberty. She is allowed to leave only for various religious festivals, and then she must be carried, as her feet must not touch the ground. When her term as Kumari has ended, the girl leaves the temple richly endowed and free to marry, but who would want to marry an ex-Goddess?

Durbar square lies close to the Temple we had just left. There is a Durbar square in most of the small towns in Nepal. You will find in each one a labyrinth of temples of different sizes. Katmandu also houses the ancient Palace. We were not inside this place, but I have a lovely slide photograph of a Gurkha soldier on guard. We found the Nepalese people very courteous and kind.

Chapter Twenty

Having just returned from India and Nepal, it was very difficult to settle down again. Fortunately for me I had most of my Advent and Christmas Services ready in outline. Because the congregation had grown over the last few years we had to have two services at Easter, Harvest and Christmas. The first service was 10.15 a.m. for the children and their parents. We always enjoyed these services, the Junior Choir sang for us, and it was a very happy time. The second service was as usual at 11 a.m. There were always the children who were not in the Sunday School and the minister's group, so there was always a young folk's address. Our Christmas tree was as usual gifted by Mr and Mrs Cameron, of the Yetts; the session clerk and his son Kenneth had the privilege of cutting it down for us each year. It was certainly in first class condition. The tree for the Stirling Hall, had to be bought. It was fortunate that we had Kenny Nicol as one of our elders, who was a fireman. It was his job to rope the Hall tree to one of the beams, as we had to make it safe. Then of course, both trees had to be decorated.

The great thing about having our Stirling Hall was the social evenings we could have. Christmas Eve we met in the hall about seven o'clock, Mums, Dads, Grannies, Grandpas, Aunties and Uncles and anyone who cared to could come, and we had a Christmas party, by the request of the minister. Everybody brought food. We played party games, we had the Grand Old Duke of York etc, and it was great fun. At about nine o'clock, tables were put down the middle of the hall, all the goodies were presented, we all enjoyed the food, and after that, the children went home to bed. The older folk, and those who were able to stay had a wee dance, and at eleven thirty, we went to the church for our Christmas Eve Service. The church was always well filled, and the parents who could get babysitters turned out for the service. Your chance of finding yourself sitting in with the choir happened every Christmas Eve. One of our young boys who played the cornet usually signalled the time of midnight. That young lad later joined the Royal Marine band; we certainly missed him.

In January of that year a Men's Fellowship came into being, there had been such an organisation many years before, but it had fallen by the wayside. I was delighted that the men of the church had decided to reform this group. It is a pity that very often there is no encouragement for the men of our churches to have the opportunity to meet with one another, and get to know each other in an informal setting.

April saw me again in the Holy Land with the Rev. James. It was his forty-fifth visit. I spoke about it to Ellen Pollock, and we decided to do something to mark the occasion. There was a German baker's shop in Tiberias, when we arrived up north, the first thing we did was go to the baker's and order a cake for James. There was no way we could get them to understand what we wanted, so we did not bother with the name. We just drew out 45; they got the message. We collected the cake from the shop on the day of the party, and the hospice put it in their fridge till night time. It was a great night, we presented the Big Boy James with the cake and he was in tears, big softy. That was my last visit with him as leader.

In 1985 the *Glasgow Herald* ran a cruise on the *MS Astor*. Three of us booked for this Greenland Adventure. I knew that James and Peggy were going with two of their grand-daughters. When Elizabeth Sutherland, a minister friend of mine who in fact was the second woman to be ordained into a parish, three months after me, heard about this adventure she said she too would like to go, but when she booked she was put in a cabin with three others she did not know. There was nothing we could do about it because I had booked with two friends and our cabin was just for three persons. However, good fortune was to shine on us; the woman who was steward of Elizabeth's cabin recognised that the other three knew each other, and that Elizabeth was the odd one out. She advised Elizabeth to apply for a shift to another cabin, because the ship was not full. This she did and got a two berth, no bunks, a super cabin. Elizabeth hot-footed it to my cabin, and asked if I would like to share. It was good for everyone concerned. It meant the two ladies I was sharing with had more room in the small cabin. I was asked to pay £50 extra, which was easy because the *Glasgow Herald* had given us a £50 pound voucher. It all turned out perfect.

We were bussed from Glasgow to Leith, to board ship; we had lots

James and cake.

of warm clothing with us. We sailed out of Leith and up the East Coast of Scotland, it was just beautiful. We were heading for the Faroe Islands. The Faroes lie in the path of the Gulf Stream, so the sea never freezes; the summer is predominantly cool, but it is daylight for almost twenty four hours a day. Our sail had been about twelve hours from Scotland. Torshavn is the capital of the Faroes. The country is made up of eighteen islands, seventeen of which are inhabited. The main industry is fishing. There are sheep in abundance. The islands are of volcanic origin and consist of black basalt rock. There are 45,000 inhabitants, and they are self governing under the Danish Crown. We had a lovely visit to the Faroe Islands, the air was clear and healthy. We walked up to the church, unfortunately it was closed. While we were ashore, I met a man, who was walking. His name was Tom Weir. It was hard going keeping up with him. It turned out Tom was married to Rhona who had worked in the office of Barr & Stroud. We were both on the works committee, I represented the West Works and Rhona the Office. We were both founder members of the Athletic Association and in the ladies hockey team ... We had not seen each other for many years, but the friendship was resumed on our cruise. After our short time on the Faroes, we set sail again, heading for Greenland. What an adventure.

We discovered very soon that the food on board *MS Astor* was absolutely wonderful. There was only one way we could cope, that was by walking round the ship or better still running round the ship. There was a very good gymnasium and a swimming pool on deck and another below deck. You will understand the swimming pool on deck was not for us: too, too, cold. You could have food any time of the day, and afternoon tea was a big temptation, the cakes were beautiful. We fell from grace, and we ate them.

The ship was indeed luxury. There were about forty *Herald* passengers, the rest were mostly German. The crew were a very caring bunch, and we were a happy group. There were various entertainments on board: the Rev. James did slide shows, Tom Weir also showed slides of wild life mostly birds. We were on board, but never bored. On our way to Greenland, there was a 10 force gale, and we were advised not to go on deck unless it was necessary. Of course it was necessary for Elizabeth and me, we were both camera buffs. Out we went and got some spectacular slides of mountainous waves, that was a bonus for us.

We reached Godthab, capital of Greenland, the world's largest island. The icecap of Greenland is 3 km thick and covers 1,833,900 square km Godthab was a very interesting place. It has only 1 per cent of the total population of Greenland, but in 1955 they built 500 tenant flats which look as if they are built on solid rock. We went off the ship to have a walk. We went with Tom Weir; again it was hard work keeping up with him, but we did gain some educative facts while with him. In 1985 the Greenlandic flag flew for the first time. They like the Faroes were also part of the Danish crown, and they have two Greenlanders in the Danish Government.

Our next port of call was Narssaq, a small town built by the USA during World War Two. It played an important role in the strategic defence of North America and Canada. The USA authorities left Narssaq in 1958. Narssaq is the centre of the sheep breeding in Greenland; there are also mink and fox farming, and a fur trade. Eskimo furs and parkas are quite famous, so also the woollen industries. Numerous flowers and bushes in beautiful colours decorate the valleys and cliffs. Poppies, harebells, Greenland orchids, blue greyish willow, birch, and juniper are found almost everywhere. There are

Icebergs.

snow-buntings, grouse, puffins, guillemots, white-tailed eagles, peregrine falcons and snowy owls. Seals and whales are common mammals in the fjords around Narssaq. We had to depart this very interesting place all too soon; it was getting a wee bit foggy and it was time to go back to the ship.

Our Captain for our cruise was Master Mariner, Commodore Ivan Currie. But the nearer we got to the Arctic Circle, navigation was very important, because of the icebergs. The ship had to take on board Captain Jenson, a Greenland ice-pilot of twenty years experience, who joined the ship for the most dangerous part of our cruise. Our ship had the honour of being the first passenger ship of its size to travel to the Arctic Circle. Our highlight was the day we entered Disco Bay, with the sparkling icebergs, the height of a three storey tenement. They were like sculptured pieces of ice cream. Looking ashore we could see a village, our last port of call in Greenland: atop the rocks was Jacobshavn, and looking further over was the biggest glacier in the world. It was just marvellous to have the privilege of seeing the beauty of this part of the world. When we reached the Arctic Circle, there was to be a ceremony. Elizabeth said she had volunteered the two of us to take part. This seemingly involved sitting in a swivel chair, being covered with washable paint like gunge, then being dumped into the deck pool to meet Neptune. I was having none of it, so scarpered up to the next deck where I was able to get pictures of Elizabeth going through the ordeal. When my name was called, there was no reply, so they put an Officer in the chair in place of me; his white uniform was in a bit of a mess. I got the photos, that was more important for me.

Over the Tannoy came the voice of a crew member: if you wished you could go round the icebergs in a small boat. Elizabeth and I were down for the boat as fast as possible. We had a wonderful time, and took many pictures. We couldn't believe our luck, until we got back on board, to be told it had all been a mistake, the wee boats should not have gone so near the icebergs. We felt that it was worth the trip, surely it's a true saying, ignorance is bliss.

We had a whole day ashore, and like most of the passengers, we made our way to the glacier. We were hoping to walk on it, but found it too dangerous. I suppose we could have risked it out of bravado, but we played safe. We were told the glacier moves 100 ft a day. The movement sounds like thunder when it moves and huge chunks float into the sea causing the ice-bergs to form.

When we entered the harbour of Jacobshavn, we were most surprised to see a great amount of activity going on. The natives looked like Eskimos, but they now preferred to be called Greenlanders. They were very friendly folk, and I think a wee bit overawed at the number of folk invading their town. We could hardly believe that there was a supermarket available. There was also a chemist shop selling coloured film, and you could buy ice-cream, but I don't remember buying ice-cream. I admired the huskies; I did not try to stroke one, but they looked quite tame. One of Jacobshavn's own personalities was Kurt Rasmussen, explorer, adventurer, and writer.

We stood on the deck that night and watched the sun set, then waited about an hour, to see it rise again. Marvellous cruise altogether. Next day we left; the ship made its way through the islands of icebergs, to continue our journey.

We sailed to Heimaey Island which is part of Iceland. There had been a volcanic eruption there in 1973. The whole island was evacuated in one night, and not one person was lost; every little boat, plus fishing boats were used on that night. Most of the island was covered in lava. The folk of Heimaey were taken to Iceland; they were supposed to make their homes there, but they wanted back to their beloved island.

They went back and rebuilt the place. It's a beautiful island and is heated by underground pipes laced through the still hot lava. These islanders know that there could be another eruption any time, but they are prepared to risk it.

Iceland itself was our next port of call. It too is volcanic, Hecla being the oldest volcano in the world. Reykjavik is the capital of the island and there are many tours round the country, but we only had a limited time ashore. We were taken to see the Gullfoss, the queen of Iceland's waterfalls. It's spectacular, just to watch millions of tons of water drop below you. One day is not long enough to see Iceland, but they did their best. Off we went to see the hot geysers, which spouted about 30 ft or more into the air, every two to three minutes. Because of the hot springs in Iceland, there is natural hot water piped into every home, central heating is also the order of the day. We were told by our guide that Reykjavik did not have any trees, but that's not quite true because I did find one and have a slide of it.

We sailed from Iceland, on our way to the Shetlands. Up to this moment in time the weather had been wonderful, we did not really need all the warm clothing, and had lots of beautiful sunshine and little or no wind, but as we neared the Shetlands, we were advised that we could not call in there because the weather was too rough. Ironicly, we did learn when we got home that we had better weather in the Arctic Circle than they had in Scotland while we were away. It was a wonderful eventful cruise; the slides turned out just great, the memories go well with the pictures. The Arctic Circle is a place of scenic beauty unspoiled by man.

At the end of 1986 the Sunday School presented their first Nativity play in the Stirling Hall. It was a huge success, and the children were well tutored by the Sunday School staff. It was just a pity we were not able to extend the production over a longer period of time.

We were heading fast to 1987. It was to turn out a very eventful year for the Church, for me, and lots of other folk. It's just as well, we can't make predictions, because we would try to change things, and that would be quite wrong. Our church would celebrate its centenary in 1988, so we were all beginning to look forward to that event. Every organisation would be involved; we had to begin to look forward. To plan, to enlist the congregation in the enthusiasm for the future days.

Chapter Twenty-one

The following words were written by me for our Church magazine in 1987. A dream had been accomplished.

'I was justly proud on Friday 23 January last when I was able personally to hand over to the Church Extension Committee the final cheque in repayment of our debt. The Stirling Hall was ours. I was justly proud of you as the congregation of Milton of Campsie Parish Church, and I remembered a text which helped me from the beginning of my training for the Ministry and still guides me today.

'Trust in the Lord with all your heart, never rely on what you think you know. Remember the Lord in everything you do, and He will show you the right way, Proverbs 3:5.6.' The following is an extract from the minutes of the Church of Scotland Extension Committee of 11 February 1987: 'The Congregation of Milton of Campsie Parish Church has repaid the loan of £47,500 plus 8% interest. The committee wish to congratulate the congregation of said Church for their prompt repayment of the loan and are much encouraged by this congregation's health and commitment. It should be noted that the loan was paid off in five years not the seven years anticipated by the Church Extension Committee.'

The wee Church in the centre of the village could now go forward in good heart. There was no debt, the fabric of our church was in good condition, and we looked forward with anticipation to 1988 when we would celebrate a hundred years of witness and service to the folk of our village. Every organisation was busy, planning what they could do for their church. Enthusiasm was running high; it was a great joy to be part of the preparations. A committee had to be formed, ideas were sought and found, and it was not long before the practicalities were up and running.

There is no way one can keep reiterating the story of one congregation. I could never exaggerate just how fortunate I was to be the minister of such a caring committed people. There were never any qualms about giving, sharing, or caring. The congregation supported every effort made by elders and office bearers. They supported me as their minister at all times, especially when bereavement hurt the manse family. Don't run away with the idea that there were never any problems, and it was not everybody who liked having this wee woman as their parish minister, but that was just too bad for them, because I had no intentions of leaving. There was once a vacancy committee in the church one Sunday morning. I was told they were from Portobello. I had been warned that they were coming. I asked Alex if he would like to go to Portobello, he said if I really wanted to go, it would be all right with him. Just like a man, can't make decisions. I asked my mother: her swift reply was that I hadn't asked her about Milton of Campsie, and she would rather stay where she was. The morning the vacancy committee turned up, my session clerk Bob told them I was not available; they were wasting their time. I saw these folk after the service;, and more or less said the same. They said it was all right; they had already been told by the session clerk. That was the end of the matter. If they had really been interested they would have dug their heels in.

In March 1987, the Rev. Elizabeth Sutherland was taking a group to the Holy Land. Although Elizabeth had been to Israel before, she had not taken a party of her own. I went as her assistant. It was a very good group, there were about thirty-eight all told. We had with us Elizabeth's auxiliary minister, Robert McKenzie Smith, who was a bachelor. He was very good to all the old ladies in the parish, but if he thought for one moment that he might be sought after as a good catch, he would have been off like a rocket. He lived in Dennistoun, in his own little flat. He had a nice new cooker which he kept his cakes in, because he never needed to cook. Robert had a different house to go to each night of the week, and at lunch time he went to Stobhill Hospital canteen.

When the group moved from Jerusalem to Tiberias, the Ron Beach Hotel were sorting out the rooms. The room for Elizabeth and me was ready, the others were to wait in the lounge until they were given their keys. Our room had three beds in it. Two were at the top of the room; you could not see them from the door, because the bathroom had been installed and blocked the top part of the room. But the other bed was visible from the door, and gave the impression that there was only one bed in the room. Elizabeth's face lit up. 'Let's play a trick on Robert,

I'll go and tell him his room is ready, then we will tell him he has to share, the clergy have to share.' Away she went. They were back very quickly, Robert entered the room.

'Oh, I'm very grateful, Elizabeth, this is a wonderful room, how did you manage to do this for me?'

I popped my head round the bathroom wall. 'Did she not tell you that the clergy have to share? Our beds are up this end, so remember and stay down where you are, and no lying in a hot bath for an hour, especially in the morning, there's three of us to get ready for breakfast.'

The case fell, the jaw dropped, he was totally at a loss for words; poor soul believed every word. Elizabeth had spilled the beans to some of her congregation; they burst into the room and saved Robert from any more embarrassment. But it had been a bit of fun and he had a good laugh with the rest of us.

Back home, I was having trouble with my eyesight, and had some terrible headaches. That puzzled me because I was not in the habit of having headaches. My eyes had not been tested for some time. I was beginning to see double on the television and I could not focus my camera. I made an appointment to have my eyes tested. The appointment was for 11 a.m. one morning. The practice that I normally went to was run by two sisters, who were both very good opticians so it did not matter who did the test. One of the sisters began the test. She stopped and told me that she could not carry on with the test, she would like her sister to have a look. Sister had a look, and decided that I needed to see a doctor. She phoned the practice, gave me a letter, and sent me over to see the doctor. Doctor Harrison was waiting for me. He had a look at whatever the sisters had seen, he lifted the phone and made an appointment for 2 o'clock that afternoon. By this time I was in a panic.

Dr Harrison said, 'Don't worry,'

I said to him, 'Don't worry, I go for an eye test at eleven, see you at twelve and I've to be at Stobhill at 2 p.m., and you say don't worry. what's wrong?'

'We think you have glaucoma, but it will have to be verified, and then you will need treatment right away.'

It was verified at Stobhill. I was given drops for night and morning, and would receive word from my doctor. I was waiting for these results when the Rev. James Currie had his heart attack. In February 1987, Rev. James phoned me, and asked me to go to the Holy Land with him in April. He said he needed me on the trip, even although he only had one bus. I told him I could not go because I was already going three times and could not take more than my six weeks holidays. I was not prepared to ask my Kirk Session for extra time. It turned out, James had already been on the phone to Dr McIlroy, saying that he needed her also.

At the end of February, I had a meeting in the manse, and we had just finished the business. My Session Clerk was helping to clear up, when the doorbell rang. Bob Gemmill opened the door and shouted to me that I had a visitor. In walked James. He said he was just passing: one doesn't just pass Milton of Campsie. Bob Gemmill made a mug of tea for James. He turned to Bob, and said. 'Please allow your minister to come to the Holy Land with me in April, I need her.' Again I refused to be bulldozed into this trip with him, and he left very disappointed. While I was in the Holy Land with Elizabeth in March, I kept thinking about James and his request. Why did he need me with only one bus of people. It was very much out of character. Why was he so adamant. I was to know soon enough. James and Peggy had gone to his beloved Arran for a few days. On Good Friday morning, he ploughed a field, Peggy saw him on the boat early afternoon, he had his Good Friday Service to take at Dunlop, Peggy remained in Arran. He did take that Service, had some folk back to the manse as usual. They left after eleven, James did not feel very well, after midnight, he phoned Kilmarnock Hospital and told them he was having a heart attack. He walked into the ambulance. They did get James to the hospital, but he let go of life in the early hour of the morning. Rev. James Currie had been due to fly out to The Holy Land on the following Tuesday.

McCabe Travel phoned me early Saturday morning. Alistair McCabe said, 'Everything is ready for Tuesday, you know James better than anyone, he would not want this tour to be cancelled, and you are the only one who has been with him to Jordan and Israel, think about it.' I phoned the Session Clerk, he said, we will have a Kirk Session meeting in the morning before the service, in the meantime I will phone all the elders and give them the bad news, you phone McCabe travel and tell them you will be there. I did not argue, The Kirk Session did meet on the Sunday morning, Easter Day. There was no problem, the folk on my session remembered all that the Rev. James had done for our wee church over the years.

That Easter Sunday morning service was very difficult, I could see the face, I could hear the man. I knew there was a hard job to do in the Holy Land. I could not fill his boots, but at least I knew that he wanted me there. One thing I would not be able to do, be present at the great man's funeral. I do believe he made the choice for me from the beginning of February ... After I got word on the Saturday morning, I phoned Dr Harrison and told him about the situation with James, and the fact I had no word from the hospital regarding my eyes. He said he would come to the manse after Sunday morning service, and he would have it worked out for me. He knew the predicament there would be for the folk on this trip if I could not go. Dr Eileen McIlroy had come up for the funeral of James, and it turned out that my Dr Harrison and Eileen had known each other when they were studying medicine. Dr Harrison had made arrangements for me to see a Mr Fawzi who was a consultant at the McAlpine Private Hospital on Easter Monday. The consultant did all the tests, and asked a lot of questions, like, 'Did you not notice a difference in your sight?'

'Yes, I was seeing two people on the TV instead of one.'

'What did you do about it.'

'I bought a better aerial, which did not help much.'

'What else.'

'I could not focus my camera.'

'And what did you do about that?'

'I just bought an automatic camera, and that was just fine.'

He was shaking his head by this time, must have thought I was a proper loony.

'Dr Harrison tells me you are a Reverend, you are going to the Holy Land on Tuesday. You must take care of your sight, you certainly have glaucoma, and it must be looked after. You will be on these drops night and morning, and you must not miss them. Glaucoma is a life sentence, there is no cure, but we can save your sight if you do exactly what you are told. You will have to see me once per month. Where will it be, here, or Stobhill?' I said Stobhill; I knew I could not afford the cost of going private every month.

Mr Fawzi did save my sight. I saw him once per month, then it was every three months, then six months. Later on Dr Harrison told me I'd need to think about retiring. Glaucoma tends to get worse if the patient is under a lot of pressure. That news was rather a shock. I just said there would be no way I would retire before the Centenary of the church, was over in 1988. The matter was left till later on.

Dr McIlroy went with me on what was known as The Rev. James Currie Memorial Holy Land Tour. Eileen said, 'I'll put the drops in your eyes for you.' I declined the offer, because when I returned to Milton I would be on my own, and have to put the drops in myself. Ours was rather a sad tour, because nearly everywhere we went we had to break the news that Father Currie, as he was known, would not be coming back. The man Avrahim, who owned the wee shop at Bethany where James used to go behind the counter and sell the produce, turned up at the Pilgrims Palace Hotel to see if it was true that James had died. He completely broke down, he was crying like a child and shaking all over. Dr Eileen had to give him a sedative, and get him home in a taxi. The wee boy who always gave James his orange juice for nothing, would not believe that Father Currie was not hiding from him; when it did sink in that the big man was really not there, he went off crying his eyes out.

The group went as usual to the Kibbutz Ein Gev. The leader of the Kibbutz was called Ben Joseph; he was getting a bit frail, but he came to speak to the group, expecting to see James. When he heard the news, he excused himself and went back home, he just could not speak. We often went to a restuarant in Haifa. The owner's father used to come to meet James, and when we were all settled the old boy would come round the tables to say, 'If you are all good, and eat up your main course, we will give you a sweet.' When he heard about James, he went home to bed. One of the guides in Jordan was in the airport when we were ready to fly home. He ran over to me,where is Father Currie, once more we had to break the news, Joseph, a big strong man broke down, he walked away devastated by the news.

Yes, the Rev. James Currie was a well loved character, I think because he was a down to earth human being. He had many faults, and he was aware of his own shortcomings, but people were very important to him, he endeared himself, to the needy and to the elderly. His faith was his life, he gave of his time and his talents and supported, many, many charities. We still miss him, the larger than life big boy.

Later on in July 1987, I was back in Israel with the Rev. Charlie McMillan with a group from his church, Ladywell, Bannockburn. Again it was a lovely group, and everything went well. The new camera was a great help to me; it meant I did not have to worry about focusing the lens at all. If there is one thing that really gets me down, it's having slides or prints returned to me out of focus. Photography was my hobby, not just abroad, but wherever I went, the camera went with me. My Dad started my interest in the camera with a Box Brownie, I bought a Halina which was my first single lens reflex camera. When I was first married Alex set up a darkroom for me, and I was able to develop my own black and white films. Later on, when coloured photographs were popular, the black and white films were out of date. Now it seems that slides are almost out of date today, but one can still give talks with slides, they help to illustrate the subject, bringing a greater understanding of other lands and their peoples.

1987 had been quite a hectic year; time goes on very quickly, and our church was really getting excited about the year ahead. Centenaries don't come along all that often. Everyone was looking forward. For me, in the background, I was wondering what to do about the eyesight. At the beginning of the autumn I was advised not to drive in the dark. I did go round the parish evening visiting, as I felt it was OK to drive locally, and did manage without mishap. But Dr Harrison's warning was never far from my mind. Church activities went on as usual, the drops in the eyes stopped the headaches. I was still very fit, and did not want to retire.

The Nativity Play of the year before had been so successful, it was decided to have another play this year of 1987. I was very happy about that because the children loved doing it, and it certainly helps to put the Christmas story into the minds of the young better than anything else. On the Sunday afternoon of the Nativity, the hall was full to capacity; the children were even better the second time round. I think the staff of the Sunday School revelled in the production themselves; it was a great way to bring 1987 to a close, New Year had still to come, what would it bring for our congregation?

Chapter Twenty-two

January 1988 started off well. I had been asked to assist the Rev. George McCabe on a visit to the Holy Land. We were taking what was known as a familiarisation group, to teach them how to be leaders. The groups would be composed of ministers who had never been to the Holy Land before. They would get their trip for half price, because of the time of year, when hotels would be quiet, and if they succeeded in getting a group from their church they would get their money back. It really was a bargain offer. George and I had forty-five ministers on that group. Have you ever tried to get that number of ministers to stick to an itinerary? It was more difficult to keep them together than all the other groups we had ever known. But you see ministers are all individualists, so we had a few laughs and got on with it.

We had snow in Israel for the first time for me; I'd never been to the Holy Land in January before. The snow did not lie for any length of time, glad to say. When it was time to go up north to Galilee, we certainly realised how much the snow was needed. Mount Hermon was a picture, with its covering of snow. I don't suppose we ever realised just how important the snow on Mount Hermon was to the livelihood of Israelis, and Jordanians. When the snow melts, the water runs into three rivers, the Dan, the Hatsbani, and the Baniyas; these three rivers feed the River Jordan, which is used by Israel and Jordan for irrigation purposes. The Jordan flows into the Sea of Galilee, so if there is no snow on Hermon, no water for the Sea of Galilee. The Jordan river flows out the other end of the Sea of Galilee and makes its way down to the Dead Sea.

The Sea of Galilee produces the water for every household in Israel, for every hotel, etc. One year there was a terrible shortage of water; the Sea of Galilee literally shrank in size. It was 1986. Between Kibbutz Ginossar and Migdol, on the shore of the Sea of Galilee, an ancient boat was discovered by the members of the Kibbutz. The sea bed clay had protected the remains for many centuries.

George and Molly McCabe, Island of Samos.

The Israeli Department of Museums, assisted by volunteers, conducted a rescue operation. The boat was cleared of mud, covered with polyurethane foam and floated up the shore to the Yigal Allon Centre. It rested in a conservation pool. The boat is dated to the period covering the first century BCE until the the first century BCE. During this period, the lakeside communities witnessed the ministry of Jesus and his disciples. Could this boat have been one of the fishing boats used by Jesus on his many crossings of the Sea of Galilee? The boats now used to take pilgrims on their outings across the Sea of Galilee are built on similar lines to the ancient boat and are called the Jesus boats.

No matter when you visit the Holy Land, whether it be for a one-off experience or like me over and over again, you always, without fail, learn something new, and definitely see the past revealed before your eyes. The Bible becomes an open book, and the reality of Jesus ever new and challenging.

I did enjoy my visits to Israel with George McCabe. His knowledge of the Holy Land was tremendous. We did share quite a number of these Fam trips. George's wife Molly came with us very often; she had a great sense of fun, and knew her way about the place like it was Edinburgh, her home town. One January we had a Burns Supper in

Holy Land. McCabe group.

the Church of Scotland's Hospice. I don't know how they managed to get the haggis on the plane, or even get it off at Tel Aviv, but they did. It was a great night, Molly replied to the toast to the lassies, and it was just a hilarious evening all together.

Having thought long and hard about the eye situation, and been a bit frustrated about driving in the dark, I decided that the risks of having an accident were too great. If the phone went at night, I always answered the call. Over the last months of 1987 I did not have any call-outs, which was very fortunate for me. It came to me that there was no way I wanted to be a part time minister, so I paid a visit to Dr Harrison. His advice was still the same. You must retire. I agreed to take his advice, but not till after the centenery of the church, which was to take place during the first week of May.

The next step was presbytery. I had to retire on health grounds because I had not reached the age of sixty-five years, I was one year short. Our Presbytery Clerk, Rev. Alex Cunningham was very helpful; he set the wheels in motion, and we set the date, which was to be 28 August 1988. It just happened to be my birthday. The Kirk Session were next to be told. It was a bit of a shock for them, but they did understand the situation. Having set the ball rolling, I pushed the situation to the back of my mind and got on with the job of ministering. At least the congregation got plenty time to think about the situation.

Glad to say, it was going to be a busy year, which helped to soften the blow, and gave me the time to get used to the idea. The family were looking to a happy day in April of 1988. My nephew Crawford married Frances at St Gabriel's Church; it was a great pleasure for me, and an honour to be invited to share in the service. I read one of the lessons and took one of the prayers. It was a lovely day, and a very happy event for both families.

Our committee for the centenary celebrations of our church had worked very hard and all was ready. A little booklet had been printed telling the history of Milton of Campsie Parish Church from 1888–1988, I was glad to have the opportunity to write the foreword. The following words were written with a great deal of humility, being a very fortunate person indeed to share in Milton's marvellous history.

'The booklet you now have in your hand tells a little of the history of Milton of Campsie Parish Church from 1888–1988. One hundred years of work, witness and service in the Name of Jesus Christ our Saviour.

Over the years the little church at the corner has served the parish of Milton of Campsie, through its services week by week, dispensing the Sacraments of Holy Communion and Baptism, rejoicing with the young folk who have been joined together in marriage, and sharing the sadness of many a family in their mourning time. One hundred years of work, witness and service is not a cut off time, it is merely a preparation for the next hundred years.

Church is people, vitally alive in giving, sharing and caring for all who seek help and comfort. The Church, the people, have a right to celebrate this time of great achievment, at the same time pledging total commitment for tomorrow. We pass this way but once, let our passing be an inspiration to those who will follow. Lift up your hearts, rejoice, in the Name of Christ Jesus our Lord and Saviour. May His Gospel be the focal point of our every commitment in the future days.

The little booklet was a great success, it sold well, and as far as I know was sent to many friends and relatives to places far afield. Our centenary dinner was held on 30 April 1988 in our own Stirling Hall. The Rev. Alex Barr, MA, BD, Moderator of the Presbytery of Glasgow and his wife, attended the dinner, and was our preacher on Sunday 1 May. There were many speeches although we tried to keep that part to the minimum. The ministry was well represented. Rev. Bill Stewart, wee Bill, our assistant of a by gone era was there; it was lovely to see him, he had not grown any bigger. There was a very good colleague, Rev. Alastair McLachlan of Kilsyth, six feet four, who went through Trinity College with me, we shared a hymn book at many a service ... Alastair had agreed to be the Interim Moderator in the vacancy that lay ahead. I was particularly pleased about that because I knew he would seek the best for my people. Many other friends were there on this very special evening, and the entertainment was provided by Alastair McDonald, with guitar. The church family did enjoy their evening, the hall was absolutely full. I was particularly happy to have Miss Betty Stirling and her sister, Mrs Marigold Langley as guests. Miss Betty was the one who made it possible to have the hall built in the first place.

Some of our guests of the Saturday evening were present on the Sunday and took part in the service. Rev. Dr Alex Morrison, retired minister of the High Church of Campsie led us in prayer. The following guests read the Scriptures Rt. Hon. Tom Clark, Provost Robert M. Coyle, Councillor Mr Charles Kennedy. The prayers of Intercession were my own. Before the last hymn, I had the privilege of sharing a prayer of Dedication with the congregation, it ran as follows.

Heavenly Father,

Today we rejoice – 100 years of witness and worship in Milton of Campsie. We the Elders, Office Bearers, members and adherents of this congregation and parish reaffirm our commitment to the proclamation of the Gospel of our Lord Jesus Christ. As we dedicate ourselves afresh this day, we pray for your continuing presence with us, grant strength of character, wisdom, compassion, and love, that we may truly be worthy of our great calling. Help us to keep our eyes fixed upon Jesus, let us glorify Him in all our endeavours. And so we do present and rededicate ourselves this day in the Name of Our Saviour, Jesus Christ our Lord, Amen ...

There were many gifts presented to our church, to mark this very special occasion. The Women's Guild and the Young Women's Group gifted a stained glass window, representing the Church, Glorat House, the bridge over the Glazert, the flowers, the BB, and the Girl Guides, with doves in a blue sky, a very beautiful window. A communion table cover came from the Sunday School, hand embroidered by one of the SS Staff. The Badminton Club gave new hymn books. Craighead Primary School presented us with a crystal bowl. Brass flower vases were the gift of Strathkelvin District Council. Milton of Campsie Community Council presented a hand carved vestibule table. And from Presbytery Clerk, Rev. Alex Cunningham, a poker tooled picture of Milton of Campsie Parish Church. From the Boy's Brigade, a beautiful pulpit fall in blue. All these gifts were received with grateful thanks; each one of them enhanced our wee church, beautiful gifts from beautiful people.

The following Sunday there was a congregational meeting after the morning service. Rev. Alastair McLachlan took charge of this meeting, and a vacancy committee was formed. This was to allow the vacancy committee to be out looking for a new minister, while I was still there. This option was open to a minister who promised the presbytery that they would not interfere in the selection of a minister. This I was glad to promise, so that there would not be a long vacancy. I did not want my congregation to deteriorate, as usually happens in long vacancies. I learned in time who were on the committee by the absence of some very good members. It was a good way of doing things.

A retiral date was planned for the end of August 1988. Meanwhile I shot off to the Holy Land with another group at the end of May. It was a good thing to do, there were too many commiserations for me to cope with. When I came home the congregation were getting used to the idea that I was retiring; they had had some months to think about it, but had pushed it to the back of their minds. We all had to face facts. I believed God had called me to this Parish, now time was up and God was saying to me, it's time to go. Once I had accepted the situation, it became easier for me and for the congregation.

June, July and August went very slowly, I could not understand what was wrong with me, then it dawned: usually in these months I was preparing for the start of the new session's work. Hymns were organised, and so was I. Now retirement had really begun. I went out visiting, what else to do? I tried to visit as many of my house-bound as possible, then the elderly; it was hard going but it had to be done. Arrangements had been made for me to go and live in Erskine with my brother Douglas and his wife. When you leave the ministry, it is difficult to set up home; it would have been different if Alex had still been with me. When we moved to Milton of Campsie, we sold our own home, and the cash went to furnish and carpet the manse, we never had any regrets. On retirement I could have got a council house in Milton, but that would not have been fair to a new minister, so decided I'd be all right with the family.

It was bad enough trying to keep myself busy, prior to retiring; what was it going to be like when I did retire. Nothing to do all day, every day, did not seem to be very attractive for me. My health was particularly good, I had plenty of energy, but life was going to be very lonely. Oh how I wished for Alex, he would have understood.

The great day of retirement was bearing down on me; there was no escape. Everyone was wishing me well: look at all the free time you will have, it was not really for me, but I was not complaining. My farewell evening came very quickly. The congregation had done me proud, there was a lovely meal, then there were the speeches etc. During the speeches I wondered who they were talking about. If I'd known I meant so much to them I would never have left. I was given a large cheque, which went into the bank, which was to be used for something special. The Sunday Service was a kind of nightmare. I could see the hankies coming out of the pockets. I knew if I let go, it would end up a 'greetin meetin', so I gritted my teeth and got on with it. At the end of the service I went to the door as usual, there were hugs aplenty, tears as well, and how I got through I'll never know, but then I did know: God was there in the midst, and I should not have been worried. Sometimes we are so enmeshed in our own problems we don't see the hand of God, guiding, sustaining and providing, but He is always there.

I was leaving the manse on the Tuesday. Rev. Diane Stewart, who had been my assistant for two years, was going to have my desk and chair, a library of books, and some furniture. I was limited to what I could take with me to Erskine; one room does not have elastic walls. My bookcase would be housed in the living room, with some of my special books. Diane had hired a van. It could not have been a worse day, it was pouring with rain, a right dreich afternoon. The door was open as Diane organised her removal. The doorbell rang, and standing on the doorstep was a monument of misery, namely the undertaker. he was in his best blacks, plus black umbrella, he said, 'Mrs Irvine, I have a wee box here for you,' I wanted to laugh, but invited him in instead. He was the undertaker from the Co-op Funeral Directors in Kilsyth. He handed the wee box to me with the compliments of the Co-op, and hoped I would have a happy retirement. I opened the box to find a very lovely carriage clock, which I still have. Was time short for me, or would time hang heavy on my hands? My future was in the hands of my Father in Heaven, but the clock made me think.

Chapter Twenty-three

Retirement is the strangest feeling. To begin with I was a wee bit busy. My room had been decorated for me, my new furniture was in place, but I had to find places for all my bits and pieces, not an easy task. I was given the room with a lovely view to the Old Kilpatrick hills, it reminded me of the Campsies. I knew it was going to take me some time to fit in.

Never mind, while my wee church was ordaining their new minister I was off on a five day trek in the Himalayas. Rev. George McCabe was our leader. What a wonderful escapade. I thought. I was usually quite good on my feet, but this trip was to be a lot different. On 5 November we flew to Delhi. We did a bit of sight-seeing in New Delhi, and in the morning we took the Taj express train to Agra for another look at the Taj Mahal, then a rickshaw ride round some marble factories. We flew from Varanasi Airport to Katmandu, booking into the Shangrila Hotel, which was sumptuous.

In the afternoon we went to visit a Buddha's Stupa (a Temple-like building), at Swayambunath, and the evening we relaxed and had a briefing session for the trek. We were up very early the next morning, as we had an eight hour journey to Pokhara on a bus that did not look as if it would make the journey. The roads were terrible, and we began to think the bus had square wheels, but the scenery was spectacular. We transferred on arrival to the Fishtail Lodge beside Lake Phewa. Legend has it that the lake covers an ancient settlement, erased by an earthquake. The fishermen's long canoes are carved out of tree trunks. The view of the Annapurna range of the Himalayas is breathtaking. On our first day of the trek, it seemed very easy. We were walking through the valley from Pokhara, there was a rapidly flowing river on our right, it was very pleasant. Halfway through the valley we stopped for lunch; the sherpas had it ready for us. Some of the trekkers bathed their feet in the stream. As we sat having lunch, we watched the mule trains, weighed down with produce for the villages high in the hills.

Ramsay and Effie in tent.

They were sure footed animals, they needed to be as they climbed up the Himalayas. It turned out we would have to be just as sure footed. Lunch over, we continued through the valley. Soon enough the easy part was over, there was an arrow pointing. I could swear it was pointing upwards to Dhampus. That day we were on the trek for five hours. Another lady called Margaret and I were last to reach the camp. We had been climbing upwards, on what are known as the staircases, on and up, only the staircases were rocks, about two feet high. My wee short legs were really struggling. The sherpas had given each person a pole to assist us on the walk; I now understood why. When we eventually reached the camp, all the tents were up, and the tented dining room was ready, even a tented latrine was waiting for us. I just wanted to lie down. Our tents were two-man affairs, and my companion was Ramsay Jackson; we had been in the Holy Land and Oberammergau together. Ramsay was very tall, her sleeping bag only reached to her oxters, I was OK I could snuggle down in mine.

I was not very hungry on that first night, but I did eat something, then I had a word with George McCabe. I said to him that I didn't think I could do the trek, I was so tired. George quickly replied that if I wanted to go back, I'd need to to go back in a sherpa's basket. I went to bed. We were called in the morning with bed tea; it tasted like nectar. We washed with wet wipes, stepped out of the tent, to a beautiful sunrise, and decided to carry on with the trek. Believe it or not we had very good porridge for breakfast, I did enjoy it, and very soon we were on our feet ready for the day's trek.

We had reached Naudanda the night before. The day's trek was to take six hours on the same kind of terrain. We were still heading for Dhampus, then to Landrung for our next campsite. Margaret and I decided that we would not even try to keep up with the advance party, we would just go at our own pace. This we did, and when we reached Dhampus for lunch, we were last but we felt good and relaxed. One could say we were beginning to enjoy ourselves. We had reached a village, and while we waited for our lunch, the village children came out to meet us. Rev. Moses Donaldson had his mouth organ with him. The kids were fascinated. So were we; in the short time we were in the village Moses taught these kids to do the actions of the song 'If I were not upon a stage something else I'd like to be'. Actions speak louder than words. Then it was off to find our campsite Landrung. When we entered the campsite, last of course, Margaret and I got a clap. We said in unison, 'It was a piece of cake.' We did enjoy our dinner, hunger had set in. There was lots of fun and banter that night. Our journey of that day was the longest, so we knew we could all cope, or so we thought.

When morning came, we realised that the rising sun did not touch our campsite; we were in the shade of the towering mountains. It was Sunday morning, and Rev. George, and Rev. Moses were preparing for a Communion Service. It was very cold. The sherpas were preparing our porridge, and while the service went on the cooks were watching us; possibly they had never seen Christians having Communion before. The sherpas were Hindu. We had with us a young gym teacher with us called Elaine. By the time the service was over we were all quite cold. Immediately after the Benediction, Elaine said, 'On your feet.' She put us through a warm-up exercise. We discovered, later that the Sherpas thought it was part of the service. The porridge was particularly good that morning.

We were soon on our way to another staircase ascent to a scenic village location. It was only supposed to take us two hours, but it was about four hours. The people of the village were very welcoming, the children especially ... George McCabe was able to speak with the

Annapurna south.

villagers in Hindi; the kids were swarming all round George. It's wonderful what happens when strangers can speak with one another. The houses in the villages were mostly the same: upstairs where the family lived, and downstairs where the cooking was done, and some of the animals were kept. They were all thatched roofs. We were always offered hospitality, but managed to refuse graciously.

Our own Sherpas prepared our lunch, we had to be careful about hygiene. After lunch we were on our way to the highest point of our trek, Ghandrung. We were much later than anticipated, but when we got to the campsite it was worth every aching minute. The tents were placed in a row, on a ridge, and all around was the beauty of the Himalayas. Annapurna and the Fishtail Mountain seemed to be immediately above us, but of course they were many miles away. We had ascended about 11,000 feet, we had all lost weight but felt very fit. It was wonderful: there were nineteen persons on our trek and not one person had been unwell, that was indeed a bonus. Says a lot for our sherpa cooks. The sunset that evening was a brilliant red; we were so high up, the air was clear and fresh. It could be quite cool in the night hours, and in the mornings.

It was marvellous how we could stay reasonably clean with a little

Fishtail Mountain.

water and wet wipes. We each had a plastic bag for our socks. I can't tell you the smell that came from my sock bag as I put yet another pair of socks away for the laundry. We scrambled out of our tents that morning at Ghandrung, but breakfast was kind of forgotten, when we caught sight of Annapurna South, with the Fishtail Mountain on the right. The sun had risen, we were totally engrossed in the sight of that view. Annapurna was covered in snow, and the sun was changing the colour of the mountain every few seconds. It was white, gold, even tinged with blue, what a sunrise. We were indeed privileged that morning, to see the work of our creator before our very eyes. We set off up the hill to get the best picture. We had to be quick because the sun moves very fast. The sherpas thought we were mad. I suppose we were just a bit mad, we had never seen anything like this before. Spectacular, yes. Brilliant, yes, breathtaking, yes, and much, much more. It was worth all the struggling, the tiredness, just to be there. No wonder folk want to climb mountains. Suddenly, and I was not the only one, I felt quite dizzy (more than usual). We realised it was altitude sickness, we had to sit down and I went back down the hill on my bottom. Never mind, we got the pictures; sadly we would be heading back down the Himalayas today.

There was not much breakfast eaten that morning, We began our descent. It was to be a five hour trail to Birethanti, and the poles came in very handy on the way down. Going down these staircases makes your legs shake. We had to be very careful, the rocks were slippy. The sherpas were all right, they did it all in their bare feet. We got down so far, then we would find ourselves climbing up to other ridges, that's just how it is. We were doing not so badly, until we were facing one of these rope bridges. You know the kind. Below there was a river with plenty of rocks, the water was swirling; we had to cross that bridge, there was no other way. The sherpa's showed us how to do it, one at a time, walk like a model, so that the bridge would not sway. It scared me rigid, there seems to be nothing between you and the rocks. I am glad to say we all reached the other side of the bridge, safe but a wee bit shaky. We were soon in Birethanti, and were now on the other side of the valley. Annapurna was still facing us. We had had a long day; all we wanted was a sleep, but dinner came first. After a bit of banter, we crawled into our tents and off to sleep. Although the ground was hard, we had no problem sleeping. The only problem was getting up.

Birethanti, in the morning, was bathed in sunshine, again the mountains stood out in all their glory. Breakfast was enjoyed, we were now feeling our legs just a wee bit tired. Going down is definitely worse than going up. The next port of call was to be Kaski, another four hour trek. This would be our last night on the Himalayas. We all felt a bit sad. We had had a wonderful time, hard graft, but it was a good group, we had all got on well together; but all good things must come to an end. Although we were still quite high up on the hills, we could now see the oxen treading the grain down below us, going round in a circle. a beautiful pastoral scene.

The walk to Kaski was without incident, just going downhill all the way. We could now see the valley we had walked through on our first day. On the other side of the ridge Lake Phewa was visible, we always stopped for pictures. It was great to think that not one of us had had any stomach problems. Some had blistered feet, but my feet were in very good shape, in fact it surprised me no end that I felt so good and fit. One thing we did know was that we lost weight, all of us. Ramsay, my tent companion had a good laugh when we listened to a conversation from the next tent. Rev. Moses was saying to Alister Gibson he had to put cotton wool inside his jaws to help him to shave, because his jaws were clapped in.

Eventually we reached Pokhara, where were taxis waiting for us. We arrived at the hotel, a little dishevelled, a wee bit grubby, but very happy. The hotel had plenty of hot water, we had showers galore. Then into bed. In the morning we were flown back to Katmandu and the luxury of the Shangrila Hotel. It had been a dream experience, we all survived. We had one more day in Katmandu. We were supposed to take the little plane along the Himalayas, but the mountains were covered in mist. Most of our group were very disappointed, I was lucky I had done that flight before. On Saturday 19 November we flew back to Heathrow. It had indeed been a great adventure.

Back home I had to find a Church. It had been in mind to try various places. My sister-in-law was an elder in her Church at Erskine; I did not want to be a burden to her. One Sunday morning I went to Bishopton Parish Church. At the door were two elders; one was Mr Rob Fleming, and the second was Mr Alex Jack. I was early, I usually am, for everything. These two men welcomed me, recognised I was a stranger, and set about making me feel at home.

Mr Fleming furnished me with a hymn book, then he said to Mr Jack, 'Could you take the lady into Church and to a seat.' Into Church we went. 'I think you should sit in this pew, there will be a Mrs Margaret Taylor here shortly, I'll tell her you are a visitor.' Off he went.

That was a very good impression. I had made up my mind that no one would know I was a minister, I wanted to be accepted by people for myself not because I was a minister. Mrs Margaret duly arrived. She too was a very welcoming character. She asked me where I came from; I told her I was retired and staying with my family in Erskine. Thankfully she never asked what I had retired from. Another lady came into the pew on the other side of me, a Mrs McDonald; she too gave me a welcome. It was a lovely feeling, and I thought, I'll just stay in this church for now. I had come to hear the minister, Rev. Douglas Alexander, but unfortunately he was on holiday.

The next week I went back to Bishopton Church. The minister was still on holiday. For the next two Sundays I was doing pulpit supply. When I went back to Bishopton. Margaret told me she thought I was not coming back, I managed to put her off the scent by saying I was just attending other Churches, which was true. The minister was present that morning, and I found him very interesting.

I was enjoying the services and decided to stay at Bishopton, but was not even thinking of joining at that time. I had been going for about three months, was off some Sundays doing pulpit supply, but always went back to Bishopton. One Sunday there was one of the ministers from 121 George St, Edinburgh Church of Scotland Offices, he was to be preaching that morning. I knew him well. When I came out of church, the visiting minister, said to the Rev. Douglas, 'She will be a good help to you.' Douglas looked at him as if he had horns. 'This is the Rev. Effie Irvine.'

I left the church, and in the middle of the week the Rev. Douglas was on the doorstep.

'How would you like to share a service with me?' I said I'd be delighted. On the Sunday I was missing from my seat, Mrs Margaret thought I might be unwell, so had decided to visit me. When I entered the church, in robes, Mrs Margaret, said, 'Oh the wee besom, she never let on.'

Rev. Douglas introduced me by saying, 'We've blown her cover, she's a minister.'

I shared many services with Douglas after that, and did pulpit supply, I joined Bishopton Church, and have been happy there ever since.

It took me a wee while to settle down at Bishopton Church. Many Sundays I was absent from my pew because I did quite a lot of pulpit supply; it was quite an experience being in a different church Sunday by Sunday. Sometimes I was asked back again, so got to know a few different congregations. In January 1989 I was back in the Holy Land with George McCabe, and with my own group in the April. We managed to fit in a cruise up the Nile with McCabe Travel. The retirement was working out quite well. I did not really have much free time. in fact i had preached in 21 different churches in 1989. Each day was a bonus for me, I had never wanted to retire. I was kept very busy without the worry of a parish. But I still missed my people of Milton of Campsie.

Chapter Twenty-four

In January I was off to the Holy Land with George McCabe; we had another group of ministers to cope with. At this time, so early in the year, I was not to know just how busy I was going to be in 1990.

In the February I did another minister's group tour with McCabe Travel; this time I was not working. It was great to relax and just enjoy the trip. We visited the seven Churches of Asia, or to be more correct, the sites of most of the churches started by St Paul on his famous missionary journeys. In Ephesus, the guide was Turkish and looked Turkish, but he had a broad Glasgow accent. When I managed to get a wee word with him, I said, 'How do you manage to speak like a Glaswegian?'

He said 'Scotland is my second home, my wife is a Glaswegian, I love the city and the people, so I decided to learn the Glasgow accent.'

Quite amazing. I asked him where he was from in Turkey. He said Kusadasi, I remembered Sumer Erdum, our guide on our Eastern Turkey adventure. I asked the Scottish Turk if he knew Sumer: of course, we work for the same company. I asked him to remind Sumer about Effee ...

In March 1990 George McCabe was going back to India; there was to be an extra tour for those who were interested in visiting the School in India. You will remember Hari Krishnan Sharma, the little boy sponsored by Milton of Campsie Parish Church. He had now reached the age of sixteen, his education had been completed and he would be going back to his family in Nepal very soon. There were four of us who had become sponsors, and we were asked if we would like to go out and live in the James Harvey Memorial School for nine days, then meet up with George's group and do more travels in India. Remember I had been given a cheque from Milton Church when I retired; now it was going to be used. I decided to go to the School to see Hari for the last time. All four of us decided to go on the trip. Margaret McCabe, George's sister, was going with us to be our translator. She was born in India, and spoke Hindi. We flew to Delhi. This time we would be away for twenty-two days, just marvellous. Andrew McCabe met us in Delhi.

We stayed in the Krishna Hotel overnight. Our journey from Delhi to Gonda would be by train. It would take all of ten hours to get there. We were not to worry, everything would be all right, famous last words. Our seating accomodation on the train was fine; we were booked first class. We also had sleeping accomodation, which turned out to be the seats we were sitting on. The blankets were a bit tacky but we were able to pay some rupees for a pillow, and were advised to sleep with our hand luggage tied to our feet. Not very comfortable.

The toilet was worst of all; it was just a hole in the floor of the train, one had to squat down holding on to a pole on either side, pray and do your best. One of our ladies said she could not manage to go in there, but when she realised she had a ten hour journey, she had no option. It turned out good for me, I was nearer the floor than the other four. By the time we reached Gonda it was quite dark. Andrew had sent word to Nawabgunge, all of 26 miles away, saying what time we would arrive in Gonda. He expected someone to meet us off the train with some sort of transport. The transport did not arrive. The town of Gonda was two miles from the station. Andrew hired six rickshaws, one for each of us, as we had luggage with us for twenty-two days. We went in style, Indian style, all the way to Gonda; these rickshaw boys can fairly run.

We got to Gonda all right, but there was still that twenty-six miles to Nawabgunge and the School. It was a good job for us that Andrew was with us in Gonda. He went down the street and managed to hire a jeep. We tried everything to get us plus luggage into that jeep, but it just would not take all of us. The next vehicle was a minibus. It had no petrol in it, and we had to help push the bus down to the garage. Andrew paid for the petrol. At the last minute Andrew noticed that the bus did not have a spare wheel, so the man hiring out the bus just took a wheel from another bus. We set off for Nawabgunge; it was getting late.

About ten miles on the road, we were stopped by the police. We had to drive into the police compound. We thought we were in trouble. There was a lad there with a motor bike. It turned out he came from Nawabgunge, where we were going. He had had his television stolen from his home, but the police had recovered it, and the idea was that we would take the TV to Nawabgunge on the roof of the bus and the boy would follow on his motor bike. It turned out that was the best thing we had done that night. We were about eight miles from our destination when one of the wheels sheered off the mini-bus. We would have been stranded except for the boy on the bike. He offered to drive back to Gonda for another vehicle. While he was away our bus driver lit a fire and produced his tea. But Andrew told us later, the fire was lit for our safety, there were a few bandits in that area. I was glad he did not tell us at the time.

You'll never believe it, the transport the boy brought back was the jeep we tried the first time around. We now had two drivers. The bus had to be left at the side of the road. This time, the luggage was put in first, under the seats, and on the seats; we had to be prepared for a rough journey. It certainly was, we were perched on luggage with our heads about an inch from the roof. We did get to to the School about 3 a.m. The gates were locked and the night watchman was sleeping, so one of the drivers had to climb some very high railings. The letter Andrew had sent by hand had never arrived at the School; it did come eventually, two days later.

We did manage to get some sleep. Three of us were billeted in what had been an office. We did not investigate our rooms that night but just fell into bed. In the morning we were looking for the shower, there was none just the tin bath, with the pot; one stood in the tin bath and poured the water over oneself. We never did manage to find out why the light went out when we flushed the toilet. We breakfasted in Andrew's home, and had all our meals there. Andrew's wife was an American lady, who looked after us very well. This gave us a chance to see what life was like for a missionary family.

It was Sunday morning and we would be going to church. That was a great experience. There were 130 boarders at the School; it is a Christian School. All the boys came to church, the oldest ones in white trousers, blue shirts and navy pullovers, the Juniors in short grey trousers and blue checked shirts, and the wee ones the same. They were all very smart. The singing was in Hindi, but we recognised the tunes. The sermon was given in Hindi and in English. We received a very warm welcome from the Pastor.

The School was started by a young British Army Officer. He was stationed in Feizabad, and saw the plight of the many deprived children,

Hari Krishnan Sharma with me.

especially orphans. He resigned his Commision, went back to India and started the school. He died in 1922 at the age of thirty-six years. His wife Esther carried on with the work, and the School grew from one hut to what it is today. Children from the villages of Nawabgunge come to Day School, both boys and girls. The daily pupils pay some rupees to be taught.

We then did a tour of the School, and met some of the teachers. The dormitories had no frills or fancies, holes in the walls were used as storage space; the accommodation was simple but adequate for the needs of the boys.

Football was of prime importance. The final of the football was to take place while we were there. Our Hari was captain of one of the teams. He so wanted to win, because we were there, but sad to say, they lost the cup. It was tough match, the majority of the boys played in their bare feet. We played skipping ropes with the girls, and 'O'Grady Said', with boys and girls of the primary school. We were happy to see that all the teachers were Indian, that was great for the children. We hired a working elephant, so that we could have fun with not only the boys of the School but invited some of the village children who don't as a rule have many elephant rides; they loved it, it was great to hear them laugh. We also had a snake charmer come to visit us. I

Pupil and Hari Krishnan Sharma.

think the snakes were sleeping; they are lovely creatures to touch, not at all cold or slimy; but warm and beautifully marked.

We were taken to visit a sugar factory in Nawabgunge, we watched the oxen bring the canes of sugar to the factory; it was dropped into a conveyer belt and hauled up to the boilers. On the way up the cane was stripped from the sugar, and inside the factory the process was then started for the making of white sugar. It was the dirtiest place imaginable. The boilers were covered with asbestos, and the fact that the sugar came out white was certainly not because of hygiene. The poor souls who worked there seemed to be undernourished. There was no sickness benefit, no holiday pay. If you went off sick, or were off for any length of time, there was always someone to take your place. I am sure the pay would be peanuts, but it was a job. The villages were poor in the extreme: mud brick houses with thatched roofs and earthen floors, no toilet or washing facilities, this was the real India, not the tourist trail, but wherever we went we got a welcome. The people we met were kindly and seemed glad to see us. It was a great privilege to meet them, and spend some time with them. The boys of the school were our translaters. We met up with some gypsies, who are outcasts from society, but we were invited to watch two monkeys dance to music. The first one was dressed in a dance costume, its owner sang and had a drum, the monkey was very good and of course this was a way of making money. The second monkey refused to get dressed, and refused to dance. It sat on a big tin can, shook its head, and said no. We laughed our heads off at the antics of the second monkey, and we paid for the entertainment. These two monkeys just acted like children.

Our next visit was to a leprosy hospital in Feizabad. Leprosy is a terrible diseas;, it robs people of their limbs, and their eyesight. It is not infectious, but it was always feared that it was. It is caused by a bug getting into the bloodstream via a break in the skin. Most people don't wear shoes in warm countries. They get cuts on their feet, or burn their fingers. Once leprosy gets into the system the person has no feelings in feet or hands; it's called an analgesic illness. Eventually gangrene sets in and limbs are lost. When a doctor is checking to see if someone has leprosy, they touch them with a feather; if there is no response, the chances are the person has leprosy. Fortunately there is a cure if the person is diagnosed early enough. One of the worst things to see is the leper whose eyesight has been destroyed. The sockets of the eyes become white. We had been in the wards of the hospital seeing some young folk who were being cured of their leprosy; some had had operations, so that they would be able to use their hands again.

After our visit to the wards, the almoner, a very lovely Indian lady, took us outside to see this group of five men who were blind. This lady's English was perfect. She explained about the eyes. One very small man was sitting on a bench alone. He spoke in Hindi, I asked the almoner what he was saying.

She said, 'I have explained to the group that you are visiting the School at Nawabgunge, he is blessing you for taking the time to visit them.'

This small man had feet with no toes, and stumps of hands with no fingers, plus white eyes, but he was sitting very straight. I asked the almoner how we could communicate when none of us could speak Hindi.

She said to me, 'Touch him and give him a blessing, I will translate.'

Touch him, that was the last thing I wanted to do. Again she said, 'Touch him, he knows that you are a Christian minister.'

Where could I touch him. He had a shock of white hair, that's it I thought, so I laid my hand on his head, and gave the blessing. When I had finished, he put the stumps of what was left of his hands up and

Blind leper in hospital.

took my hand in his stumps, held on tightly, and thanked me for the blessing. It was then I remembered the story of the leper who came to Jesus and asked for healing, he said to Jesus. 'If you would, you can make me clean.' Jesus not only healed the man, but he touched him. Here was me, almost denied my Lord. I walked away from the wee man with tears flowing free, feeling humbled, I have never forgotten that episode in my life, I did learn a great lesson that day.

Our nine days sojourn with the boys was over. We had to leave, it was very difficult, Hari knew we would not be seeing each other again, and I was thinking just how difficult it was going to be, saying goodbye. Hari was now sixteen years, he had taken an agricultural course and was going back to Nepal to help his Dad on the croft. I have since learned that Hari's Dad died soon after Hari went home. Hari is now married and has two children. Rev. Andrew is retired, but still at his beloved school, he visits his boys as often as possible, and sends home the information, I am sure Rev. Andrew will never give up India.

We flew back to Delhi, to a lovely hotel; we had to wait a day for the other group to begin the rest of our tour. The next day we all departed for Kashmir. I never realised that the mountains round Kashmir would be covered with snow, they just looked like the Alps. We were not aware either that there was a war going on in Kashmir. When we arrived in the airport, we had to accept an armed escort for our safety, I laughed, we all did when we noticed that the gun had a bent barrel; it could only shoot round corners, if it could shoot at all. It was possibly a deterrent. Our destination was Lake Dal, and we would be staying in a house boat on the lake. When we did get there we discovered we were the only tourists on Lake Dal. The house boat was based in the everglade. Everyone has a boat there, because there are no roads, the waterways are the roads, its a very eerie place but very beautiful, with the snow covered mountains and a lake like glass, but it was too quiet. There were dozens of house boats the others were empty. We were booked for four days. At night we could hear the drums being banged. I really believed we were in quite a dangerous situation, others were quite naive about it all. I was glad to return over the snow covered mountains to civilisation.

We picked up our bus for the journey to Mussoorie, this was where the Rev. George had been educated. It was uphill all the way. The hotel we went into could have taken over a thousand guests at the time of the British Raj. We were a very small group. The hotel had not been used for some time. The mattresses were damp, so we took them off the beds. There were open fires and plenty of wood, so we lit the fires and tried to dry off the mattresses. We did not sleep very well. The next day George got us moved to a different hotel. We visited George's School which brought back memories for him, and we found it very interesting. Then on to Dehra Dun to the Dunoltie Breeze Hotel; we wondered why it was called Dunoltie Breeze, until we learned it was just as breezy inside the hotel as it was outside. We did a bit of trekking from there; we only had two days, and were proposing to leave in the late afternoon, but the weather had changed for the worse and we decided to leave after breakfast. It was just as well we did.

The bus was made ready; we decided to leave as quickly as possible because of the weather. We were doing very well, making good time, until we turned a corner, and were stopped in our tracks, there was no road. There had been a landslide, and there was absolutely no way through. Men were trying to clear the road with shovels; we would have been there for days. The driver said that the only way out was via the taxi run, which was very narrow, but it was the only option. First the bus had to be turned on a ledge that had about a yard in front and the same at the back. It was not a very nice situation for the driver. Our driver did manage to turn that bus, it was not a three point turn: but about a ten point turn, one slip and the lot would have been over the edge. The taxi run was another nightmare for the driver; we were in between houses with about an inch to spare on both sides of the bus, again our driver was first class.

We did the journey at 15 miles per hour.

We got back to Delhi, having had a most marvellous journey, twenty two days of excitement, good fun and good company. These journeys bring out the best in people. I have certainly learned that that is true. 1990 was beginning to be busy, there were lots more experiences still to come.

Chapter Twenty-five

April 1990 saw me back in the Holy Land with my own group; it was small but the folk involved were very happy, and a good collection of people. We did our usual visits, important to the Ministry of Jesus, sometimes it's better with a small group as there is more time at each place visited, and very important, more free time. I had a rest in May, except for some pulpit supply.

Come early June, one Saturday afternoon I was relaxing at home. The phone rang, it was Alistair McCabe. 'How would you like to come to Oberammergau and give me a hand?'

I said, 'Sure, when do you want me?'

Alistair said, 'Monday, your tickets will be waiting for you at Glasgow Airport, and also at Heathrow for Munich, I'll be waiting for you at the airport in Munich.'

It was the year of the Passion Play at Oberammergau, which takes place every ten years, fulfilling a vow the folk of the village made in 1633. There had been a plague in Europe, and when it reached Oberammergau, the Elders and the Priests met with the village people and promised that if God stopped the plague, the folk of the village would perform a Passion Play every ten years. After the vow was taken the village had no more recorded cases of the plague. The Passion Play was first performed in 1634. Only twice has the play not taken place, once in 1770 and during the Second World War. There was an extra performance in 1984 to mark the 350th anniversary of the play.

The Passion Play of Oberammergau tells the story of the entrance into Jerusalem of Jesus on a donkey. It traces the story of the Passion of Jesus right through to the trial, Crucifixion, His Resurrection and Ascension. The Easter Story is brought to life in a most wonderful way. The play lasts from May through to October, with five performances in each week. People come from all over the world to see this play. In 1990 there had been a ticket scam; some persons had offered tickets that did not exist to various groups of people. When the time of the opening was drawing near, it was discovered that a whole lot of people had no tickets. People from as far away as Australia, America and France had travelled to the village to find that their tickets did not exist.

McCabe Travel found themselves in that predicament. They were better off than some travel agencies, because they had purchased most of their tickets direct from Oberammergau, but there was still the problem of getting tickets for those who had been let down. Alistair invited me out to help in the situation. My new found job was to meet the buses coming into the village each morning of the play, at 7 a.m., and in the afternoons at 2 p.m. to give out tickets, and take the afternoon bus groups to their various hotels. Those coming in on the morning buses were only there for the day of the play. I had to meet a young German called Wolfgang, at the Magic Bar, each evening and he would have the tickets needed for the next day. He never let me down, but I was always worried in case we would be short of the number of tickets required.

Alistair did meet me in Munich. Outside the airport was a new black Volkswagen car. Alistair said, 'That's your car.' I near had a fit, I'd never driven a left hand drive before.

'No problem,' said Alistair. 'I'll drive it to Oberammergau, and then you can get started tomorrow.'

The next day we went round the villages where some of our people would be staying for the play. Alistair left on the Wednesday, the office needed him.

I had a room in one of the villager's houses. It was lovely, it had a balcony with the usual floral displays; I was very comfortable. The lady could not speak English, I could not speak German, but we did manage to communicate. I fed myself, except when I had to take some folk for dinner in a hotel. I had been given an envelope full of local currency, the local currency. I was there for three weeks in June, and loved every minute of it. I had a map of the village and got to know it very well. If someone was unable to use their ticket for the play, I could use it. That meant I was in the playhouse a few times. If there were two tickets I sold them back to the box-office; there was always a queue for these tickets.

After I got our people into the playhouse in the morning, I would go and get what I needed for the day, food for lunch and dinner. Then I went to the stationer's, got my newspaper, which was two days old,

Holy Land. My own group.

and then went to the ice-cream shop. The folk in each of these establishments got to know me quite well. Some days it was a bit lonely, but I filled in the time pretty well.

I returned home at the end of June. Alistair's Dad, George, took my place. I had managed to keep the car in good nick, so had no worries. I had enjoyed the experience. Believe it or not I came home to take my own group to Oberammergau. We were booked for one week's holiday in a little Austrian village called Maria Alm, very beautiful, with the mountains all round, great for hill-walking. From there we visited Salzburg, where *The Sound of Music* was filmed, a beautiful but expensive town. Our group enjoyed the peace of Maria Alm, but were looking forward to the Passion Play. It's not enough to say that you enjoy this play, for it makes a great impression on all who are privileged to see it. We must keep reminding ourselves that the people of Oberammergau are fulfilling a vow; it is a very serious commitment for them.

In August 1990, I was back in the Holy Land with Rev. Charlie McMillan. We did our usual pilgrimage; it's great to be involved with these groups, one gets to know a lot of people. Some of them had been saving up for a long time to walk in the footsteps of Jesus. I can honestly say I have never met anyone who was disappointed. As for me, the land of Jesus is like home. I always feel particularly well there no matter the season, and always leave with a wee bit of sadness, hoping to go back.

September, again Alistair phoned: would I go back to Oberammergau to relieve his Dad George? Of course I went. It was the usual drill: meet Wolfgang at the Magic Bar. I got a phone call from the office in Salzburg to ask me to be at the railway station one morning. A train would be in with tickets and I had to get thirty-six of these, for the group coming in that morning. There was a queue and when my turn came there were only thirty-two tickets down for me. I tried to tell them at the station, but no-one was listening. Horrors, the unthinkable had happened, I was four tickets short.

I had to meet this group at 8.30 a.m. with their tickets, I rushed up to the Playhouse, where they were waiting patiently. I asked for the leader of the group and broke the news to her, that four would not get in. We asked for volunteers. Four women who had seen the play many years ago came forward and said they would stand aside. I was very grateful. The others went in to the Playhouse and we went to a café. I bought them coffee and asked them to give me time to phone Salzburg, and they agreed. I went back to my wee room and phoned the office, told them the story, and was advised to phone back at eleven that morning. When I phoned at eleven I was asked if the ladies involved were retired; if they were could they remain in Oberammergau, at the expense of McCabe Travel, and they would try and sort something out. Happily for me and them they were all retired and decided to stay on. While the group, including my four ladies were at lunch, I set to work.

Dinner was organised at the Poste Hotel, for the four ladies and myself. McCabe said, 'Get them booked into a hotel, we will try and get them tickets for tomorrow.' Everything was arranged and these very gracious ladies did get to see the Passion Play: they had had a bonus. The morning after the play, they were taxied to Munich Airport and flew back to Heathrow. I said, well done, McCabe Travel. The nightmare experience had turned out OK. At the end of the play in September, I was happy to go home because it was getting dark in the evenings.

There was one last thing I wanted to do in Oberammergau before I went home. In the church of Peter and Paul there is a Crucifix.

According to tradition, during the plague of 1633 the vow to perform the Passion Play was made before this Gothic Cross which is now above a side altar in the Parish Church. I wanted a picture of that Crucifix. Tuesday was more or less the deadline. That was the day of rest for the cast of the play, and all was quiet in the village. I made my way to the church, unusually the door was shut. I pushed open the outside door of the church, then I heard the singing. I knew instinctively that it was the Oberammergau Choir, so I pushed open the second door. The church was full, and the choir were singing "Ave Maria", I've never heard anything so beautiful. I stayed in the church to the end of the service. This service had been conducted in German, so I had no idea what it was all about. Later I discovered it was a memorial service for one of the cast of the play, one of the soldiers, who had died of a heart attack during the season. In other words the cast of the Passion Play were in mourning for one of their own, but they had to rise above their own grief, the "Vow" had to come first. I waited in the church until it was almost empty, and I did get my picture.

In 1994, I was asked if I would stand in as Chaplain for three months at Lennox Castle Hospital, The minister at Lennoxtown had given up his charge. I knew the place quite well, so agreed to do it for three months only. The remit was to visit the hospital three days a week; it took three weeks to visit all the wards in rotation. The three months became six months, eventually it was one year and three months. Having stood in over the winter months of 1994 to the first three months of 1995 I decided enough was enough and resigned. Lennoxtown had a new minister, so it was time to give up.

I left the Lennox Castle Hospital on the Friday, and on the Sunday the Rev. Douglas Alexander asked me if I'd like to be an associate minister at Bishopton Church. I agreed, so became officially employed by the church. I did enjoy the parish work again, visiting the elderly and the many homes where the older, infirm folk of the parish were located. I had more or less a free hand to visit where needed, I just gave Rev. Douglas a note of what I had done during the week. I was also available to help out with funerals etc. It worked very well, I enjoyed my time as associate until Rev. Douglas retired in April 1998.

1995 was the only year I did not go to the Holy Land, but I did manage to go for Christmas 1999. What a marvellous experience that was. Our group were in Bethlehem on the day before Christmas. We watched the celebrations in Bethlehem square, lots of young Palestinians involved in the festivities. Cubs, Scouts, Brownies and Guides all paraded. There were pipe bands playing, and they were playing Scottish tunes. It was a lovely day, the sun was shining. We waited in a long queue to enter the Church of the Nativity, so that once again we would see the place where the baby Jesus was born. Bethlehem was a place of great joy that Christmas; how thrilled we were to be there. That evening, some of us went to St Andrew's Church of Scotland at about 9.30 p.m. We were entertained by the staff of St Andrew's Hospice, then we went into church for a Christmas Eve Service, how lovely.

We moved up to Galilee to celebrate the Millenium. The leader of our group for this tour was a vicar from England, Rev. Peter Hammersly, a quiet gentle type of person. We were not sure how we would be celebrating the New Year, especially this particular one. A party surely, after midnight, but we should not have worried, a Jesus boat came to the Hotel Ron Beach at 11.30 p.m., and we sailed out into the Sea of Galilee. It was as calm as a mill pond, on a beautiful night, azure blue sky, the myriads of stars shining. The Jesus boat was anchored in the middle of the lake, and the only sound was the lapping of the water of the Sea of Galilee against the sides of the boat.

Rev. Peter had prepared a Communion Service. He spoke with a gentleness and sincerity that came from the heart of the man. He had a sermon which simply said, 'Two thousand years ago Jesus came walking on the water of the Sea of Galilee, He stepped into a boat, not unlike this one, and into the hearts of His disciples. Tonight, Jesus may come walking on the water, may your hearts be open to receive Him,' then we shared Communion. As we sailed back to the hotel, there was no one interested in having a party; we had stepped into a New Year, in the best possible way. After a service such as we had, there was nothing left to say or do. We had sailed out of 1999 and sailed into 2000. We went to bed, at peace with the world and with one another, thinking of our loved ones at home, very much aware just how privileged we had been.

Twice I've been booked to take a group out to the Holy Land for my fortieth visit. Twice it has been cancelled, because of the trouble which has erupted over the months. I weep for the Land of Jesus, and for its people, both Palestinian and Israeli. Peace can only come when both sides realise their need for one another; peace must surely come, but at what price?

The Passion Play at Oberammergau was again produced by the faithful people of that village. The Rev. Elizabeth Sutherland and I took three groups out in the year 2000. I don't suppose I'll be there in 2010, but I think I've had a fair innings; all good things must come to an end.

Looking back over my life, I realise how good God has been to me. I remember the wee lassie of Medwyn Street who never had a holiday until she was thirteen, but I have really made up for that. I've been to Italy, been at the Vatican, stood in the Colisseum, where the Christians were persecuted. Greece, and that great city of Athens, where Paul preached his sermon to an Unknown God, for the philosophers of that time. Eastern and Western Turkey, where the Gospel of Christ was brought to all peoples, again by St Paul.

Egypt the Land of the Pharoahs, the place of the Exodus: today, the landmarks of a bygone age. The Pyramids, the Sphinx, Obelisks, Temples to all kinds of gods. Sailing up the Nile: a happy pastime, stopping off to see the Valley of the Kings and the relics of Tutankhamun. Egypt, where Christianity came early and the Coptic Church is still alive today. India and Nepal, poor countries with friendly, kindly people who have so little of this world's goods but can still smile and welcome visitors to their countries.

Greenland and Iceland, beautiful islands, nature at its best. Icebergs sculpted by the wind and the waves, polar bears, seals and whales. Hardy folk live there; each day in the winter, they fight for survival.

Morocco, again a poor country where life is cheap, and making a living is hard. The tanneries stink to high heaven, but the men who work there make beautiful leather goods that last a lifetime. Norway, the land of the midnight sun, fjords and mountains, all the way to the North Cape, and round to Murmansk and Russia with its concrete blocks of houses, no shops with windows. A harsh way of life, cold and cheerless. Austria with its high mountains its snows where skiing can take place all the year round, spotlessly clean, beautiful food. Germany, with lovely villages, the mountains in the background and the Oberammergau Passion Play. Cruising on the Rhine, seeing these wonderful castles of a bygone era.

Malta, the George Cross Island of the Second World War, where they almost starved to death: the island that housed the Knights of the Order of St John. Valletta was founded by the Knights of St John. The Grand Harbour sheltered many British navy ships during the last war. The Mosta Church, a rotunda building, during the Second World War: a bomb was dropped on the Church which went clean through the roof, it landed on the floor and never exploded. It is still housed in the Mosta Church today. Syria, whose claim to fame is again St Paul, who met with Jesus on the Damascus road. The place where that meeting is said to have taken place is barren indeed, and the ancient city of Palmyra, where travellers from the east had to pass through that town to come to the west. Jordan, the Hashemite Kingdom of the Middle East, which includes the rose-red city of Petra, where the buildings are carved out of solid rock, a magical unbelievable place to visit. When we went to Petra, the only way in was through a defile in the rocks. We learned to sit on the backs of Arab horses very quickly, there was a great deal of laughter and fun. Of course Scotland, England and Ireland have been well and truly visited, as has Canada. Not bad for a not very well educated Glaswegian. I've had a wonderful life. It's only half time now, I'll be happy when the full time whistle blows, but there is still a lot to do before then.

In Bishopton we had a very fine young minister ordained and inducted to our Church in November 1999. Her name is Gayle Taylor. It's been a great pleasure to work with her. I just help out when needed. There is only one thing wrong with the lass, she is 5 feet 10 inches in height; I am only 4 feet 10 inches. I warned her about working too hard: I told her I was her height when I started in the ministry. Seriously, she is a first class minister. I no longer want to do pulpit supply; I am happy to sit in the church and listen. Every Sunday is a bonus for me. The Gospel is preached, the young folk are cared for, the older folk are cared for; the men and women in Erskine Hospital, Erskine Mains Home, and Ailsa Lodge are certainly cared for, this young woman is a naturally gifted minister. Anyone needing pastoral care, in sickness, in bereavement, this dedicated minister copes with the lot. We would pray that the Rev. Gayle will be with us for a long time. God has certainly called her to Bishopton Parish Church; we are all benefiting from the good Lord's wisdom.

I will let you into a wee secret. I was ordained before Gayle was born; I'm old enough to be her grandmother. Her generous spirit allows me still to be active in her parish. I'm now in my 78th year, but not ready to hang up my spurs yet. The good Lord called me to serve many years ago. I believed that then, I still believe it today, and I believe he will gently tell me when time is up.

I've been touched by many personalities throughout my journey of life. The one that touched me most was the little scrap of humanity I met in a leper hospital in India: you know the story, the man I did not want to touch, has touched me deeply. His face will always be etched in my heart. A shock of white hair was my escape route: touch him. I can still see my little friend, there on the wood bench, feet minus toes, hands minus fingers, a friendly face, white eyes. I failed in what I was doing, but he saved me from myself, he touched me, by taking my hand in his. When my time is up, I pray that Jesus will take my hand in His, just as the leper did, I believe Jesus was there that day, prompting both of us.

THE END